Study Guide and Workbook

for

Managerial Accounting

Fourteenth Edition

Ray H. Garrison
Professor Emeritus
Brigham Young University

Eric W. Noreen
Professor Emeritus
University of Washington

Peter C. Brewer
Miami University

McGraw-Hill Irwin

McGraw-Hill
Irwin

Study Guide and Workbook for
MANAGERIAL ACCOUNTING
Ray H. Garrison, Eric W. Noreen, and Peter C. Brewer

Published by McGraw-Hill/Irwin, an imprint of The McGraw-Hill Companies, Inc., 1221 Avenue of the
Americas, New York, NY 10020. Copyright © 2012, 2010, 2008, 2006, 2003 by The McGraw-Hill Companies, Inc. All rights
reserved.

1 2 3 4 5 6 7 8 9 0 QDB/QDB 1 0 9 8 7 6 5 4 3 2 1

ISBN: 978-0-07-731784-3
MHID: 0-07-731784-X

www.mhhe.com

Preface

To The Student

This study guide supplements the thirteenth edition of *Managerial Accounting* by Ray Garrison, Eric Noreen, and Peter Brewer. Each chapter of the study guide contains three major sections:

1. The *Chapter Study Suggestions* help you study more efficiently.
2. *Chapter Highlights* summarize in outline form the essential points in a chapter.
3. *Review and Self Test* questions and exercises test your knowledge of the material in the chapter. Solutions are provided. *Caution:* If you want to score well on exams, you *must* work out each solution on your own and *then* check to see whether your solution is correct by comparing it to the solution in the study guide. You cannot learn the material by simply reading the solution provided in the study guide. This does not work.

This study guide can be used as an integral part of the process of learning the material in a chapter. When used for this purpose, we recommend that you follow the steps below:

1. Read the *Chapter Study Suggestions* in this study guide.
2. Read the textbook chapter.
3. Read the outline in the *Chapter Highlights* section of the study guide. If you run across anything in the outline you don't understand, refer back to the textbook for a more detailed discussion.
4. Work the questions and exercises in the study guide and then compare your answers to those given in the study guide. If you find something you don't understand, refer to the textbook for help.
5. Work the homework problems assigned by your instructor.

Alternatively, the study guide can also be used as a very effective way to study for exams. Before reading the chapter in your textbook, read the *Chapter Study Suggestions* in this study guide. Then lay the study guide aside until it is time to prepare for an exam. The *Chapter Highlights* section of the study guide can then be used to review the essential material covered in the chapter. The *Review and Self Test* questions and exercises are excellent practice for exams. The questions and exercises in the study guide are particularly effective used in this way since they are likely to be similar to the questions and exercises your instructor will ask on an exam.

Remember, the study guide is not a substitute for the textbook. Rather, its purpose is to *supplement* the textbook by helping you to learn the material.

Ray H. Garrison
Eric W. Noreen
Peter C. Brewer

Contents

Chapter 1

Managerial Accounting: An Overview

Chapter Study Suggestions

This chapter contrasts financial and managerial accounting and discusses important features of the current business environment as they relate to managerial accounting.

CHAPTER HIGHLIGHTS

A. *Managerial accounting* is concerned with providing information to managers inside the organization for the purposes of planning, directing, and controlling operations. *Financial accounting* is concerned with providing information to individuals outside the organization such as stockholders, creditors, and others. Financial and managerial accounting differ from each other in a number of ways. In contrast to financial accounting, managerial accounting:

1. Focuses on providing data for internal uses.

2. Places more emphasis on the future.

3. Emphasizes relevance and flexibility rather than objectivity, verifiability, and precision.

4. Emphasizes the segments of an organization, rather than just the organization as a whole.

5. Is not governed by Generally Acceptable Accounting Practices.

6. Is not mandatory.

B. Managers carry out three major activities: planning, controlling, and decision making.

1. *Planning* involves establishing goals and specifying how to achieve them. These plans are often expressed in the form of *budgets*.

2. *Controlling* involves gathering feedback to ensure that the plan is actually carried out and is appropriately modified as circumstances change. *Performance reports* provide *feedback* that signals whether operations are on track.

3. *Decision making* involves selecting a course of action from competing alternatives.

C. A *strategy* is a plan that enables a company to attract customers by distinguishing itself from competitors. The focal point of a company's strategy should be its target customers. A *customer value proposition* is a reason for customers to choose a company over its competitors. Successful customer value propositions tend to fall into the following three broad categories:

1. *Customer intimacy*. A company that adopts this strategy is saying to its target customers: "The reason that you should choose us is because we understand and respond to your individual needs better than our competitors."

2. *Operational excellence*. A company that adopts this strategy is saying to its target customers: "The reason that you should choose us is because we can deliver products and services faster, more conveniently, and at a lower price than our competitors."

3. *Product leadership*. A company that adopts this strategy is saying to its target customers: "The reason that you should choose us is because we offer higher quality products than our competitors."

D. In many industries, a company that does not continually improve will find itself losing out to competitors. To effectively compete, managers have found that they must focus on improving *business processes*, which are a series of steps that are carried out to perform a task. They must also effectively manage the company's *value chain,* which consists of the major business functions that add value to a company's products and services. The text discusses two major approaches for improving business processes—Lean Production and the Theory of Constraints (TOC). These approaches can be combined.

E. Before discussing modern approaches to improving business processes, we should say a few words concerning the traditional approach to managing manufacturing operations.

1. In the traditional approach, as many units as possible are produced in order to spread the costs of investments in equipment and other assets over as many units as possible—even if those units cannot be sold in the immediate future. Units are *pushed* through the production process regardless of whether they can be sold. This creates a number of problems—the most obvious of which is large amounts of unsold inventory. These inventories consist of the following three broad classes:

a. *Raw materials* are the materials used to make a product.

b. *Work in process* consists of units that are only partially complete.

c. *Finished goods* consist of units that have been completed and are ready for sale.

2. With the traditional push approach, all three classes of inventories tend to increase and become very large over time. While not obvious, in addition to tying up money, these excessive inventories encourage inefficient and sloppy work with too many defects and dramatically increase the amount of time required to make a product.

F. *Lean Production* is a modern approach to manufacturing that is based on producing only what the market demands. Units are *pulled* through the production process only as they are demanded by customers. This single change dramatically reduces inventories and leads to a number of improvements in operations that are discussed in the text.

1. The *lean thinking model*, an integral part of Lean Production, is a five step management approach that is discussed in some detail in the text and is summarized in Exhibit 1-6.

2. The lean thinking model can be used in *supply chain management*—the process of coordinating business processes across companies to better serve customers.

G. The *Theory of Constraints (TOC)* is based on the idea that every organization has at least one constraint that prevents it from obtaining more of its objective. For example, if a company is unable to satisfy the demand for its products, the constraint might be a specific machine that cannot process units fast enough. To increase its sales and profits, the company must focus its improvement efforts on this constraint. Improvement efforts will be largely wasted if focused on machines or other business processes that are not constraints.

H. Ethics plays a vital role in an advanced market economy.

1. If people were generally dishonest, it would become more difficult for companies to raise investment funds, the quality of goods and services would decline, fewer goods and services would be available for sale, and prices would be higher.

2. The Institute of Management Accountants has issued a code of conduct that is a useful, practical guide for general managers as well as management accountants. The code of conduct is reproduced in Exhibit 1-7 in the text.

Chapter 2

Managerial Accounting and Cost Concepts

Chapter Study Suggestions

This chapter introduces cost terms that will be used throughout the book. The reason for so many different cost terms is that costs are classified in many ways, depending on how the costs will be used. To fit the cost terms into a framework, you should frequently refer to Exhibit 2-13 as you go through the chapter.

CHAPTER HIGHLIGHTS

A. *Manufacturing costs* are the costs involved in making a product and consist of direct materials, direct labor, and manufacturing overhead.

  1. *Direct materials* are those materials that become an integral part of a finished product and whose costs can be conveniently traced to it.

    a. The battery in a new Ford auto is an example of direct materials.

    b. Materials such as glue are classified as *indirect materials* rather than direct materials. It is too costly and inconvenient to trace such small costs to individual units of output.

  2. *Direct labor* consists of labor costs that can be easily traced to individual units of product. Direct labor is sometimes called *touch labor*.

    a. The worker who installs overhead lights in the passenger cabin in a Boeing aircraft is an example of direct labor.

    b. Other labor costs, such as supervisors and janitors, are considered to be *indirect labor* rather than direct labor. These costs cannot be traced to individual units of product.

  3. *Manufacturing overhead* consists of all manufacturing costs except direct materials and direct labor. Manufacturing overhead includes indirect materials, indirect labor, and other manufacturing costs such as factory rent, factory utilities, and depreciation on factory equipment and facilities.

  4. The terms prime cost and conversion cost are also used to categorize manufacturing costs.

    a. *Prime cost* consists of direct materials plus direct labor.

    b. *Conversion cost* consists of direct labor plus manufacturing overhead.

B. The two main categories of *nonmanufacturing costs* are selling costs and administrative costs.

  1. *Selling costs* include all costs associated with marketing finished products such as sales commissions, costs of delivery equipment, costs of finished goods warehouses, and advertising.

  2. *Administrative costs* include all costs associated with the general administration of an organization, including secretarial salaries, depreciation of general administrative facilities and equipment, and executive compensation.

C. For purposes of preparing external financial reports, costs can be classified as product costs or period costs.

  1. *Product costs* are matched with units of product and are recognized as an expense on the income statement only when the units are sold. Until that time, product costs are considered to be assets and are included on the balance sheet as inventory.

  2. *Period costs* are expensed on the income statement in the period in which they are incurred. (By incurred, we mean the period in which the cost is accrued, not necessarily when it is paid. Remember from financial accounting that items such as salaries are counted as costs when the company incurs the liability to pay them rather than when they are paid. Continue to use the rules you learned in financial accounting.)

  3. In a manufacturing company, product costs include direct materials, direct labor, and manufacturing overhead. All other costs are period costs.

  4. In a merchandising company such as Macy's or WalMart, product costs consist solely of the costs of products purchased from suppliers for resale to customers. All other costs are period costs.

D. For purposes of predicting cost behavior, costs are often classified as fixed or variable. A *variable cost* is a cost that varies, in total, in proportion to changes in the level of activity. Variable costs are constant on a *per unit* basis.

  1. Activity is often measured in terms of the volume of goods produced or services provided by the organization. However, other measures of activity may be used for specific purposes such as patients admitted to a hospital, number of machinery setups performed, number of sales calls made, and so on.

  2. The first graph in Exhibit 2-2 illustrates a variable cost. Note that a variable cost is represented as a sloping straight line that goes through zero (i.e., the origin) on the graph.

E. A *fixed cost* is a cost that is constant in total within the relevant range. The second graph in Exhibit 2-2 illustrates a fixed cost.

  1. Because the *total* fixed cost is constant, the *average* fixed cost drops as the activity level increases.

2. Fixed costs can be classified as committed or discretionary fixed costs.

    a. *Committed fixed costs* relate to investments in facilities, equipment, and the basic organization of a company. These costs are difficult to adjust in the short-term.

    b. *Discretionary fixed costs* result from annual decisions by management to spend in certain areas, such as advertising, research, and management development programs. These costs are easier to adjust than committed fixed costs.

3. Even committed fixed costs may change if the change in activity is big enough. Exhibit 2-4 illustrates this idea. However, within the band of activity known as the relevant range, total fixed cost is constant.

F. The relevant range and curvilinear costs.

1. For simplicity, we usually assume that the relation between cost and volume is strictly linear—i.e., the graph of the cost is a straight line. However, many cost relationships are curvilinear, such as illustrated in Exhibit 2-3.

2. The straight-line assumption is reasonable because any small portion of a curvilinear cost can be approximated by a straight line. The *relevant range* is the range of activity within which a particular straight line is a reasonable approximation to the curvilinear cost.

G. A *mixed cost* contains both variable and fixed cost elements. Exhibit 2-6 illustrates a mixed cost. Note that in the case of a mixed cost, the straight line representing the relation between total cost and activity does not go through zero (i.e., the origin). Examples of mixed costs include electricity, costs of processing bills, costs of admitting patients to a hospital, and maintenance.

H. Cost formula for a mixed cost.

1. The fixed and variable elements of a mixed cost can be expressed in the form of the following *cost formula*, which can be used to predict costs at all levels of activity within the relevant range:

$$Y = a + bX$$
where:
    Y = The total mixed cost
    a = The total fixed cost (the vertical intercept)
    b = The variable cost per unit of activity
          (slope of the line)
    X = The level of activity

2. In the above formula, X is known as the *independent variable* and Y is known as the *dependent variable* because the total mixed cost (Y) *depends* on the level of activity (X).

3. Each of the methods discussed below can be used to estimate the variable cost per unit, *b*, and the total fixed cost, *a*, based on data from prior periods. Then with the use of the cost formula, the expected amount of total cost, Y, can be computed for any expected activity level, X, within the relevant range.

I. The analysis of a mixed cost begins with records of past cost and activity. The first step is to plot the cost and activity data on a *scattergraph*. The cost is represented on the vertical, Y, axis and activity is represented on the horizontal, X, axis. If the scattergraph plot indicates that the relation between cost and activity is approximately linear (i.e., a straight line), the analysis can proceed to the next stage of estimating the variable cost per unit of activity and the fixed cost per period using the high-low method or least-squares regression method.

J. The *high-low method* of analyzing a mixed cost is based on using just the data at the highest and lowest levels of activity.

1. The high-low method uses the "rise over run" formula for the slope of a straight line. The change in cost observed between the two extremes (i.e., the rise) is divided by the change in activity (i.e., the run) to estimate the amount of variable cost. The formula is:

$$\frac{\text{Variable cost}}{\text{per unit of activity}} = \frac{\text{Change in cost}}{\text{Change in activity}}$$

2. The estimated variable cost per unit of activity is then used to estimate the fixed cost as follows:

Total cost at the high activity level ..	$XXX
Less variable portion:	
High activity level × variable cost.	<u>XXX</u>
Fixed portion of the mixed cost........	<u>$XXX</u>

3. The high-low method is quick, but it is not reliable because it is based on costs and activity for only two periods—the periods with the highest and lowest levels of activity. Other data are ignored. Moreover, the periods with the highest and lowest levels of activity tend to be unusual and unrepresentative of typical cost behavior.

K. The *least-squares regression method* of analyzing a mixed cost fits a straight line, called a *regression line*, to cost and activity data using a formula explained in the appendix to the chapter.

1. The least-squares regression formula calculates the slope and intercept of the straight line that minimizes the sum of the squared errors from the regression line. Because the computations are fairly complex, it is a good idea to use statistical software or a spreadsheet to do the calculations.

2. *Multiple regression* analysis should be used when more than one factor causes a cost to vary.

L. Two different formats for merchandising company income statements are covered in the chapter—the traditional format and the contribution format.

1. The *traditional format* for an income statement groups expenses into two categories—cost of goods sold and selling and administrative expenses:

Sales	$XXX
Cost of goods sold	XXX
Gross margin	XXX
Selling and administrative expense	XXX
Net operating income	$XXX

2. The *contribution format* emphasizes cost behavior. Expenses on this income statement are categorized as variable or fixed.

Sales	$XXX
Variable expenses	XXX
Contribution margin	XXX
Fixed expenses	XXX
Net operating income	$XXX

3. Variable expenses are often broken down into cost of goods sold, variable selling expenses, and variable administrative expenses. Fixed expenses are often broken down into fixed selling expenses and fixed administrative expenses.

4. The contribution approach is very useful in internal reports because it emphasizes cost behavior. As you will see in later chapters, this is very important in planning, budgeting, controlling operations, and in performance evaluation. However, the traditional format that emphasizes cost by function must be used in external reports.

M. Managers often want to know how much something (e.g., a product, a department, or a customer) costs. The item for which a cost is desired is called a *cost object*.

1. A *direct cost* is a cost that can be easily and conveniently traced to a particular cost object. For example, the salaries and commissions of salespersons in a department store's shoe department are direct costs of the shoe department.

2. An *indirect cost* is a cost that cannot be easily and conveniently traced to the cost object. For example, the salary of the manager of a department store is an indirect cost of the shoe department and other departments.

N. For purposes of making decisions, the following cost terms are often used: differential costs, opportunity costs, and sunk costs.

1. Every decision involves choosing from among at least two alternatives. A difference in cost between two alternatives is called a *differential cost*. Only the differential costs are relevant in making a choice between two alternatives. Costs that are the same for the two alternatives are not affected by the decision and should be ignored.

2. An *opportunity cost* is the potential benefit given up by selecting one alternative over another. Opportunity costs are not recorded in accounting records. They represent a lost benefit rather than an out-of-pocket cost.

3. A *sunk cost* is a cost that has already been incurred and that cannot be changed by any decision made now or in the future. Sunk costs are never differential costs and should always be ignored when making decisions.

REVIEW AND SELF-TEST
Questions and Exercises

True or False

Enter a T or an F in the blank to indicate whether the statement is true or false.

___ 1. Raw materials are basic natural resources, such as crude oil and iron ore.

___ 2. A supervisor's salary is classified as direct labor.

___ 3. Nonmanufacturing costs consist of selling costs and administrative costs.

___ 4. All selling and administrative costs are period costs.

___ 5. The terms product cost and manufacturing cost are synonyms.

___ 6. A fixed cost is constant per unit of product.

___ 7. A variable cost is a cost that changes, in total, in proportion to changes in the activity level.

___ 8. In cost analysis, activity is the dependent variable and cost is the independent variable.

___ 9. Within the relevant range, the higher the activity level, the lower the average fixed cost per unit.

___ 10. Contribution margin and gross margin mean the same thing.

___ 11. Discretionary fixed costs arise from annual decisions by management to spend in certain areas.

___ 12. Advertising is a committed fixed cost.

___ 13. A mixed cost is a cost that contains both manufacturing and non-manufacturing costs.

___ 14. In order for a cost to be variable, it must vary with either units produced or services provided.

___ 15. The contribution approach to the income statement organizes costs according to behavior, rather than according to function.

___ 16. Manufacturing overhead is an indirect cost with respect to units of product.

___ 17. Sunk costs can be either variable or fixed.

___ 18. Property taxes on factory land and insurance on a factory building are examples of manufacturing overhead.

Multiple Choice

Choose the best answer or response by placing the identifying letter in the space provided.

___ 1. Which of the following costs is not a period cost? a) indirect materials; b) advertising; c) administrative salaries; d) shipping costs; e) sales commissions.

___ 2. If the activity level increases, one would expect the fixed cost per unit to: a) increase; b) decrease; c) remain unchanged; d) none of these.

___ 3. If the activity level drops by 5%, variable costs should: a) increase per unit of product; b) drop in total by 5%; c) remain constant in total; d) decrease per unit of product.

___ 4. A company's cost formula for maintenance is $Y = \$4,000 + \$3X$, where X is machine-hours. During a period in which 2,000 machine-hours are worked, the expected maintenance cost would be: a) \$12,000; b) \$6,000; c) \$10,000; d) \$4,000.

___ 5. The costs associated with a company's basic facilities, equipment, and organization are known as: a) committed fixed costs; b) discretionary fixed costs; c) mixed costs; d) variable costs.

___ 6. Last year, Barker Company's sales were \$240,000, its fixed costs were \$50,000, and its variable costs were \$2 per unit. During the year, 80,000 units were sold. The contribution margin was: a) \$200,000; b) \$240,000; c) \$30,000; d) \$80,000.

___ 7. Which of the following is an example of a discretionary fixed cost? a) depreciation on equipment; b) rent on a factory building; c) salaries of top management; d) items a, b, and c are all discretionary fixed costs; e) none of the above.

___ 8. In March, Espresso Express had electrical costs of \$225 when the total volume was 4,500 cups of coffee served. In April, electrical costs were \$227.50 for 4,750 cups of coffee. Using the high-low method, what is the estimated fixed cost of electricity per month? a) \$200; b) \$180; c) \$225; d) \$150.

___ 9. All of the following are product costs for financial reporting except: a) indirect materials; b) advertising; c) rent on factory space; d) idle time.

Exercises

Exercise 2-1.   Classify each of the following costs as either period costs or product costs. Also indicate whether the cost is fixed or variable with respect to changes in the amount of output produced and sold.

		Period Cost	*Product Cost*	*Variable Cost*	*Fixed Cost*
Example	Rent on a sales office	X	___	___	X
Example	Direct materials...........................	___	X	X	___
a.	Sales commissions	___	___	___	___
b.	Rent on a factory building..............	___	___	___	___
c.	Headquarters secretarial salaries.....	___	___	___	___
d.	Assembly line workers...................	___	___	___	___
e.	Product advertising	___	___	___	___
f.	Cherries in a cannery	___	___	___	___
g.	Top management salaries................	___	___	___	___
h.	Lubricants for machines.................	___	___	___	___
i.	Shipping costs via express service..	___	___	___	___
j.	Executive training program............	___	___	___	___
k.	Factory supervisory salaries............	___	___	___	___

Exercise 2-2.   Data concerning the electrical costs at Doughboy Corporation follow:

	Machine-Hours	*Electrical Cost*
Week 1	6,800 hours	$1,770
Week 2	6,000 hours	$1,650
Week 3	5,400 hours	$1,560
Week 4	7,900 hours	$1,935

a. Plot the data on the following scattergraph:

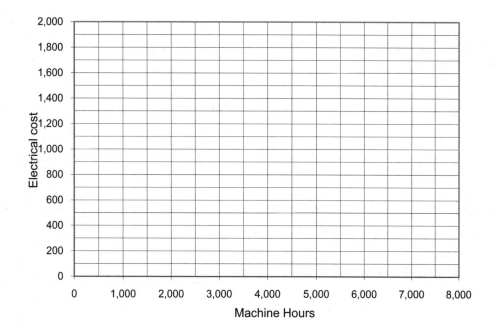

b. Is the relation between machine-hours and electrical costs approximately linear? Explain.

_____

_____

_____

_____

Exercise 2-3.   Refer to the data for Doughboy in the previous exercise.

a. Using the high-low method of cost analysis, what is the variable cost per machine-hour at Doughboy?

	Cost	Machine Hours
High activity level..........	$_____	_____
Low activity level...........	_____	_____
Change	$_____	_____

$$\frac{\text{Change in cost}}{\text{Change in activity}} = \frac{\text{_____}}{\text{_____}} = \$\text{_____}\text{ per machine hour}$$

b. Using the high-low method of cost analysis, what is the total fixed cost?

Total cost at the high activity level .... $_____

Less variable cost element:

_____............   _____

Fixed cost element............................. $_____

c. Express the cost formula for electrical costs in the form $Y = a + bX$: _____

Exercise 2-4.   Cramer's, Inc., is a wholesale distributor of a unique business software application. The company's traditional income statement for the month follows:

Cramer's, Inc.
Traditional Format Income Statement
For the Month Ended July 31

Sales...		$50,000
Cost of goods sold......................................		30,000
Gross margin..		20,000
Selling and administrative expenses:		
Selling..	$11,000	
Administrative	7,000	18,000
Net operating income.................................		$ 2,000

Redo the company's income statement for the month in the contribution format using the form on the following page. A total of $3,000 of the selling expenses and $1,000 of the administrative expenses are variable; the remainder are fixed.

Cramer's, Inc.
Contribution Format Income Statement
For the Month Ended July 31

Sales.. $_____

Variable expenses:

_____ .... $_____

_____ .... _____

_____ .... _____   _____

Contribution margin.................................   _____

Fixed expenses:

_____ .... _____

_____ .... _____   _____

Net operating income............................. $_____

Exercise 2-5.   Harry is considering whether to produce and sell classic wooden surfboards in his spare time. He would build the surfboards in his garage, which was constructed at a cost of $12,000 several years ago. The garage would be depreciated over a 20-year life. Each surfboard will require $30 of wood. He would hire students to do most of the work and would pay them $35 for each surfboard completed. He would rent tools at a cost of $400 per month. Harry can draw money out of savings to provide the capital needed to get the operation going. The savings are earning interest at 6% annually. An ad agency would handle advertising at a cost of $500 per month. Harry would hire students to sell the surfboards and pay a commission of $20 per board.

Required:

Classify each cost as a variable cost, fixed cost, selling and administration cost, product cost, manufacturing overhead cost, sunk cost, opportunity cost, and/or differential cost (a single item may be identified as many types of costs). A cost should be classified as variable if it is variable with respect to the number of surfboards produced and sold. A cost should be classified as a differential cost if it differs between the alternatives of producing or not producing the surfboards.

	Variable cost	Fixed cost	Selling and administrative cost	Product cost	Manufacturing overhead cost	Sunk cost	Opportunity cost	Differential cost
Original cost of garage..	____	____	____	____	____	____	____	____
Depreciation on the garage......................	____	____	____	____	____	____	____	____
Wood for each surfboard	____	____	____	____	____	____	____	____
Student workers	____	____	____	____	____	____	____	____
Tool rental....................	____	____	____	____	____	____	____	____
Interest on savings	____	____	____	____	____	____	____	____
Advertising costs	____	____	____	____	____	____	____	____
Sales commissions........	____	____	____	____	____	____	____	____

Answers to Questions and Exercises

True or False

1. F Raw materials are materials used to make a product—including parts or subassemblies produced by a supplier. They are not necessarily basic natural resources.

2. F Supervisors do not work directly on products and therefore are not classified as direct labor.

3. T True by definition.

4. T Selling and administrative costs are period costs because they are charged against income in the period in which they are incurred.

5. T These two terms are synonyms.

6. F A fixed cost is constant in total amount; on a per unit basis, it varies inversely with changes in the level of activity.

7. T This is the definition of a variable cost.

8. F Activity is the independent variable and cost is the dependent variable. Cost depends on activity, not the other way around.

9. T The average fixed cost per unit becomes progressively smaller as the level of activity increases.

10. F Contribution margin is sales less variable expenses; gross margin is sales less cost of goods sold.

11. T Discretionary fixed costs are reevaluated each year by management.

12. F Advertising is a discretionary fixed cost because the company's advertising budget is typically reevaluated on an annual basis.

13. F Mixed costs contain both variable and fixed cost elements.

14. F Activity can be measured in many ways besides units produced and units sold. Examples of other activity measures include miles driven, number of beds occupied in a hospital, and number of flight hours.

15. T The contribution approach groups variable costs together and fixed costs together; thus, the income statement is organized according to cost behavior.

16. T Manufacturing overhead cost is an indirect cost; only direct materials and direct labor are direct manufacturing costs.

17. T A sunk cost is a cost that has already been incurred and can be variable or fixed. If obsolete materials have already been purchased, for example, then the cost of the materials is a sunk cost.

18. T Manufacturing overhead consists of all production costs except direct materials and direct labor.

Multiple Choice

1. a Indirect materials are part of manufacturing overhead and thus are classified as a product cost.

2. b The fixed cost per unit should drop as activity increases because a constant amount is spread over more units.

3. b By definition, total variable cost changes in proportion to changes in the activity level.

4. c

Fixed cost......................................	$ 4,000
Variable cost:	
2,000 hours × $3 per hour	6,000
Total cost	$10,000

5. a Committed fixed costs relate to basic facilities, equipment, and organization.

6. d

Sales...	$240,000
Less variable cost:	
80,000 units × $2 per unit	160,000
Contribution margin........................	$ 80,000

7. e All of the listed costs are generally considered to be committed fixed costs.

8. b

	Cost	*Cups*
High activity level..	$227.50	4,750
Low activity level ..	225.00	4,500
Change	$ 2.50	250

$$\frac{\text{Change in cost}}{\text{Change in activity}} = \frac{\$2.50}{250 \text{ cups}} = \$0.01 \text{ per cup}$$

14

Total cost at the high activity $227.50
Less variable cost element:
   4,750 cups × $0.01 per cup............   47.50
Fixed cost element............................ $180.00

9. b   Advertising is a period cost rather than a product cost.

Exercises

Exercise 2-1.

		Period Cost	*Product Cost*	*Variable Cost*	*Fixed Cost*
a.	Sales commissions..........................	X		X	
b.	Rent on a factory building		X		X
c.	Headquarters secretarial salaries.....	X			X
d.	Assembly line workers		X	X	
e.	Product advertising.........................	X			X
f.	Cherries in a cannery		X	X	
g.	Top management salaries	X			X
h.	Lubricants for machines		X	X	
i.	Shipping costs via express service..	X		X	
j.	Executive training program	X			X
k.	Factory supervisory salaries		X		X

Exercise 2-2.

a. The scattergraph plot looks like this:

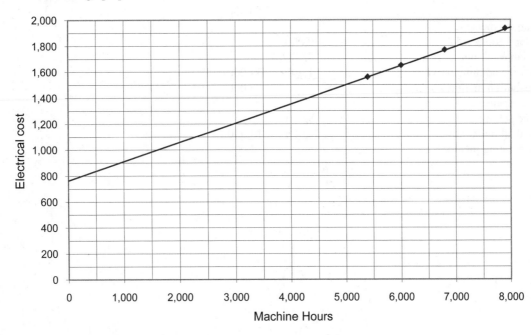

b. The relation between machine-hours and electrical costs is almost perfectly linear—a straight line can be drawn through all of the points on the scattergraph.

Exercise 2-3.

a. Variable cost per machine-hour:

	Cost	Machine Hours
High activity level............	$1,935	7,900
Low activity level............	1,560	5,400
Change	$ 375	2,500

$$\frac{\text{Change in cost}}{\text{Change in activity}} = \frac{\$375}{2,500 \text{ machine-hours}} = \$0.15 \text{ per machine-hour}$$

b. Total fixed cost:

Total cost at the high activity level	$1,935
Less variable cost element:	
7,900 hours × $0.15 per hour	1,185
Fixed cost element.............................	$ 750

c. The cost formula for electrical costs is $750 per period, plus $0.15 per machine-hour, or
$$Y = \$750 + \$0.15X$$

Exercise 2-4.

Cramer's, Inc.
Contribution Format Income Statement
For the Month Ended July 31

Sales..		$50,000
Variable expenses:		
Cost of goods sold	$30,000	
Variable selling...............................	3,000	
Variable administrative....................	1,000	34,000
Contribution margin...........................		16,000
Fixed expenses:		
Fixed selling	8,000	
Fixed administrative	6,000	14,000
Net operating income.........................		$ 2,000

16

Exercise 2-5.

	Variable cost	Fixed cost	Selling & administrative cost	Product cost	Manufacturing overhead cost	Sunk cost	Opportunity cost	Differential cost
Original cost of garage..						X		
Depreciation on the garage.........................		X		X	X			(1)
Wood for each surfboard	X			X				X
Student workers	X			X				X
Tool rental......................		X		X	X			X
Interest on savings							X	(2)
Advertising costs		X	X					X
Sales commissions	X		X					X

(1) This is not a differential cost if the depreciation on the garage is the same regardless of whether it is used to make surfboards or is used as a residential garage.

(2) This may be considered to be a differential cost, although some would say that it is not because it is a foregone benefit rather than a cost *per se*.

Appendix 2A

Least-Squares Regression Computations

APPENDIX HIGHLIGHTS

A. The formulas for computing the variable cost per unit, b, and total fixed cost, a, using the least-squares regression method are:

$$b = \frac{n\left(\sum XY\right) - \left(\sum X\right)\left(\sum Y\right)}{n\left(\sum X^2\right) - \left(\sum X\right)^2}$$

$$a = \frac{\left(\sum Y\right) - b\left(\sum X\right)}{n}$$

where n is the number of observations; X is the activity; and Y is the cost.

B. The appendix illustrates how to use built-in functions in Microsoft Excel to do a regression analysis.

REVIEW AND SELF-TEST
Questions and Exercises

Exercise

Exercise 2A-1.   Data concerning activity in the shipping department of Osan, Inc. are given below:

	Units Shipped	Shipping Cost
Monday	12	$595
Tuesday	17	$640
Wednesday	10	$555
Thursday	7	$500
Friday	9	$545
Saturday	5	$480

a. Estimate the fixed shipping cost per day. (Use statistical software or see Appendix 2A for instructions concerning how to use Excel to compute this value.)

   a = _____

b. Using the least-squares method, estimate the variable cost per unit shipped. (Use statistical software or see Appendix 2A for instructions concerning how to use Excel to compute this value.)

   b = _____

c. Express the cost formula for shipping costs in the form Y = a + bX: _____

Answers to Questions and Exercises

Exercise

Exercise 2A-1.

    a. Using statistical software or Excel will yield an estimate of the fixed cost of about $413 per day.

    b. The least-squares regression estimate of the variable cost is about $13.92 per unit shipped.

    c. The cost formula is Y = $413 + $13.92X.

Appendix 2B

Cost of Quality

APPENDIX HIGHLIGHTS

A. The term quality is used in many ways. It can mean a luxurious product with many features or it can mean a product that is free of defects. We use the term quality in the latter sense. *Quality of conformance* is the degree to which a product or service meets its design specifications and is free of defects or other problems that might affect appearance or performance.

B. Defects (i.e., poor quality of conformance) result in costs that can be classified as prevention costs, appraisal costs, internal failure costs, and external failure costs.

 1. Internal failure costs and external failure costs result from defects that occur in products.

  a. *Internal failure costs* result from correcting defects in products before they are shipped to customers. Internal failure costs include scrap, reworking of defective units, and downtime.

  b. *External failure costs* result when a defective product is delivered to a customer. These costs include warranty repairs, exchanges, returns, and loss of future sales. It is best to detect defective goods before they get into the hands of customers. A dissatisfied customer will not buy from the company in the future and is likely to tell others of his or her dissatisfaction.

 2. Prevention costs and appraisal costs are incurred to prevent defects and reduce the likelihood of external failures.

  a. *Prevention costs* are incurred to reduce or eliminate defects. Prevention is often simple and inexpensive. For example, a simple metal shield can prevent drilling a hole in the wrong place. Prevention costs include the costs of quality engineering and quality improvement projects.

  b. *Appraisal costs* are incurred to identify defective products prior to shipping them to customers. These costs include wages of inspection workers and the costs of testing equipment.

C. In most companies, the total cost of quality (the sum of prevention costs, appraisal costs, internal failure costs, and external failure costs) decreases as the defect rate improves—at least until very low levels of defect rates occur. (A higher quality of conformance means a lower defect rate.) Exhibit 2B-2 illustrates this relation between total cost of quality and defect rates.

 1. Reducing the defect rate (e.g., defects per million parts) involves spending more on prevention and appraisal. However, this additional spending is usually more than offset by reductions in the costs of internal and external failures caused by defects.

 2. Most companies would benefit from putting more effort into prevention. This reduces the need for appraisal and decreases the incidence of internal and external failures.

D. Quality costs are summarized for management on a *quality cost report* such as in Exhibit 2B-3.

 1. The report classifies the costs of quality into the four categories discussed above.

 2. The report should summarize costs associated with defective products and services throughout the organization—all the way from research and development through customer service. The report should not be limited to just manufacturing costs.

 3. Such a report helps managers see the financial significance of defects and it aids managers in diagnosing whether their quality costs are poorly distributed (e.g., too much external failure cost relative to prevention cost).

REVIEW AND SELF-TEST
Questions and Exercises

True or False

Enter a T or an F in the blank to indicate whether the statement is true or false.

___ 1. A product containing defects has a poor quality of conformance.

___ 2. The best quality systems are those that put their emphasis on appraisal costs.

Multiple Choice

Choose the best answer or response by placing the identifying letter in the space provided.

___ 1. The cost of quality training is an example of a(n): a) prevention cost; b) appraisal cost; c) internal failure cost; d) external failure cost.

___ 2. The cost of warranty repairs is an example of a(n): a) prevention cost; b) appraisal cost; c) internal failure cost; d) external failure cost.

___ 3. The cost of rework labor is an example of a(n): a) prevention cost; b) appraisal cost; c) internal failure cost; d) external failure cost.

___ 4. The cost of supplies used in testing and inspection is an example of a(n): a) prevention cost; b) appraisal cost; c) internal failure cost; d) external failure cost.

___ 5. The cost of lost sales due to a reputation for poor quality is an example of a(n): a) prevention cost; b) appraisal cost; c) internal failure cost; d) external failure cost.

Exercise

Exercise 2B-1.   The management of Jehrol Fantasy Products would like for you to compile a quality cost report using the following data:

Net cost of scrap...	$90,000
Disposal of defective products	$17,000
Maintenance of test equipment.........................	$61,000
Rework labor and overhead...............................	$69,000
Depreciation of test equipment	$28,000
Systems development..	$40,000
Quality training	$82,000
Warranty repairs and replacements	$89,000
Liability arising from defective products	$61,000

The company's total sales for the year were $10,000,000.

Prepare the company's quality cost report using the form below:

Jehrol Fantasy Products
Quality Cost Report

	Amount	Percent of Sales
Prevention costs:		
_____	$_____	_____ %
_____	_____	_____ %
Total prevention cost...................................	_____	_____ %
Appraisal costs:		
_____	_____	_____ %
_____	_____	_____ %
Total appraisal cost.....................................	_____	_____ %
Internal failure costs:		
_____	_____	_____ %
_____	_____	_____ %
_____	_____	_____ %
Total internal failure cost	_____	_____ %
External failure costs:		
_____	_____	_____ %
_____	_____	_____ %
Total external failure cost............................	_____	_____ %
Total quality cost	$_____	_____ %

Answers to Questions and Exercises

True or False

1. T   Quality of conformance indicates how well a product meets its design specifications and is free of defects and other problems.

2. F   The best quality systems emphasize prevention costs.

Multiple Choice

1. a   See Exhibit 2B-1.

2. d   See Exhibit 2B-1.

3. c   See Exhibit 2B-1.

4. b   See Exhibit 2B-1.

5. d   See Exhibit 2B-1.

Exercise

Exercise 2B-1.

Jehrol Fantasy Products
Quality Cost Report

	Amount	Percent of Sales
Prevention costs:		
Systems development	$ 40,000	0.40%
Quality training	82,000	0.82%
Total prevention costs	122,000	1.22%
Appraisal costs:		
Depreciation of test equipment	28,000	0.28%
Maintenance of test equipment	61,000	0.61%
Total appraisal cost	89,000	0.89%
Internal failure costs:		
Rework labor and overhead	69,000	0.69%
Net cost of scrap	90,000	0.90%
Disposal of defective products	17,000	0.17%
Total internal failure cost	176,000	1.76%
External failure costs:		
Warranty repairs and replacements	89,000	0.89%
Liability arising from defective products	61,000	0.61%
Total external failure cost	150,000	1.50%
Total quality cost	$537,000	5.37%

Job-Order Costing

Chapter Study Suggestions

This chapter expands on the concepts introduced in Chapter 2 and provides more details concerning how product costs are determined. The chapter covers a costing method called *job-order costing*. Exhibit 3-5 provides an overall view of the flow of costs in a job-order cost system. Pay particular attention to the section in the chapter titled "Applying Manufacturing Overhead." *Overhead application is a key concept.*

Exhibits 3-6, 3-7, and 3-8 show how direct materials, direct labor, and overhead costs are assigned to jobs. Study these exhibits with particular care—these concepts are likely to show up in homework. Exhibits 3-10 and 3-11 summarize the cost flows and illustrate the statements of cost of goods manufactured and cost of goods sold. Study and then *restudy* the section titled "Underapplied and Overapplied Overhead," paying particular attention to how underapplied and overapplied overhead is computed.

CHAPTER HIGHLIGHTS

A. *Job-order costing* is used in situations where many different products or services are produced each period. Examples include special-order printing, custom furniture manufacturing, and a consulting company.

B. When materials are purchased, their costs are recorded in the Raw Materials inventory account, which is an asset. If the materials are paid for with cash, the journal entry would look like this:

Raw Materials	XXX	
Cash		XXX

1. When a job is started, materials are withdrawn from storage. The document that authorizes this withdrawal is called a *materials requisition form*. This form lists all the materials required to complete a specific job. The journal entry to record withdrawal of materials from the storeroom for use in production is:

Work in Process	XXX	
Manufacturing Overhead	XXX	
Raw Materials		XXX

Materials that are traced directly to jobs are classified as *direct materials* and are debited to Work in Process. Any materials that are not directly traced to jobs are classified as *indirect materials* and are debited to a special control account called *Manufacturing Overhead.*

2. When materials are placed into production, they are also recorded on a *job cost sheet*, which summarizes all production costs assigned to a particular job. Exhibit 3-2 in the text illustrates a job cost sheet.

C. Labor costs are recorded by employees on *time tickets*. These documents list the amount of time each employee works on specific jobs and tasks.

1. Labor time spent working directly on specific jobs is *direct labor*. Labor time spent working on supportive tasks (e.g., supervision, maintenance, janitorial) is *indirect labor*. The entry to record labor costs is:

Work in Process	XXX	
Manufacturing Overhead	XXX	
Salaries and Wages Payable		XXX

Direct labor costs are debited to Work in Process. Indirect labor costs are debited to the control account Manufacturing Overhead.

2. Direct labor costs are added to the individual job cost sheets at the same time they are recorded in the formal accounts.

D. As explained in Chapter 2, manufacturing overhead consists of *indirect* manufacturing costs that cannot be easily traced to individual products or jobs. Manufacturing overhead costs are assigned to jobs using a *predetermined overhead rate*.

1. The predetermined overhead rate is computed *before* the period begins and is based on estimated data. The formula is:

$$\text{Predetermined overhead rate} = \frac{\text{Estimated total manufacturing overhead cost}}{\text{Estimated total amount of the allocation base}}$$

An *allocation base* is a measure of activity, such as direct labor-hours, direct labor cost, or machine-hours that all jobs have in common. Ideally, the allocation base should actually cause variations in manufacturing overhead costs, but in practice this ideal is often ignored.

2. To assign overhead costs to a job, the predetermined overhead rate is multiplied by the actual amount of the allocation base incurred by the job. For example, suppose that a particular job incurs 20 direct labor-hours and the predetermined overhead rate is $40 per direct labor-hour. Then $800 (20 direct labor-hours × $40 per direct labor-hour) of overhead cost would be *applied* to that job. This $800 is called *overhead applied*. Note that this is not actual overhead spending on the job. The $800 may have little to do with any overhead that is actually caused by the job. It is simply a way of distributing the overhead costs that were estimated at the beginning of the year among the jobs worked on during the year.

3. The overhead that is applied to a job is entered on its job cost sheet and is recorded in the company's formal accounts with the following journal entry:

Work in Process	XXX	
Manufacturing Overhead		XXX

Note that in this case, the Manufacturing Overhead control account is credited rather than debited.

4. Actual overhead costs are *not* charged to Work in Process. Instead, they are charged to the Manufacturing Overhead control account as we saw in the entries for indirect labor and indirect materials above.

Note that *actual overhead costs all appear as debits to Manufacturing Overhead.*

E. When jobs are completed, their costs are transferred from Work in Process to Finished Goods. The journal entry is:

Finished Goods	XXX	
Work in Process		XXX

When completed products are sold, their costs are transferred from Finished Goods to Cost of Goods Sold. The journal entry is:

Cost of Goods Sold	XXX	
Finished Goods		XXX

F. This section describes the computation of cost of goods manufactured, cost of goods sold, and preparation of the income statement.

    1. Computing the cost of goods sold for a manufacturing company involves a number of steps. These steps rely on the following basic model that describes flows into and out of any inventory account.

        Basic inventory flows:
        Beginning balance
  + Additions to inventory
  = Available
  − Ending balance
  = Withdrawals from inventory

    2. To compute the raw materials used in production, this basic model is written as follows:

        Beginning balance raw materials
  + Purchases of raw materials
  = Total raw materials available
  − Ending balance raw materials
  = Raw materials used in production

The raw materials used in production may include both direct materials and indirect materials.

    3. The next step is to compute the total manufacturing cost for the period. This is the sum of direct materials, direct labor, and manufacturing overhead costs:

        Direct materials
  + Direct labor
  + Manufacturing overhead applied
  = Total manufacturing cost

    4. The next step is to compute the *cost of goods manufactured*, which is the cost of the goods that were *finished* during the period.

        Beginning balance, work in process
  + Total manufacturing cost
  − Ending balance, work in process
  = Cost of goods manufactured

    5. The final step in the computation of cost of goods sold is also based on the inventory flow model:

        Beginning balance, finished goods
  + Cost of goods manufactured
  = Cost of goods available for sale
  − Ending balance, finished goods
  = Unadjusted cost of goods sold

The unadjusted cost of goods sold will be adjusted for any overhead that is overapplied or underapplied as described later in this outline.

    6. The income statement in a manufacturing company may or may not show the computation of the cost of goods sold as shown above. Ordinarily, at least in external financial reports, only the summary cost of goods sold and selling and administrative expense are shown as follows:

        Sales
  − Cost of goods sold
  = Gross margin
  − Selling and administrative expenses
  = Net operating income

G. Generally, the amount of overhead cost *applied* to Work in Process will differ from the amount of *actual* overhead cost incurred. This difference is reflected in a debit or credit balance in the Manufacturing Overhead account.

    1. If overhead applied is less than the actual overhead costs incurred, then overhead has been *underapplied.* In this case, the Manufacturing Overhead account will have a debit balance.

    2. If overhead applied to Work in Process exceeds the amount of overhead cost actually incurred, then overhead has been *overapplied.* In this case, the Manufacturing Overhead account will have a credit balance.

    3. At the end of a period, underapplied or overapplied overhead may be closed out to Cost of Goods Sold or it may be allocated among Work in Process, Finished Goods, and Cost of Goods Sold.

      a. Closing out any balance to Cost of Goods Sold is simpler than the allocation method. If overhead has been underapplied, the entry would be:

Cost of Goods Sold	XXX	
Manufacturing Overhead		XXX

If overhead has been underapplied, not enough overhead cost was applied to jobs during the period, and therefore costs are understated in the accounts. The journal entry above adjusts Cost of Goods Sold so that it is no longer understated.

If overhead has been overapplied, the journal entry would be:

Manufacturing Overhead	XXX	
Cost of Goods Sold		XXX

If overhead has been overapplied, too much overhead cost was applied to jobs during the period, and therefore costs are overstated in the accounts. The above journal entry adjusts Cost of Goods Sold so that it is no longer overstated.

b.   Allocating any underapplied or overapplied overhead among inventory accounts and Cost of Goods Sold is more complex, but is considered to be more accurate. The allocation is based on the amount of the overhead applied during the current period that remains in the ending balances of the Work in Process, Finished Goods, and Cost of Goods Sold accounts. Assuming that overhead is underapplied, the journal entry would be:

Work in Process	XXX	
Finished Goods	XXX	
Cost of Goods Sold	XXX	
Manufacturing Overhead		XXX

H. For simplicity, the chapter assumes that a single "plant-wide" overhead rate is used. Many companies use *multiple overhead rates* rather than a single plant wide rate. In such a system, each processing department, work center, or business activity has its own predetermined overhead rate. These more complex systems will be investigated in a later chapter.

REVIEW AND SELF-TEST
Questions and Exercises

True or False

Enter a T or an F in the blank to indicate whether the statement is true or false.

____ 1. A company producing many different kinds of furniture would probably use a job-order cost system.

____ 2. Most manufacturing overhead costs are direct costs that can be easily traced to specific jobs.

____ 3. The predetermined overhead rate is computed using estimates of overhead cost and the amount of the allocation base for the upcoming period.

____ 4. The cost of indirect materials used in production is added to the Manufacturing Overhead account rather than added directly to Work in Process.

____ 5. A job cost sheet is used to accumulate the costs charged to a particular job.

____ 6. Actual manufacturing overhead costs are charged directly to the Work in Process account as the costs are incurred.

____ 7. Selling and administrative expenses are charged to the Manufacturing Overhead account.

____ 8. Cost of goods manufactured is an expense in a manufacturing company.

____ 9. Factory depreciation is included in assets on the balance sheet if goods are uncompleted or unsold at the end of a period.

____ 10. If more manufacturing overhead is applied to Work in Process than is actually incurred, then overhead cost is overapplied.

____ 11. A debit balance in the Manufacturing Overhead account at the end of a period means that overhead was underapplied for the period.

____ 12. Any balance in the Work in Process account at the end of a period should be closed to Cost of Goods Sold.

____ 13. Underapplied or overapplied overhead is computed by finding the difference between actual overhead costs and the amount of overhead cost applied to Work in Process.

Multiple Choice

Choose the best answer or response by placing the identifying letter in the space provided.

____ 1. In a job-order costing system, the basic document for accumulating costs for a specific job is: a) the materials requisition form; b) the job cost sheet; c) the Work in Process inventory account; d) the labor time ticket.

____ 2. Suppose $30,000 of raw materials are purchased. What account is debited? a) Work in Process inventory; b) Raw Materials inventory; c) Cost of Goods Sold; d) Manufacturing Overhead.

____ 3. Suppose $20,000 of raw materials is withdrawn from the storeroom to be used in production. Of this amount, $15,000 consists of direct materials and $5,000 consists of indirect materials. What account or accounts will be debited? a) Work in Process $15,000 and Raw Materials $5,000; b) Raw Materials $15,000 and Manufacturing Overhead $5,000; c) Manufacturing Overhead $15,000 and Work in Process $5,000; d) Work in Process $15,000 and Manufacturing Overhead $5,000.

____ 4. Suppose $70,000 of wages and salaries is earned by employees. Of this amount, $20,000 consists of direct labor; $10,000 consists of indirect labor; and $40,000 consists of administrative salaries. What account or accounts will be debited? a) Work in Process $20,000 and Manufacturing Overhead $10,000 and Administrative Salary Expense $40,000; b) Direct Labor $20,000 and Indirect Labor $10,000 and Administrative Salary Expense $40,000; c) Work in Process $20,000 and Manufacturing Overhead $50,000; d) Direct Labor $20,000 and Manufacturing Overhead $50,000.

____ 5. Suppose jobs are completed whose job cost sheets total to $120,000. What account will be debited? a) Manufacturing Overhead $120,000; b) Cost of Goods Sold $120,000; c) Work in Process $120,000; d) Finished Goods $120,000.

____ 6. Suppose a total of $30,000 of overhead is applied to jobs. What account will be debited? a) Manufacturing Overhead $30,000; b) Cost of Goods Sold $30,000; c) Work in Process $30,000; d) Finished Goods $30,000.

___ 7. The term used to describe the cost of goods transferred from work in process inventory to finished goods inventory is: a) cost of goods sold; b) raw materials; c) period cost; d) cost of goods manufactured.

___ 8. Manufacturing cost is synonymous with all of the following terms except: a) product cost; b) inventoriable cost; c) period cost; d) direct materials, direct labor, and manufacturing cost.

___ 9. Walston Manufacturing Company has provided the following data concerning its raw materials inventories last month:

Beginning raw materials inventory	$ 80,000
Purchases of raw materials.................	$420,000
Ending raw materials inventory	$ 50,000

The cost of the raw materials used in production for the month was: a) $500,000; b) $450,000; c) $390,000; d) $470,000.

___ 10. Juniper Company has provided the following data concerning its manufacturing costs and work in process inventories last month:

Raw materials used in production	$270,000
Direct labor	$140,000
Manufacturing overhead	$190,000
Beginning work in process inventory.	$ 50,000
Ending work in process inventory......	$ 80,000

The cost of goods manufactured for the month was: a) $730,000; b) $630,000; c) $600,000; d) $570,000.

___ 11. Vonder Inc. has provided the following data concerning its finished goods inventories last month:

Beginning finished goods inventory...	$110,000
Cost of goods manufactured...............	$760,000
Ending finished goods inventory........	$ 70,000

The cost of goods sold for the month was: a) $800,000; b) $720,000; c) $950,000; d) $280,000.

___ 12. Last year, a company reported estimated overhead of $100,000, actual overhead of $90,000, and applied overhead of $92,000. The company's manufacturing overhead cost for the year was: a) underapplied, $10,000; b) underapplied, $8,000; c) overapplied, $2,000; d) overapplied, $10,000.

___ 13. Jurden Company bases its predetermined overhead rates on machine-hours. At the beginning of the year, the company estimated $60,000 of manufacturing overhead and 40,000 machine-hours for the year. Actual manufacturing overhead for year amounted to $65,100 and the actual machine-hours totaled 42,000. Manufacturing overhead for the year was: a) underapplied by $2,100; b) overapplied by $3,000; c) underapplied by $3,000; d) overapplied by $5,100.

___ 14. On January 1, Hessler Company's Work in Process account had a balance of $18,000. During the year, direct materials costing $35,000 were placed into production. Direct labor cost for the year was $60,000. The predetermined overhead rate for the year was set at 150% of direct labor cost. Actual overhead costs for the year totaled $92,000. Jobs costing $190,000 to manufacture according to their job cost sheets were completed during the year. On December 31, the balance in the Work in Process inventory account was: a) $13,000; b) $18,000; c) $15,000; d) $8,000.

___ 15. Cost of Goods Manufactured represents: a) the amount of cost charged to Work in Process during the period; b) the amount transferred from Work in Process to Finished Goods during the period; c) the amount of cost placed into production during the period; d) none of these.

___ 16. If overhead is overapplied for a period, it means that: a) the predetermined overhead rate used to apply overhead cost to Work in Process was too low; b) the company incurred more overhead cost than it charged to Work in Process; c) too much cost has been assigned to jobs; d) none of these.

___ 17. Malt Company's Manufacturing Overhead account showed a $10,000 underapplied overhead balance on December 31. Other accounts showed the following amounts of overhead applied from the current period in their ending balances:

Work in Process...........	$ 40,000
Finished Goods	$ 60,000
Cost of Goods Sold......	$ 100,000

If the company allocates the underapplied overhead among Cost of Goods Sold, Work in Process, and Finished Goods, the amount allocated to Work in Process was: a) $2,000; b) $4,000; c) $1,600; d) $1,800.

Exercises

Exercise 3-1.   Bartle Company uses a job-order cost system and applies overhead with a predetermined overhead rate based on direct labor-hours. At the beginning of the year the estimated total manufacturing overhead for the year was $150,000 and the estimated level of activity was 100,000 direct labor-hours. At the end of the year, the actual manufacturing overhead costs totaled $160,000 and 105,000 direct labor-hours had been worked.

a. The predetermined overhead rate for the year was $_____

b. Manufacturing overhead cost applied to work in process during the year was $_____

c. The amount of underapplied or overapplied overhead cost for the year was $_____

Exercise 3-2.   The following selected account balances are taken from the books of Pardoe Company as of January 1 of the most recent year:

Cash	Work in Process	Accounts Payable	Sales
12,000	40,000	75,000	

Accounts Receivable	Finished Goods	Salaries and Wages Payable	Cost of Goods Sold
48,000	100,000	12,000	

Prepaid Insurance	Accumulated Depreciation		
8,000	120,000		

Raw Materials	Manufacturing Overhead		
30,000			

The following data relate to the activities of Pardoe Company during the year:
1. Raw materials purchased on account, $150,000.
2. Raw materials issued to production, $145,000 (all direct materials).
3. Advertising cost incurred for the year, $50,000 (credit accounts payable).
4. Utilities cost incurred for the factory, $35,000 (credit accounts payable).
5. Salaries and wages costs incurred: direct labor, $250,000 (30,000 hours); indirect labor, $75,000; selling and administrative, $140,000.
6. Depreciation recorded for the year, $20,000, of which 75% related to manufacturing and 25% related to selling and administrative functions.
7. Other manufacturing overhead costs incurred for the year, $30,000 (credit accounts payable).
8. Other selling and administrative expenses incurred for the year, $25,000 (credit accounts payable).
9. Prepaid insurance of $4,000 expired during the year; all of this is related to the factory.
10. The company applies manufacturing overhead on the basis of direct labor-hours at $5.50 per hour.
11. The cost of goods manufactured for the year totaled $550,000.
12. Goods that cost $540,000 according to their job cost sheets were sold on account for $800,000.
13. Collections on account from customers during the year totaled $790,000.
14. Cash disbursed during the year: on accounts payable, $300,000; for salaries and wages, $460,000.

Required:
a. Post the above entries directly to Pardoe Company's T-accounts on the previous page. Key your entries with the numbers 1-14.
b. Compute the ending balance in each T-account.
c. Is overhead underapplied or overapplied for the year? Close the balance to Cost of Goods Sold. (Key the entry as #15.)
d. Prepare an income statement for the year using the form that appears below.

Pardoe Company
Income Statement

Sales .... $_____

Cost of goods sold................................. _____

Gross margin .... _____

Selling and administrative expenses:

_____ .... $_____

_____ .... _____

_____ .... _____

_____ .... _____ _____

Net operating income .... $_____

Exercise 3-3.   The following data were taken from the Precision Milling Machine, Inc., cost records for the current year. Compute the amount of raw materials used in production during the year:

Raw materials inventory, beginning	$ 10,000
Raw materials inventory, ending	$ 15,000
Purchases of raw materials...........................	$145,000

_____

_____

_____

_____

_____

_____

_____

_____

Exercise 3-4.   Suppose all of the raw materials used in production by Precision Milling Machine in the preceding exercise were direct materials. The company has supplied the following additional information:

Direct labor cost..	$240,000
Manufacturing overhead applied	$ 90,000
Work in process inventory, beginning	$ 60,000
Work in process inventory, ending	$ 75,000

Compute the cost of goods manufactured for the year.

_____

_____

_____

_____

_____

_____

_____

_____

Exercise 3-5.   Using the following data and the form that appears below, prepare a Schedule of Cost of Goods Manufactured.

Direct labor	$ 90,000
Sales commissions	$ 24,600
Purchases of raw materials	$120,000
Work in process, beginning	$ 16,000
Work in process, ending	$ 11,500
Raw materials, beginning	$ 15,000
Raw materials, ending	$ 5,000
Manufacturing overhead	$ 30,300

Schedule of Cost of Goods Manufactured
(See Exhibit 2-6 in the text for the proper format)

Direct materials:

_____ ..... $_____

_____ ..... _____

_____ ..... _____

_____ ..... _____

_____ .... $_____

Direct labor .... _____

Manufacturing overhead .... _____

_____ .... _____

_____ .... _____

_____

_____ .... _____

Cost of goods manufactured .... $_____

Exercise 3-6.   Precision Milling Machine Company has supplied the following additional information. Use this data together with your answer to exercise 3-4 above to compute the (adjusted) Cost of Goods Sold for the company. Close out any balance in Manufacturing Overhead to Cost of Goods Sold.

Actual manufacturing overhead incurred.....	$ 88,000
Finished goods inventory, beginning...........	$120,000
Finished goods inventory, ending................	$145,000

Exercise 3-7.   **Critical thought writing exercise:** Quality Foods, Inc., is a major producer of canned vegetables, fruits, and other goods. This year the company planned a normal year of producing canned goods and set its predetermined overhead rate the same as in other years. However, during the year a major freeze in key growing areas wiped out much of the expected fruit crop and the company was able to do little canning of fruit. A large amount of the manufacturing overhead cost associated with producing canned goods consists of depreciation and other fixed costs. Would you expect Quality Foods, Inc., to have underapplied or overapplied manufacturing overhead cost this year? Explain.

Answers to Questions and Exercises

True or False

1. T Job-order costing is used when many different kinds of products are made.

2. F Only direct materials and direct labor are direct costs; manufacturing overhead cannot be easily traced to specific jobs.

3. T Estimates are used because the rate is developed before the period begins.

4. T Indirect costs are charged to the Manufacturing Overhead account.

5. T A separate job cost sheet is prepared for each job which is used to accumulate costs as they are charged to the job.

6. F Actual manufacturing overhead costs are charged to the Manufacturing Overhead account—not to Work in Process.

7. F Selling and administrative expenses are period costs, not product costs.

8. F Cost of goods manufactured is not an expense. It is the amount transferred from work in process to finished goods inventory when goods are completed. This is a subtle, but important, point.

9. T Manufacturing costs such as factory depreciation are assigned to units during production. If these units are not complete or not sold at the end of a period, then the manufacturing costs incurred to date are included as part of Work in Process or Finished Goods inventories which are assets on the balance sheet.

10. T This is true by definition.

11. T A debit balance in Manufacturing Overhead means that more overhead cost was incurred than was applied to Work in Process. Thus, manufacturing overhead was underapplied.

12. F Any balance in the Manufacturing Overhead account (not Work in Process) should be closed to Cost of Goods Sold or allocated among ending inventories and Cost of Goods Sold.

13. T By definition, this is how underapplied or overapplied overhead cost is computed.

Multiple Choice

1. b The job cost sheet is used to accumulate direct materials, direct labor, and overhead costs.

2. b The journal entry would be:

Raw Materials	30,000	
Cash or Accounts Payable		30,000

3. d The journal entry would be:

Work in Process	15,000	
Manufacturing Overhead	5,000	
Raw Materials		20,000

4. a The journal entry would be:

Work in Process	20,000	
Manufacturing Overhead	10,000	
Administrative Salaries Expense	40,000	
Wages and Salaries Payable		70,000

5. d The journal entry would be:

Finished Goods	120,000	
Work in Process		120,000

6. c The journal entry would be:

Work in Process	30,000	
Manufacturing Overhead		30,000

7. d Goods that are completed and ready for sale move out of work in process and into finished goods. The cost of such goods is termed cost of goods manufactured.

8. c A period cost is charged against the period in which the cost is incurred; it has nothing to do with manufacturing a product.

9. b The computations are as follows:

Beginning raw materials inventory	$ 80,000
Add: Purchases of raw materials	420,000
Raw materials available for use	500,000
Deduct: Ending raw materials inventory	50,000
Raw materials used in production	$450,000

10. d   The computations are as follows:

Raw materials used in production...	$270,000
Direct labor	140,000
Manufacturing overhead	190,000
Total manufacturing costs	600,000
Add: Beginning work in process inventory	50,000
	650,000
Deduct: Ending work in process inventory	80,000
Cost of goods manufactured	$570,000

11. a   The cost of goods sold is computed as follows:

Beginning finished goods inventory	$110,000
Add: Cost of goods manufactured ..	760,000
Cost of goods available for sale	870,000
Deduct: Ending finished goods inventory	70,000
Cost of goods sold	$800,000

12. c   Underapplied or overapplied overhead represents the difference between actual overhead cost and applied overhead cost. The computation in this case is:

Actual overhead cost	$ 90,000
Applied overhead cost	92,000
Overapplied overhead cost.	$ (2,000)

13. a   The predetermined overhead rate is $60,000 ÷ 40,000 hours = $1.50 per hour.

Actual overhead cost	$65,100
Applied overhead cost (42,000 hours × $1.50 per hour)	63,000
Underapplied overhead cost	$ 2,100

14. a   The solution would be:

Work in Process

Balance	18,000	Finished	190,000
Direct materials	35,000		
Direct labor	60,000		
Overhead applied*	90,000		
Balance	13,000		

*$60,000 × 150% = $90,000

15. b   The cost of goods manufactured represents the costs of goods completed during the period; thus, it is the amount transferred from Work in Process to Finished Goods.

16. c   If overhead is overapplied, then more overhead cost has been added to jobs than has been incurred. Therefore, too much overhead cost will have been assigned to jobs.

17. a   The computations are:

Work in Process	$ 40,000	20%
Finished Goods	60,000	30%
Cost of Goods Sold	100,000	50%
Total cost	$200,000	100%

20% × $10,000 = $2,000.

Exercises

Exercise 3-1.

a. $\dfrac{\$150,000}{100,000 \text{ DLHs}} = \$1.50$ per DLH

b. 105,000 DLHS × \$1.50 per DLH = \$157,500 applied

c.
Actual overhead cost..................	\$160,000
Applied overhead cost..............	157,500
Underapplied overhead cost......	\$ 2,500

Exercise 3-2. a. & b.

Cash			
Bal.	12,000	(14)	760,000
(13)	790,000		
	42,000		

Accumulated Depreciation			
		Bal.	120,000
		(6)	20,000
			140,000

Sales			
		(12a)	800,000

Accounts Receivable			
Bal.	48,000	(13)	790,000
(12a)	800,000		
	58,000		

Manufacturing Overhead			
(4)	35,000	(10)	165,000
(5)	75,000		
(6)	15,000		
(7)	30,000		
(9)	4,000		
(15)	6,000		6,000

Cost of Goods Sold			
(12b)	540,000	(15)	6,000
	534,000		

Prepaid insurance			
Bal.	8,000	(9)	4,000
	4,000		

Salaries Expense			
(5)	140,000		

Raw Materials			
Bal.	30,000	(2)	145,000
(1)	150,000		
	35,000		

Accounts Payable			
(14)	300,000	Bal.	75,000
		(1)	150,000
		(3)	50,000
		(4)	35,000
		(7)	30,000
		(8)	25,000
			65,000

Advertising Expense			
(3)	50,000		

Work in Process			
Bal.	40,000	(11)	550,000
(2)	145,000		
(5)	250,000		
(10)	165,000		
	50,000		

Depreciation Expense			
(6)	5,000		

Finished Goods			
Bal.	100,000	(12b)	540,000
(11)	550,000		
	110,000		

Salaries and Wages Payable			
(14)	460,000	Bal.	12,000
		(5)	465,000
			17,000

Other Selling and Administrative Expenses			
(8)	25,000		

c. Overhead is overapplied by \$6,000.

d.

Pardoe Company
Income Statement

Sales		$800,000
Cost of goods sold ($540,000 – $6,000).		534,000
Gross margin		266,000
Selling and administrative expenses:		
Advertising expense............................	$ 50,000	
Salaries expense.................................	140,000	
Depreciation expense..........................	5,000	
Other expenses...................................	25,000	220,000
Net operating income		$ 46,000

Exercise 3-3.

Raw materials inventory, beginning......................	$ 10,000
Add: Purchases of raw materials	145,000
Total	155,000
Deduct: Raw materials inventory, ending	15,000
Raw materials used in production	$140,000

Exercise 3-4.

Direct materials	$140,000
Direct labor...	240,000
Manufacturing overhead applied	90,000
Total manufacturing cost......................................	470,000
Add: Beginning work in process inventory	60,000
	530,000
Deduct: Ending work in process inventory	75,000
Cost of goods manufactured.................................	$455,000

Exercise 3-5.

Schedule of Cost of Goods Manufactured

Direct materials:		
Raw materials inventory, beginning..............	$ 15,000	
Add: Purchases of raw materials....................	120,000	
Raw materials available for use....................	135,000	
Deduct: Raw materials inventory, ending	5,000	
Raw materials used in production		$130,000
Direct labor...		90,000
Manufacturing overhead		30,300
Total manufacturing cost...............................		250,300
Add: Work in process, beginning...................		16,000
		266,300
Deduct: Work in process, ending		11,500
Cost of goods manufactured...........................		$254,800

Note: Sales commissions and depreciation on office equipment are not manufacturing costs.

Exercise 3-6.

Finished goods inventory, beginning	$120,000
Add: Cost of goods manufactured	455,000
Cost of goods available for sale	575,000
Deduct: Finished goods, ending	145,000
Unadjusted cost of goods sold	430,000
Deduct: Overapplied overhead (see below)	2,000
Adjusted cost of goods sold	$428,000

Actual manufacturing overhead cost incurred	$ 88,000
Applied manufacturing overhead cost	90,000
Overapplied overhead cost	($ 2,000)

Exercise 3-7.   Quality Foods, Inc. would probably have underapplied manufacturing overhead cost for the year. Because a large amount of the manufacturing overhead cost associated with producing canned goods is fixed, the company's *actual* manufacturing overhead costs would be about as planned. However, the company's *applied* manufacturing overhead costs would be less than planned because less productive activity would take place in the plant due to the loss of the fruit crop. Thus, with a large amount of *actual* overhead cost and less than planned *applied* overhead cost, the company would end the year with an underapplied balance in its Manufacturing Overhead account.

Appendix 3A
The Predetermined Overhead Rate and Capacity

APPENDIX HIGHLIGHTS

A. Traditionally, the predetermined overhead rate is based on the *estimated* total amount of the allocation base for the next year.

$$\text{Predetermined overhead rate} = \frac{\text{Estimated total manufacturing overhead cost}}{\text{Estimated total amount of the allocation base}}$$

This traditional approach can lead to some potential problems.

1.   If demand falls due to a recession or other reason, the estimated total amount of the allocation base is likely to fall. For example, in a recession total sales are likely to fall and the company may use less overtime or lay off workers so that the total amount of direct labor-hours declines as well. Because manufacturing overhead cost tends to be relatively fixed, the predetermined overhead rate will rise as the general level of activity falls. This will result in higher product costs and may lead managers to attempt to increase prices—which would be unwise in a recession.

2.   Under the traditional method, products and services are charged for the resources they *don't* use as well as the resources they do use. Suppose, for example, that a particular product uses 10% of the capacity of a machine. Under the traditional method, if the machine is expected to be idle 50% of the time, the product will be charged for 20% of the cost of the machine. In effect, the product will be charged 10% of the total cost of the machine for the time it uses and 10% of the total cost of the machine for the idle capacity it does not use.

B. An alternative to the traditional method is to base the predetermined overhead rate on the total amount of the allocation base and the estimated total manufacturing overhead cost at capacity. For example, suppose that the estimated amount of machine-hours for the upcoming year is 80,000 hours even though the plant has capacity for 100,000 hours. Under this approach, the predetermined overhead rate would be based on the capacity of 100,000 hours rather than on the expected usage of 80,000 hours. This method has a number of advantages:

1.   Product costs are stable and do not increase as the level of activity declines and decrease as the level of activity rises.

2.   Products are charged only for their share of the costs of the resources they actually use.

C. When the predetermined overhead rate is based on the total amount of the allocation base at capacity, overhead will ordinarily be underapplied. This is because of idle capacity. Rather than closing out this underapplied overhead to Cost of Goods Sold or allocating it among inventories and Cost of Goods Sold, the underapplied overhead is treated as a period expense and is separately disclosed as "Cost of Unused Capacity." This treatment makes the costs of idle capacity much more visible than under the conventional approach.

Appendix 3B
Further Classification of Labor Costs

APPENDIX HIGHLIGHTS

A. Labor costs can be broken down into five main categories: direct labor, indirect labor, idle time, overtime premium, and labor fringe benefits. As mentioned earlier:

    1.   Direct labor consists of factory labor costs that can be easily traced to products.

    2.   Indirect labor consists of factory labor costs that are supportive or supervisory. These include the costs of supervisors, custodians, maintenance persons, and others who do not work directly on the product.

B. This appendix explains three new terms:

    1.   *Idle time* refers to the costs of direct labor workers who are unable to perform their assignments due to material shortages, power failures, and the like. Idle time is treated as part of manufacturing overhead.

    2.   *Overtime premium* consists of any amount paid above an employee's base hourly rate for working beyond normal working hours. An overtime premium ordinarily is not charged to specific jobs, but rather is included as part of manufacturing overhead. An exception is when a customer specifically requests a rush job that results in having to work overtime. In such a case, the overtime premium might be charged directly to that job.

    3.   *Labor fringe benefits* include employment-related costs paid by the employer, such as insurance, retirement plans, etc.

       a.   Many companies include such costs as part of manufacturing overhead.

       b.   The preferred method is to include only the labor fringe benefits relating to indirect labor as part of manufacturing overhead and treat the fringe benefits relating to direct labor as added direct labor costs.

REVIEW AND SELF-TEST
Questions and Exercises

True or False

Enter a T or an F in the blank to indicate whether the statement is true or false.

___   1.   An overtime premium is ordinarily charged to the specific jobs worked on during overtime periods.

Multiple Choice

Choose the best answer or response by placing the identifying letter in the space provided.

___   1.   A machinist earns $10 per hour. During a given week he works 40 hours, of which he is idle 5 hours. For the week: a) $400 cost should be charged to direct labor; b) $50 cost should be charged to overtime premium; c) $50 cost should be charged to overhead; d) $425 cost should be charged to direct labor, and $25 cost should be charged to overhead.

Exercise

Exercise 3B-1.   Sally Anderson worked 47 hours last week. She was idle 3 hours and spent the remaining 44 hours making products. Sally is paid $8 per hour and time-and-a-half for work in excess of 40 hours per week. Allocate her week's wages between direct labor and manufacturing overhead using the form that appears below.

Direct labor.. $_____

Manufacturing overhead:

  Idle time .... $_____

  Overtime premium ....   _____   _____

Total earnings.. $_____

Answers to Questions and Exercises

True or False

1. F Overtime premium is ordinarily added to manufacturing overhead cost and spread over all jobs worked on during the period rather than charged to the specific jobs worked during overtime hours.

Multiple Choice

1. c All of the cost of idle time is charged to manufacturing overhead. Thus, $10 per hour × 5 hours = $50.

Exercise

Exercise 3B-1.

Direct labor (44 hours × $8 per hour).............		$352
Manufacturing overhead:		
Idle time (3 hours × $8 per hour)	$24	
Overtime premium (7 hours × $4 per hour).	28	52
Total earnings..		$404

Chapter 4

Systems Design: Process Costing

Chapter Study Suggestions

The chapter is divided into five main parts. The first part compares job-order and process costing. Exhibit 4-1, which outlines the differences between the two costing methods, is the key to understanding this part. The second part of the chapter describes cost flows in a process costing system. Study Exhibit 4-3 carefully, as well as the journal entries that follow. The third part of the chapter deals with a concept known as equivalent units of production. Pay particular attention to the computations in Exhibits 4-5 and 4-6. The fourth part of the chapter is concerned with the computation of the costs of ending inventory and the costs of the units transferred out of a department.

CHAPTER HIGHLIGHTS

A. Process costing is used in industries that produce homogeneous products such as bricks, flour, and cement. It is also used in some assembly-type operations, as well as in utilities producing gas, water, and electricity.

B. Process costing is similar to job-order costing in three ways:

1. Both systems have the same basic purpose, which is to assign material, labor, and overhead costs to products.

2. Both systems use the same basic manufacturing accounts—Manufacturing Overhead, Raw Materials, Work in Process, and Finished Goods—and costs flow through those accounts in basically the same way.

C. Process costing differs from job-order costing in three ways:

1. A single product is produced on a continuous basis and each unit is essentially the same.

2. Costs are accumulated by department, rather than by job.

3. Unit costs are computed by department (rather than by job).

D. A *processing department* is any work center where work is performed on a product and where materials, labor, or overhead costs are added. Processing departments in a process costing system have two common features. First, the activity carried out in the department is performed uniformly on all units passing through it. Second, the output of the department is basically homogeneous.

E. Using a process costing system requires less effort than a job-order costing system; costs only need to be traced to a few processing departments rather than to many individual jobs.

F. Exhibit 4-3 provides a T-account model of cost flows in a process costing system. A separate work in process account is maintained for each processing department. Materials, labor, and overhead costs are entered directly into each processing department's work in process account.

G. Separate computations are made within each processing department for each cost category. The cost categories may include:

1. Costs of prior departments associated with units transferred into the department.

2. Materials costs added in the department.

3. Direct labor costs added in the department.

4. Manufacturing overhead costs applied in the department.

In process costing, direct labor costs and manufacturing overhead costs are often combined into one cost category called *conversion costs.*

H. Once the costs in each category have been totaled for a department, the department's output must be determined so that unit costs can be computed. Units that have only been partially completed pose a problem. A unit that is only 10% complete should not count as much as a unit that has been completed and transferred on to the next department.

1. *Equivalent units* are the number of whole, complete units one could obtain from the materials and effort contained in partially completed units. Equivalent units are computed using the following formula:

$$\text{Equivalent units} = \begin{array}{c}\text{Number of}\\ \text{partially completed}\\ \text{units}\end{array} \times \begin{array}{c}\text{Percentage}\\ \text{completion}\end{array}$$

2. *Equivalent units of production* is used to compute the cost per equivalent unit. Under the weighted-average method, the equivalent units of production are determined as follows:

Units transferred to the next department or to finished goods..................	XXX
+ Equivalent units in ending work in process inventory	XXX
= Equivalent units of production..............	XXX

3. The equivalent units of production are computed separately for each cost category.

I. Note the following points.

1. The equivalent units of production and the cost per equivalent unit must be computed separately for each cost category.

2. Units transferred out of the department to the next department—or, in the case of the last department, to finished goods—are always considered to be 100% complete with respect to the work done by the transferring department.

3. The first processing department does not have a cost category for the costs of units transferred in, but subsequent departments will have such a cost category. Units in process in a department are considered to be 100% complete with respect to the costs of the prior department.

J. After the equivalent units of production are computed, the next step is to compute the *cost per equivalent unit*. Under the weighted-average method, the formula is:

$$\text{Cost per equivalent unit} = \frac{\text{Cost of beginning work in process inventory} + \text{Cost added during the period}}{\text{Equivalent units of production}}$$

K. The final step is to compute the costs of the units transferred out during the period and the ending work in process inventory. These costs are determined as follows:

1. Units completed and transferred out. These units are presumed to be 100% complete. If they were not complete with respect to the work done in the department, they would not be transferred out. The costs of units transferred out are determined for each cost category within a department as follows:

	Units transferred to the next department	XXX
×	Cost per equivalent unit	XXX
=	Cost of units transferred out	XXX

This computation is made for each cost category in the department. The results are summed to determine the overall cost of units transferred out of the department.

2. Units in ending work in process inventory. The costs of the units in ending work in process inventory are determined for each cost category within a department as follows:

	Equivalent units of production in ending work in process inventory	XXX
×	Cost per equivalent unit	XXX
=	Cost of ending work in process inventory	XXX

This computation is made for each cost category in the department. The results are summed to determine the overall cost of ending work in process inventory.

L. Note that the weighted-average method combines costs from the beginning inventory with costs from the current period. It is called the weighted-average method because it averages together costs from the prior period with costs of the current period.

M. *Operation costing* is a hybrid system containing elements of both job-order and process costing. It is most commonly used when products use different materials but follow the same basic processing steps. For example, a factory that assembles personal computers might make many different models that use different components. However, all of the models go through the assembly department, testing department, and packing and shipping department.

1. In operation costing, products are handled in batches and each batch is charged with its own specific materials. In this sense, operation costing is similar to job-order costing.

2. Labor and overhead costs are accumulated by department and these costs are assigned to the batches on an average per unit basis as in process costing.

REVIEW AND SELF-TEST
Questions and Exercises

True or False

Enter a T or an F in the blank to indicate whether the statement is true or false.

____ 1. Under process costing it is important to identify the materials, labor, and overhead costs associated with a particular customer's order just as under job-order costing.

____ 2. Operation costing uses aspects of both job-order and process costing systems.

____ 3. In process costing, costs incurred in a department are not transferred to the next department.

____ 4. If beginning work in process inventory contains 500 units that are 60% complete, then the inventory contains 300 equivalent units.

Multiple Choice

Choose the best answer or response by placing the identifying letter in the space provided.

____ 1. The Mixing Department of Deerdon Company started 4,800 units into process during the month. 500 units were in the beginning inventory and 300 units were in the ending inventory. How many units were completed and transferred out during the month? a) 5,000; b) 4,600; c) 5,300; d) 5,100.

____ 2. Last month the Welding Department of Eager Company started 8,000 units into production. The department had 2,000 units in process at the beginning of the month, which were 60% complete with respect to conversion costs, and 3,000 units in process at the end of the month, which were 30% complete with respect to conversion costs. A total of 7,000 units were completed and transferred to the next department during the month. Using the weighted-average method, the equivalent units of production for conversion costs for the month would be: a) 7,900; b) 8,500; c) 9,200; d) 9,500.

____ 3. At the beginning of the month, 200 units were in process in the Stamping Department and they were 70% complete with respect to materials. During the month 2,000 units were transferred to the next department. At the end of the month, 100 units were still in process and they were 60% complete with respect to materials. The materials cost in the beginning work in process inventory was $2,721 and $39,200 of materials costs were added during the month. Using the weighted-average method, what is the cost per equivalent unit for materials costs? a) $19.06; b) $20.35; c) $20.42; d) $19.60.

____ 4. The Weaving Department of a company had $8,000 of conversion cost in its beginning work in process inventory and added $64,000 of conversion cost during the month. The department completed 37,000 units during the month and had 10,000 units in the ending work in process inventory that were 30% complete with respect to conversion cost. Using the weighted-average method, the amount of cost assigned to the units in ending inventory would be: a) $12,600; b) $4,800; c) $11,200; d) $5,400.

____ 5. The Heat Treatment Department at Northern Pipe is the third department in a sequential process. The work in process account for the department would consist of: a) costs transferred in from the prior department; b) materials costs added in the heat treatment department; c) conversion costs added in the heat treatment department; d) all of the above.

Exercises

Exercise 4-1.   Diebold Corporation has a process costing system. Data relating to activities in the Mixing Department for March follow:

	Units	Percent Complete	
		Materials	*Conversion*
Work in process, March 1	5,000	100%	60%
Units started into production during March	80,000		
Units completed during March and trans- ferred to the next department.......................	83,000	100%	100%
Work in process, March 31	2,000	100%	50%

	Materials	*Conversion*
Costs in beginning inventory............................	$ 10,000	$ 15,000
Costs added during March................................	$160,000	$405,000

a. Using the weighted-average method, determine the equivalent units of production for both materials and conversion for the month of March.

	Materials	*Conversion*
Units transferred to the next department..................	_____	_____
Work in process, March 31:		
Materials (_____ units × _____ complete)..............	_____	
Conversion (_____units × _____ complete)...........		_____
Equivalent units of production................................	_____	_____

b. Using the weighted-average method, determine the cost per equivalent unit for both materials and conversion for the month of March.

	Materials	*Conversion*
Cost of beginning work in process inventory	$_____	$_____
Costs added during March......................................	_____	_____
Total cost (a)...	$_____	$_____
Equivalent units of production (see above) (b)........	_____	_____
Cost per equivalent unit (a) ÷ (b)...........................	$_____	$_____

c. Using the weighted-average method, determine the cost of ending work in process inventory and of the units transferred out during March.

	Materials	Conversion	Total
Ending work in process inventory:			
Equivalent units of production (a)................................	_____	_____	
Cost per equivalent unit (see above) (b)........................	$_____	$_____	
Cost of ending work in process inventory (a) × (b).......	$_____	$_____	$_____
Units completed and transferred out:			
Units transferred to the next department (a)..................	_____	_____	
Cost per equivalent unit (see above) (b)........................	$_____	$_____	
Cost of units completed and transferred out (a) × (b) ...	$_____	$_____	$_____

d. Prepare the department's cost reconciliation report for March.

Mixing Department
Cost Reconciliation

Costs to be accounted for:	
Cost of beginning work in process inventory................	$_____
Cost added to production during the period..................	_____
Total cost to be accounted for	$_____
Costs accounted for as follows:	
Cost of ending work in process inventory.....................	$_____
Cost of units transferred out...	_____
Total cost accounted for	$_____

Answers to Questions and Exercises

True or False

1. **F** Because units are indistinguishable from each other, there is no need to identify costs by customer order.

2. **T** In operation costing, materials are handled as in job-order costing while labor and overhead costs are handled as in process costing.

3. **F** Costs that have been incurred in a department are transferred to the next department when processing is completed and units are transferred.

4. **T** 500 units × 60% = 300 equivalent units.

Multiple Choice

1. **a**

Beginning inventory	500
Units started into process	4,800
Total units	5,300
Less ending inventory	300
Completed and transferred	5,000

2. **a**

Units completed and transferred	7,000
Work in process, ending:	
3,000 units × 30%	900
Equivalent units of production	7,900

3. **b**

Cost in beginning work in process	$ 2,721
Cost added during the month	39,200
Total cost (a)	$41,921
Units transferred out	2,000
Equivalent units in ending work in process inventory (100 × 60%)	60
Equivalent units (b)	2,060
Cost per equivalent unit (a) ÷ (b)	$ 20.35

4. **d**

Cost in beginning work in process	$ 8,000
Cost added during the year	64,000
Total cost (a)	$72,000
Units transferred out	37,000
Equivalent units in ending work in process inventory (10,000 × 30%)	3,000
Equivalent units (b)	40,000
Cost per equivalent unit (a) ÷ (b)	$ 1.80

3,000 units × $1.80 per unit = $5,400.

5. **d** Costs in the department's work in process inventory account include costs transferred in from the previous department and any costs added in the department itself—including materials, labor, and overhead. Labor and overhead together equal conversion cost.

Exercises

Exercise 4-1.

a.

	Materials	Conversion
Units transferred to the next department..................	83,000	83,000
Work in process, March 31:		
Materials (2,000 units × 100% complete)................	2,000	
Conversion (2,000 units × 50% complete................		1,000
Equivalent units of production...............................	85,000	84,000

b.

	Materials	Conversion
Cost of beginning work in process inventory	$ 10,000	$ 15,000
Costs added during March	160,000	405,000
Total cost (a)..	$170,000	$420,000
Equivalent units of production (see above) (b)........	85,000	84,000
Cost per equivalent unit (a) ÷ (b)............................	$ 2.00	$ 5.00

c.

	Materials	Conversion	Total
Ending work in process inventory:			
Equivalent units of production (a).................................	2,000	1,000	
Cost per equivalent unit (see above) (b)........................	$ 2.00	$ 5.00	
Cost of ending work in process inventory (a) × (b).......	$ 4,000	$ 5,000	$ 9,000
Units completed and transferred out:			
Units transferred to the next department (a).................	83,000	83,000	
Cost per equivalent unit (see above) (b)........................	$ 2.00	$ 5.00	
Cost of units completed and transferred out (a) × (b) ...	$166,000	$415,000	$581,000

Mixing Department
Cost Reconciliation

Costs to be accounted for:	
Cost of beginning work in process inventory	
($10,000 + $15,000)...	$ 25,000
Cost added to production during the period	
($160,000 + $405,000)...	565,000
Total cost to be accounted for	$590,000
Costs accounted for as follows:	
Cost of ending work in process inventory.....................	$ 9,000
Cost of units transferred out...	581,000
Total cost accounted for..	$590,000

Appendix 4A

FIFO Method

APPENDIX HIGHLIGHTS

A. The *FIFO method* is more complex than the weighted-average method. The FIFO method keeps units and costs from the prior period separate from the units and costs of the current period.

B. Under the FIFO method, the equivalent units of production are determined as follows:

	Equivalent units to complete the beginning work in process inventory......	XXX
+	Units started and completed this period .	XXX
+	Equivalent units in ending work in process inventory..............................	XXX
=	Equivalent units of production	XXX

Note that the weighted-average method includes the equivalent units in beginning inventory whereas the FIFO method does not. This is most easily seen from the following alternative method of computing the equivalent units of production under the FIFO method:

	Units completed this period....................	XXX
–	Equivalent units in beginning inventory.	XXX
+	Equivalent units in ending inventory......	XXX
=	Equivalent units of production	XXX

C. Under the FIFO method, the cost per equivalent unit is computed using *only* costs added during the current period.

$$\text{Cost per equivalent unit} = \frac{\text{Cost added during the period}}{\text{Equivalent units of production}}$$

D. The computation of the cost of ending work in process inventory is handled identically under the FIFO and weighted-average cost methods, although the costs per equivalent unit will usually be different. In computing the cost of units transferred out under the FIFO method, the units in beginning work in process inventory are kept separate from the units started and completed during the current period as follows:

Computing the cost of units transferred out:

Cost of beginning work in process inventory...	$XXX
Equivalent units of production required to complete the units in beginning work in process inventory..	XXX
× Cost per equivalent unit......................	$XXX
= Cost to complete the units in beginning work in process inventory.......	$XXX
Units started and completed this period...	XXX
× Cost per equivalent unit......................	$XXX
= Cost of units started and completed this period	$XXX

For each cost category within the department, the above three costs—the cost of beginning work in process inventory, the cost to complete the units in beginning work in process inventory, and the cost of units started and completed during the period—are summed to determine the cost of the units transferred out during the period. These costs are then summed across cost categories within the department to determine the overall cost of the units transferred out of the department.

E. When comparing the weighted-average and FIFO methods, two points should be noted:

1. From the standpoint of cost control, the FIFO method is better than the weighted-average method because it separates the costs of the prior period from the costs of the current period.

2. If there are no beginning inventories, there will be no difference in costs reported using the FIFO and weighted-average methods. Because lean production reduces inventories to a minimum, adopting lean production will decrease the differences in costs computed under the two methods.

REVIEW AND SELF-TEST
Questions and Exercises

True or False

Enter a T or an F in the blank to indicate whether the statement is true or false.

___ 1. Under the FIFO method, costs in the beginning work in process inventory are not included when computing the cost per equivalent unit.

___ 2. Under the FIFO method, units in beginning work in process inventory are treated as if they were completed before any new units are completed.

___ 3. The weighted-average and FIFO methods will produce significantly different unit costs when beginning work in process inventory is zero.

___ 4. From the standpoint of cost control, the weighted-average method is superior to the FIFO method.

Multiple Choice

Choose the best answer or response by placing the identifying letter in the space provided.

___ 1. Last month the Welding Department of Eager Company started 8,000 units into production. The department had 2,000 units in process at the beginning of the month, which were 60% complete with respect to conversion costs, and 3,000 units in process at the end of the month, which were 30% complete with respect to conversion costs. A total of 7,000 units were completed and transferred to the next department during the month. Using the FIFO method, the equivalent units of production for conversion costs for the month would be: a) 8,300; b) 7,700; c) 6,700; d) 7,300.

___ 2. Mercer Corp. uses the FIFO method in its process costing system. The Cutting Department had $6,000 of materials cost in its beginning work in process inventory and $75,000 in materials cost was added during the period. The equivalent units of production for materials for the period was 20,000. The cost per equivalent unit for materials would be: a) $3.75; b) $4.05; c) $0.30; d) $3.30.

Exercise

Exercise 4A-1.   Diebold Corporation has a process costing system. Data relating to activities in the Mixing Department for March follow:

		Percent Complete	
	Units	*Materials*	*Conversion*
Work in process, March 1	5,000	100%	60%
Units started into production during March	80,000		
Units completed during March and transferred to the next department.........................	83,000	100%	100%
Work in process, March 31	2,000	100%	50%

	Materials	*Conversion*
Costs in beginning inventory............................	$ 10,000	$ 15,000
Costs added during March................................	$160,000	$405,000

a. Using the FIFO method, determine the equivalent units of production for both materials and conversion for the month of March.

	Materials	*Conversion*
To complete the beginning work in process		
Materials (_____ units × (100% − ___%))	_____	
Conversion (_____ units × (100% − ___%)).........		_____
Units started and completed during the period		
(_____ units started − _____ units in ending work in process inventory).................................	_____	_____
Ending work in process:		
Materials (_____ units × ___%)	_____	
Conversion (_____ units × ___%).........................		_____
Equivalent units of production................................	======	======

b. Using the FIFO method, determine the cost per equivalent unit for both materials and conversion for the month of March.

	Materials	*Conversion*
Costs added during March (a).................................	_____	_____
Equivalent units of production (see above) (b)........	_____	_____
Cost per equivalent unit (a) ÷ (b)............................	$_____	$_____

c. Using the FIFO method, determine the cost of ending work in process inventory and of the units transferred out during March.

	Materials	*Conversion*	*Total*
Ending work in process inventory:			
Equivalent units of production (a)	_____	_____	
Cost per equivalent unit (see above) (b)	$_____	$_____	
Cost of ending work in process inventory (a) × (b)	$_____	$_____	$_____
Units transferred out:			
Cost in beginning work in process inventory	$_____	$_____	$_____
Cost to complete the units in beginning inventory:			
Equivalent units of production required to complete the			
units in beginning inventory (a)	_____	_____	
Cost per equivalent unit (see above) (b)	$_____	$_____	
Cost to complete the units in beginning inventory			
(a) × (b)	$_____	$_____	$_____
Cost of units started and completed this period:			
Units started and completed this period (a)	_____	_____	
Cost per equivalent unit (see above) (b)	$_____	$_____	
Cost of units started and completed this period (a) × (b)...	$_____	$_____	$_____
Total cost of units transferred out			$_____

d. Prepare the department's cost reconciliation report for March.

Mixing Department
Cost Reconciliation

Costs to be accounted for:	
Cost of beginning work in process inventory	$_____
Cost added to production during the period	_____
Total cost to be accounted for	$_____
Costs accounted for as follows:	
Cost of ending work in process inventory	$_____
Cost of units transferred out	_____
Total cost accounted for	$_____

Answers to Questions and Exercises

True or False

1. **T** Costs in the beginning work in process inventory are kept separate from costs of the current period; the cost per equivalent unit for units produced during the current period reflects only current period costs.

2. **T** The FIFO method assumes that the units that are first in (i.e., in beginning inventory) are the first out (i.e., completed).

3. **F** When beginning inventories are zero, the weighted-average and FIFO methods will produce identical results.

4. **F** The reverse is true—from a standpoint of cost control, the FIFO method is superior to the weighted-average method.

Multiple Choice

1. **c**

Work in process, beginning:	
2,000 units × 40%*	800
Units started and completed**	5,000
Work in process, ending:	
3,000 units × 30%	900
Equivalent units of production	6,700

   *100% − 60% = 40%
   **7,000 units − 2,000 units = 5,000 units.

2. **a** $75,000 ÷ 20,000 units = $3.75 per unit.

Exercise

Exercise 4A-1.

a.

	Materials	Conversion
To complete the beginning work in process		
Materials (5,000 units × (100% − 100%))	0	
Conversion (5,000 units × (100% − 60%))		2,000
Units started and completed during the period (80,000 units started − 2,000 units in ending work in process inventory)....................................	78,000	78,000
Ending work in process:		
Materials (2,000 units × 100%)...............................	2,000	
Conversion (2,000 units × 50%)		1,000
Equivalent units of production...............................	80,000	81,000

b.

	Materials	Conversion
Costs added during March (a).................................	$160,000	$405,000
Equivalent units of production (see above) (b)........	80,000	81,000
Cost per equivalent unit (a) ÷ (b)............................	$ 2.00	$ 5.00

c.

	Materials	Conversion	Total
Ending work in process inventory:			
Equivalent units of production (a)	2,000	1,000	
Cost per equivalent unit (see above) (b)	$ 2.00	$ 5.00	
Cost of ending work in process inventory (a) × (b)	$ 4,000	$ 5,000	$ 9,000
Units transferred out:			
Cost in beginning work in process inventory	$ 10,000	$ 15,000	$ 25,000
Cost to complete the units in beginning inventory:			
Equivalent units of production required to complete the units in beginning inventory (a).....................................	0	2,000	
Cost per equivalent unit (see above) (b)	$ 2.00	$ 5.00	
Cost to complete the units in beginning inventory (a) × (b).........................	$ 0	$ 10,000	$ 10,000
Cost of units started and completed this period:			
Units started and completed this period (a)	78,000	78,000	
Cost per equivalent unit (see above) (b)	$ 2.00	$ 5.00	
Cost of units started and completed this period (a) × (b)...	$156,000	$390,000	$546,000
Total cost of units transferred out			$581,000

Mixing Department
Cost Reconciliation

Costs to be accounted for:	
Cost of beginning work in process inventory	$ 25,000
Cost added to production during the period ($160,000 + $405,000)..	565,000
Total cost to be accounted for	$590,000
Costs accounted for as follows:	
Cost of ending work in process inventory.....................	$ 9,000
Cost of units transferred out..	581,000
Total cost accounted for..	$590,000

Appendix 4B

Service Department Allocations

APPENDIX HIGHLIGHTS

A. Operating departments differ from service departments.

   1. *Operating departments* carry out the central purposes of the organization. Examples include the surgery department in a hospital, the shoe department in a department store, and production departments in a manufacturing company.

   2. *Service departments* provide service or assistance to other departments. Examples of service departments include the cafeteria in a hospital, the billing department in a department store, and the purchasing department in a factory.

   3. The costs of service departments are typically allocated to operating departments. These allocated costs are then added to the overhead costs of the operating departments and included in predetermined overhead rates.

B. Three major methods are used to allocate service department costs—the direct method, the step-down method, and the reciprocal method. The methods differ mainly in how they treat services that service departments provide to each other. These services are called *interdepartmental services* or *reciprocal services.*

C. The *direct method* is the simplest, but the least accurate, of the three methods. When the direct method is used, reciprocal services are ignored and service department costs are allocated directly to operating departments. For example, a hospital's custodial staff cleans administrative offices as well as operating rooms and hospital wards. However, in the direct method none of the custodial costs are allocated to the administrative department. Instead, all the custodial costs are allocated *directly* to the operating departments. See Exhibit 4B-1 in the text for an example of the direct method of allocation.

D. The *step-down method* is slightly more complex than the direct method, but it is also more accurate.

   1. In the step-down method, service department costs are allocated in a specific order. Usually, service departments are ranked in terms of the amount of service they provide to other service departments, with the service department that provides the greatest service to the other service departments allocated first.

   2. The costs of the first service department are allocated to all the other departments, both service and operating departments. After the first service department's costs have been allocated, it is ignored in subsequent allocations. Then the costs of the next service department are allocated to the *remaining* service departments as well as to the operating departments. However, any services provided by the second service department to the first service department are ignored. No costs are allocated back to the first service department.

   3. The allocation proceeds in this manner, stepping through all the service departments. In each step, a service department's costs are allocated to the remaining service departments as well as to the operating departments. After a service department's costs have been allocated, the service department is ignored.

   4. By following this procedure, the step-down method takes into account some of the reciprocal services, but not all of them. See Exhibit 4B-2 in the text for an example of the step-down method of service department allocation.

E. Under both the direct and step-down methods, the service department whose cost is being allocated is never included in the allocation base. For example, when allocating the costs of a cafeteria on the basis of meals served, the meals served to cafeteria workers are ignored.

F. The *reciprocal method* is the most complex and the most accurate method of the three methods for allocating service department costs. The reciprocal method takes all of the reciprocal services fully into account. However, the reciprocal method is seldom used in practice—probably because of its mathematical complexity. This method is covered in more advanced textbooks.

REVIEW AND SELF-TEST
Questions and Exercises

True or False

Enter a T or an F in the blank to indicate whether the statement is true or false.

____ 1. The direct method of allocating service department costs fully accounts for all reciprocal services among service departments.

____ 2. When allocating a service department's costs under the direct or step-down method, the service department being allocated should not be included in the allocation base. (e.g., The meals served to cafeteria workers should not be included in the allocation base for the cafeteria.)

____ 3. The reciprocal method is generally considered to be more accurate than the step-down method of service department allocation.

Multiple Choice

Choose the best answer or response by placing the identifying letter in the space provided.

The following data are used in multiple choice questions 1 through 6:

Oscar Company has two service departments, Personnel and Custodial, and two operating departments, A and B. Budgeted data for the current year appear below:

| | Service Departments | | Operating Departments | |
	Personnel	Custodial	A	B
Overhead costs	$800	$600	$2,000	$5,000
Employees......	2	18	30	50
Space occupied (000s of square feet) ...	20	10	40	80

Personnel costs are allocated on the basis of employees. Custodial costs are allocated on the basis of space occupied. The company makes no distinction between fixed and variable costs in its service department allocations.

____ 1. If the direct method of service department allocation is used, how much Personnel Department cost would be allocated to Operating Department A? a) $240; b) $300; c) $0; d) $800.

____ 2. If the direct method of service department allocation is used, how much Personnel Department cost would be allocated back to the Personnel Department? a) $16; b) $800; c) $0; d) $200.

____ 3. If the direct method of service department allocation is used, what would be the total overhead cost in Operating Department B after the allocations have been completed? a) $5,900; b) $900; c) $5,000; d) $6,400.

____ 4. If the step-down method of service department allocation is used and Personnel Department costs are allocated first, how much Personnel Department cost would be allocated to the Custodial Department? a) $146.94; b) $0; c) $144; d) $200.

____ 5. If the step-down method of service department allocation is used and Personnel Department costs are allocated first, how much Custodial Department cost would be allocated to the Personnel Department? a) $80; b) $0; c) $99.59; d) $150.

____ 6. If the step-down method of service department allocation is used and Personnel Department costs are allocated first, how much Custodial Department cost would be allocated to Operating Department A? a) $0; b) $150; c) $248.94; d) $171.43.

Exercise

Exercise 4B-1. Piney Company has three service departments and two operating departments. Cost and other data relating to these departments follow:

	Service Departments			Operating Departments	
	Janitorial	Cafeteria	Engineering	Assembly	Finishing
Overhead costs..................	$60,000	$42,600	$75,000	$230,000	$300,000
Square feet.......................	1,500	2,000	1,000	4,000	3,000
Number of employees.......	15	12	50	200	400

The company allocates Janitorial costs on the basis of square feet. The Cafeteria and Engineering costs are allocated on the basis of the number of employees. The company makes no distinction between variable and fixed service department costs in its allocations of service department costs.

Allocate service department costs to the operating departments using the step-down method. The company allocates service department costs in the following order: Janitorial, Cafeteria, then Engineering.

	Service Departments			Operating Departments	
	Janitorial	Cafeteria	Engineering	Assembly	Finishing
Overhead costs..	$60,000	$42,600	$75,000	$230,000	$300,000
Allocations:					
Janitorial	_____	_____	_____	_____	_____
Cafeteria		_____	_____	_____	_____
Engineering...			_____	_____	_____
Total..	$_____	$_____	$_____	$_____	$_____

Exercise 4B-2. Refer to the data in Exercise 4B-1 above. Allocate the service department costs to the operating departments using the direct method.

	Service Departments			Operating Departments	
	Janitorial	Cafeteria	Engineering	Assembly	Finishing
Overhead costs..	$60,000	$42,600	$75,000	$230,000	$300,000
Allocations:					
Janitorial	_____			_____	_____
Cafeteria		_____		_____	_____
Engineering...			_____	_____	_____
Total..	$_____	$_____	$_____	$_____	$_____

Answers to Questions and Exercises

True or False

1. F   The direct method entirely ignores recipro-cal services among service departments.

2. T   If the service department being allocated is included in the allocation base, some of the cost will be allocated back to the service department.

3. T   The reciprocal method fully accounts for all reciprocal services among service departments.

Multiple Choice

1. b   Allocation base = 30 + 50 = 80
Allocation: (30/80) × $800 = $300

2. c   Even though the Personnel Department has two employees, none of its costs are charged to itself in the direct method or in the step-down method.

3. a
Original overhead cost in Operating Department B ...	$5,000
Allocated Personnel Dept. cost: (50/80) × $800	500
Allocated Custodial Dept. cost: (80/120) × $600	400
Total	$5,900

4. a   Allocation base = 18 + 30 + 50 = 98
Allocation: (18/98) × $800 = $146.94

5. b   In the step-down method, once a service de-partment's costs have been allocated, the department is ignored in subsequent allocations.

6. c   This problem requires two steps:

Original Custodial cost	$600.00
Allocated from Personnel*	146.94
Custodial cost to be allocated	$746.94

*See the answer to question (4) above.

Allocation base = 40 + 80 = 120
Allocation: (40/120) × $746.94 = $248.98

Exercise

Exercise 4B-1.

	Service Departments			Operating Departments	
	Janitorial	*Cafeteria*	*Engineering*	*Assembly*	*Finishing*
Overhead costs	$60,000	$42,600	$75,000	$230,000	$300,000
Allocations:					
Janitorial (2/10, 1/10, 4/10, 3/10)	(60,000)	12,000	6,000	24,000	18,000
Cafeteria (50/650, 200/650, 400/650)		(54,600)	4,200	16,800	33,600
Engineering (200/600, 400/600)			(85,200)	28,400	56,800
Total	$ 0	$ 0	$ 0	$299,200	$408,400

Exercise 4B-2.

	Service Departments			Operating Departments	
	Janitorial	*Cafeteria*	*Engineering*	*Assembly*	*Finishing*
Overhead costs	$60,000	$42,600	$75,000	$230,000	$300,000
Allocations:					
Janitorial (4,000/7,000, 3,000/7,000)	(60,000)			34,286	25,714
Cafeteria (200/600, 400/600)		(42,600)		14,200	28,400
Engineering (200/600, 400/600)			(75,000)	25,000	50,000
Total	$ 0	$ 0	$ 0	$303,486	$404,114

Cost-Volume-Profit Relationships

Chapter Study Suggestions

Chapter 5 is one of the key chapters in the book. Many of the chapters ahead depend on concepts developed here. You should study several sections in the chapter with particular attention. The first of these is the section titled, "Contribution Margin." Note how changes in the contribution margin affect net operating income. The next section you should study with particular care is titled "Contribution Margin Ratio." The contribution margin ratio is used in much of the analytical work in the chapter.

Another section you should study very carefully is titled "Some Applications of CVP Concepts." Much of the homework material is drawn from this section. The section titled "Break-Even Analysis" also forms the basis for much of the homework material. Finally, the section titled "The Concept of Sales Mix" shows how to use CVP analysis when the company has more than one product.

When studying this chapter, try especially hard to understand the logic behind the solutions rather than just memorizing formulas.

CHAPTER HIGHLIGHTS

A. The contribution margin is a key concept. The *contribution margin* is the difference between total sales and total variable expenses. The *unit contribution margin* is the difference between the unit selling price and the unit variable expense.

1. Net operating income is equal to the contribution margin less fixed expenses.

Sales	$XXX
Variable expenses.............	XXX
Contribution margin	XXX
Fixed expenses	XXX
Net operating income	$XXX

2. The *break-even point* is the level of sales at which profit is zero.

3. The relation between contribution margin and net operating income provides a very powerful planning tool. It gives the manager the ability to predict what profits will be at various activity levels without the necessity of preparing detailed income statements.

    a. The contribution margin must first cover fixed expenses. If it doesn't, the company has a loss. Below the break-even point, every unit sold reduces the loss by the amount of the unit contribution margin.

    b. Once the break-even point is reached, net operating income will increase by the amount of the unit contribution margin for each additional unit sold.

B. The contribution margin ratio (CM ratio), which expresses the contribution margin as a percentage of sales, is another very powerful concept.

1. The contribution margin ratio is defined as follows:

$$\text{CM ratio} = \frac{\text{Contribution margin}}{\text{Sales}}$$

2. In a company with only a single product, the CM ratio can also be computed as follows:

$$\text{CM ratio} = \frac{\text{Unit contribution margin}}{\text{Unit selling price}}$$

3. The contribution margin ratio is used to predict the change in total contribution margin that would result from a given change in dollar sales:

	Change in dollar sales..................	XXX
×	CM ratio......................................	XXX
=	Change in contribution margin	XXX

4. Assuming that fixed expenses are not affected, an increase (or decrease) in contribution margin will be reflected dollar for dollar in increased (or decreased) net operating income.

5. The CM ratio is particularly useful when a company has multiple products. In such situations, volume is most conveniently expressed in terms of total dollar sales rather than in units sold.

C. Cost-volume-profit (CVP) concepts can be used in many day-to-day decisions. Carefully study the examples given under the heading "Some Applications of CVP Concepts" in the early part of the chapter.

1. Note that each solution makes use of either the unit contribution margin or the CM ratio. This underscores the importance of these two concepts.

2. Also note that several of the examples use *incremental analysis*. An incremental analysis is based on only those costs and revenues that *differ* between alternatives.

D. Two particular examples of CVP analysis, called *break-even analysis* and *target profit analysis*, are often used. Break-even analysis is a special case of target profit analysis, so target profit analysis is considered first below.

1. Target profit analysis is used to find out how much would have to be sold to attain a specific target profit. The analysis is based on the following equation:

Profit = Sales − Variable expenses − Fixed expenses

In CVP analysis, this equation is often rewritten as:

Profit = Unit CM × Q − Fixed expense

or

Profit = CM ratio × Sales − Fixed expense

where Q is the quantity sold and CM stands for contribution margin.

All of the problems can be worked using these basic equations and simple algebra. However, handy formulas are available for answering some of the more common questions. These formulas are discussed below.

2. Target profit analysis is used in two basic variations. In the first variation, the question is how many *units* would have to be sold to attain the target profit. In the second variation, the question is how much total

dollar sales would have to be to attain the target profit. The formulas are:

$$\text{Unit sales to attain target profit} = \frac{\text{Target profit} + \text{Fixed expenses}}{\text{Unit CM}}$$

$$\text{Dollar sales to attain target profit} = \frac{\text{Target profit} + \text{Fixed expenses}}{\text{CM ratio}}$$

E. Break-even occurs when profit is zero. Thus, break-even analysis is really just a special case of target profit analysis in which the target profit is zero. Therefore, the break-even formulas can be stated as follows:

$$\text{Units sales to break even} = \frac{\text{Fixed expenses}}{\text{Unit CM}}$$

$$\text{Dollar sales to break even} = \frac{\text{Fixed expenses}}{\text{CM ratio}}$$

F. CVP and break-even analysis can also be done graphically. Exhibits 6-1 and 6-2 show how a CVP graph is prepared and interpreted. A cost-volume-profit graph depicts the relations among sales, costs, and volume.

G. The *margin of safety* is the excess of budgeted (or actual) sales over the break-even volume of sales. It is the amount by which sales can drop before losses begin to be incurred. The margin of safety can be stated in terms of either dollars or as a percentage of sales:

Total budgeted (or actual) sales	$XXX
Less break-even sales....................	XXX
Margin of safety...........................	$XXX

$$\text{Margin of safety percentage} = \frac{\text{Margin of safety}}{\text{Total budgeted (or actual) sales}}$$

H. Cost structure—the relative proportion of fixed and variable costs—has an impact on how sensitive a company's profits are to changes in sales. A company with low fixed costs and high variable costs will tend to have a lower CM ratio than a company with a greater proportion of fixed costs. Such a company will tend to have less volatile profits, but at the risk of losing substantial profits if sales trend sharply upward.

I. *Operating leverage* refers to the effect a given percentage increase in sales will have on net operating income.

   1.   The degree of operating leverage is defined as:

$$\text{Degree of operating leverage} = \frac{\text{Contribution margin}}{\text{Net operating income}}$$

   2.   To estimate the *percentage* change in net operating income that would occur as the result of a given percentage change in dollar sales, multiply the change in sales by the degree of operating leverage.

Percentage change in dollar sales	XXX
× Degree of operating leverage.............	XXX
= Percentage change in net operating income	XXX

   3.   The degree of operating leverage is not constant. It changes as sales increase or decrease. In general, the degree of operating leverage decreases the further a company moves away from its break-even point.

J. When a company has more than one product, the *sales mix* can be crucial. The sales mix refers to the relative proportions in which the company's products are sold.

   1.   When CVP analysis involves more than one product, the analysis is normally based on the *overall contribution margin ratio*. This is computed exactly like the CM ratio is computed in a single product company except that overall figures are used for both the contribution margin and sales:

$$\text{Overall CM ratio} = \frac{\text{Overall contribution margin}}{\text{Overall sales}}$$

   2.   When the company has more than one product, the *overall* CM ratio is used in the target profit and break-even formulas instead of the CM ratio.

   3.   As the sales mix changes, *the overall CM ratio will also change*. If the shift is toward less profitable products, then the overall CM ratio will fall; if the shift is toward more profitable products, then the overall CM ratio will rise.

K. CVP analysis ordinarily relies on the following assumptions:

   1.   The selling price is constant; it does not change as unit sales change.

   2.   Costs are linear. Costs can be accurately divided into variable and fixed elements. The variable cost per unit is constant and the total fixed cost is constant.

   3.   In multi-product situations, the sales mix is constant.

   4.   In manufacturing companies, inventories do not change.

REVIEW AND SELF-TEST
Questions and Exercises

True or False

Enter a T or an F in the blank to indicate whether the statement is true or false.

____ 1. If product A has a higher unit contribution margin than product B, then product A will also have a higher CM ratio than product B.

____ 2. The break-even point occurs where the total contribution margin is equal to total variable expenses.

____ 3. The break-even point can be expressed either in terms of units sold or in terms of total sales dollars.

____ 4. If the sales mix changes, the break-even point may change.

____ 5. For a given increase in sales dollars, a high CM ratio will result in a greater increase in profits than will a low CM ratio.

____ 6. If sales increase by 8%, and the degree of operating leverage is 4, then profits can be expected to increase by 12%.

____ 7. The degree of operating leverage remains the same at all levels of sales.

____ 8. Once the break-even point has been reached, net operating income will increase by the unit contribution margin for each additional unit sold.

____ 9. A shift in sales mix toward less profitable products will cause the overall break-even point to fall.

____ 10. Incremental analysis focuses on the differences in costs and revenues between alternatives.

____ 11. If a company's cost structure shifts toward higher fixed costs and lower variable costs, the company's CM ratio will fall.

____ 12. One way to compute the break-even point is to divide total sales by the CM ratio.

____ 13. When a company has more than one product, a key assumption in break-even analysis is that the sales mix will not change.

Multiple Choice

Choose the best answer or response by placing the identifying letter in the space provided.

____ 1. Lester Company has a single product. The selling price is $50 and the variable cost is $30 per unit. The company's fixed expense is $200,000 per month. What is the company's unit contribution margin? a) $50; b) $30; c) $20; d) $80.

____ 2. Refer to the data for Lester Company in question 1 above. What is the company's contribution margin ratio? a) 60%; b) 40%; c) 167%; d) 20%.

____ 3. Refer to the data for Lester Company in question 1 above. What is the company's break-even in sales dollars? a) $500,000; b) $33,333; c) $200,000; d) $400,000.

____ 4. Refer to the data for Lester Company in question 1 above. How many units would the company have to sell to attain target profits of $50,000? a) 10,000; b) 12,500; c) 15,000; d) 13,333.

____ 5. Parker Company has provided the following data for the most recent year: net operating income, $30,000; fixed expense, $90,000; sales, $200,000; and CM ratio, 60%. The company's margin of safety in dollars is: a) $150,000; b) $30,000; c) $50,000; d) $80,000.

____ 6. Refer to the data in question for Parker Company in 5 above. The margin of safety in percentage form is: a) 60%; b) 75%; c) 40%; d) 25%.

____ 7. Refer to the data for Parker Company in question 5 above. What is the company's total contribution margin? a) $110,000; b) $120,000; c) $170,000; d) $200,000.

____ 8. Refer to the data for Parker Company in question 5 above. What is the company's degree of operating leverage? a) 0.25; b) 0.60; c) 1.25; d) 4.00.

____ 9. If sales increase from $400,000 to $450,000, and if the degree of operating leverage is 6, net operating income should increase by: a) 12.5%; b) 75%; c) 67%; d) 50%.

___ 10. In multiple product companies, a shift in the sales mix from less profitable products to more profitable products will cause the company's break-even point to: a) increase; b) decrease; c) there will be no change in the break-even point; d) none of these.

___ 11. Herman Corp. has two products, A and B, with the following total sales and total variable costs:

	Product A	Product B
Sales	$10,000	$30,000
Variable expenses......	$ 4,000	$24,000

What is the overall contribution margin ratio? a) 70%; b) 50%; c) 30%; d) 40%.

Exercises

Exercise 5-1.   Hardee Company sells a single product. The selling price is $30 per unit and the variable expense is $18 per unit. The company's most recent annual contribution format income statement is given below:

Sales	$135,000
Variable expenses..........	81,000
Contribution margin	54,000
Fixed expenses	48,000
Net operating income	$ 6,000

a. Compute the contribution margin per unit. $_____

b. Compute the CM ratio. _____%

c. Compute the break-even point in sales dollars. $_____

d. Compute the break-even point in units sold. _____ units.

e. How many units must be sold next year to double the company's profits? _____ units.

f. Compute the company's degree of operating leverage. _____

g. Sales for next year (in units) are expected to increase by 5%. Using the degree of operating leverage, compute the expected percentage increase in net operating income. _____%

h. Verify your answer to part g above by preparing a contribution format income statement showing a 5% increase in sales.

Sales..	$_____
Variable expenses	_____
Contribution margin...	_____
Fixed expenses..	_____
Net operating income......................................	$_____

Exercise 5-2.   Using the data below, construct a cost-volume-profit graph like the one in Exhibit 5-1 in the text:

Sales: 15,000 units at $10 each.
Variable expense: $6 per unit.
Fixed expense: $40,000 total.

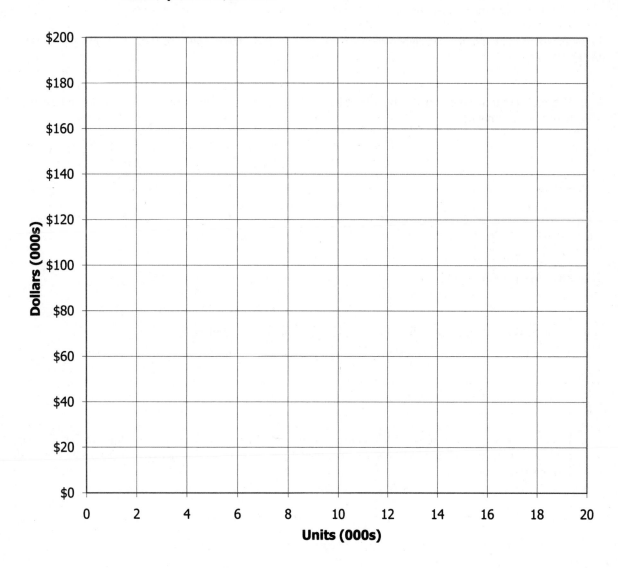

What is the break-even point in units? _____.

What is the break-even point in total sales dollars? _____.

Exercise 5-3.   Seaver Company produces and sells two products, X and Y. Data concerning the products follow:

	Product X	Product Y
Selling price per unit................	$10	$12
Variable expense per unit.........	6	3
Contribution margin per unit....	$ 4	$ 9

In the most recent month, the company sold 400 units of Product X and 600 units of Product Y. Fixed expense is $5,000 per month.

a. Complete the following contribution format income statement for the most recent month (carry percentages to one decimal point):

	Product X		Product Y		Total	
	Amount	%	Amount	%	Amount	%
Sales................................	$		$		$	
Variable expenses						
Contribution margin........	$		$			
Fixed expenses................						
Net operating income......					$	

b. Compute the company's overall monthly break-even point in sales dollars. $_____

c. If the company continues to sell 1,000 units, in total, each month, but the sales mix shifts so that an equal number of units of each product is being sold, would you expect monthly net operating income to rise or fall? Explain.

_____

_____

_____

_____

_____

_____

d. Refer to the data in part c above. If the sales mix shifts as explained, would you expect the company's monthly break-even point to rise or fall? Explain.

_____

_____

_____

_____

_____

_____

Exercise 5-4.   **Critical thought writing exercise:** Able Company and Baker Company are competing companies that sell a product at the same price. Both companies are operating above the break-even point and have similar total profits. Able Company's costs are mostly variable, whereas Baker Company's costs are mostly fixed. In a time of increasing sales, which company will tend to realize the most rapid increase in net operating income? Explain your answer.

_____

_____

_____

_____

_____

_____

_____

_____

_____

_____

_____

_____

Answers to Questions and Exercises

True or False

1. F   The CM ratio is the unit contribution margin divided by the unit selling price. One product might have a higher unit contribution than another, but its selling price may be lower.

2. F   The break-even occurs where profit is zero.

3. T   The break-even can be computed in terms of units sold or sales dollars.

4. T   A change in sales mix often results in a change in the overall CM ratio. If the overall CM ratio changes, the break-even will also change.

5. T   The CM ratio measures how much of a sales dollar is translated into increased contribution margin.

6. F   Profits should increase by 32% = 4 × 8%.

7. F   The degree of operating leverage decreases as a company moves further and further from its break-even.

8. T   At the break-even all fixed costs are covered. All contribution margin generated from that point forward increases net operating income.

9. F   The reverse is true—the overall break-even will rise because the average CM ratio will be lower as a result of selling less profitable products.

10. T   By definition, incremental analysis deals only with differences between alternatives.

11. F   The reverse is true—one would expect the company's CM ratio to rise. Variable costs would be lower and hence the CM ratio would be higher.

12. F   The break-even is computed by dividing total *fixed expenses* by the CM ratio.

13. T   This is a key assumption because a change in the sales mix will change the break-even.

Multiple Choice

1. c

Unit selling price.................	$50
Less unit variable expenses.	30
Unit contribution margin.....	$20

2. b

Unit contribution margin.....	$20
Unit selling price.................	$50
Contribution margin ratio....	40%

3. a

$$\text{Dollar sales to break even} = \frac{\text{Fixed expenses}}{\text{CM ratio}}$$

$$= \frac{\$200,000}{0.40} = \$500,000$$

4. b

$$\text{Unit sales to attain target profit} = \frac{\text{Target profit} + \text{Fixed expenses}}{\text{Unit CM}}$$

$$= \frac{\$200,000 + \$50,000}{\$20}$$

$$= 12,500 \text{ units}$$

5. c

$$\text{Dollar sales to break even} = \frac{\text{Fixed expenses}}{\text{CM ratio}}$$

$$= \frac{\$90,000}{0.60} = \$150,000$$

Margin of safety = $200,000 − $150,000
= $50,000

6. d $50,000 ÷ $200,000 = 25%

7. b

Sales	$200,000
CM ratio	× 0.60
Contribution margin	$120,000

8. d

Contribution margin	$120,000
Net operating income ...	÷ $30,000
Operating leverage	4.0

9. b   The computations are:

$$\text{Percentage change in sales} = \frac{\$450,000 - \$400,000}{\$400,000} = 12.5\%$$

Percentage change in dollar sales...	12.5%
Degree of operating leverage	× 6.0
Percentage change in net operating income	75.0%

10. b   A shift to more profitable products would result in an increase in the overall CM ratio. Thus, fewer sales would be needed to cover the fixed costs and the break-even would therefore decrease.

11. c

	Product A	Product B	Total
Sales............	$10,000	$30,000	$40,000
Variable expenses ..	4,000	24,000	28,000
Contribution margin	$ 6,000	$ 6,000	$12,000

Overall CM ratio = $12,000 ÷ $40,000 = 30%

Exercises

Exercise 5-1.

a.

	Per Unit	
Selling price...........................	$30	100%
Variable expenses.................	18	60%
Unit contribution margin	$12	40%

b. $$\text{CM ratio} = \frac{\text{Contribution margin}}{\text{Sales}} = \frac{\$54,000}{\$135,000} = 40\%$$

c.
$$\text{Profit} = \text{CM ratio} \times \text{Sales} - \text{Fixed expenses}$$
$$\$0 = 0.40 \times \text{Sales} - \$48,000$$
$$0.40 \times \text{Sales} = \$48,000$$
$$\text{Sales} = \$48,000 \div 0.40$$
$$\text{Sales} = \$120,000$$

Alternative solution:

$$\text{Dollar sales to break even} = \frac{\text{Fixed expenses}}{\text{CM ratio}} = \frac{\$48,000}{0.40} = \$120,000$$

d.   Profit = Unit CM × Q − Fixed expenses
$$\$0 = (\$30 - \$18) \times Q - \$48,000$$
$$\$0 = (\$12) \times Q - \$48,000$$
$$\$12Q = \$48,000$$
$$Q = \$48,000 \div \$12$$
$$Q = 4,000 \text{ units}$$

Alternative solution:

$$\text{Units sold to break even} = \frac{\text{Fixed expenses}}{\text{Unit contribution margin}} = \frac{\$48,000}{\$12} = 4,000 \text{ units}$$

e.   Profit = Unit CM × Q − Fixed expenses
$$\$12,000 = (\$30 - \$18) \times Q - \$48,000$$
$$\$12,000 = (\$12) \times Q - \$48,000$$
$$\$12Q = \$12,000 + \$48,000$$
$$Q = \$60,000 \div \$12$$

$$Q = 5{,}000 \text{ units}$$

Alternative solution:

$$\frac{\text{Unit sales to}}{\text{attain target profit}} = \frac{\text{Target profit + Fixed expenses}}{\text{Unit CM}} = \frac{\$12{,}000 + \$48{,}000}{\$12} = 5{,}000 \text{ units}$$

f. $$\frac{\text{Degree of operating}}{\text{leverage}} = \frac{\text{Contribution margin}}{\text{Net income}} = \frac{\$54{,}000}{\$6{,}000} = 9.0$$

g.
Percentage change in dollar sales	5%
Degree of operating leverage	× 9.0
Percentage change in net operating income	45%

h. New sales volume: 4,500 units × 105% = 4,725 units

Sales (4,725 units @ $30 per unit)	$141,750
Variable expenses (4,725 units @ $18 per unit)	85,050
Contribution margin	56,700
Fixed expenses	48,000
Net operating income	$ 8,700

Current net operating income	$ 6,000
Expected increase: $6,000 × 45%	2,700
Expected net operating income (as above)	$ 8,700

Exercise 5-2.   The completed CVP graph:

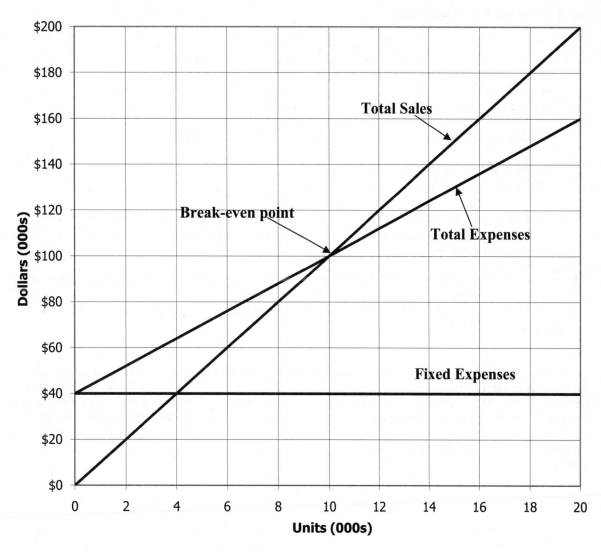

The break-even point is 10,000 units or $100,000 in sales.

Exercise 5-3.

a. The completed income statement:

	Product X		Product Y		Total	
	Amount	*%*	*Amount*	*%*	*Amount*	*%*
Sales..............................	$4,000	100	$7,200	100	$11,200	100.0
Variable expenses	2,400	60	1,800	25	4,200	37.5
Contribution margin........	$1,600	40	$5,400	75	7,000	62.5
Fixed expenses................					5,000	
Net operating income......					$ 2,000	

b. $$\text{Dollar sales to break even} = \frac{\text{Fixed expenses}}{\text{CM ratio}} = \frac{\$5,000}{0.625} = \$8,000$$

c. Monthly net operating income will fall. The shift in sales mix means that less of Product Y and more of Product X is being sold. Because Product Y has a higher contribution margin per unit than Product X, less contribution margin in *total* will be available and profits will therefore fall.

d. The monthly break-even will rise. As explained above, the shift in sales mix will be toward the less profitable Product X, which has a CM ratio of only 40% as compared to 75% for Product Y. Thus, the company's *overall* CM ratio will fall, and the break-even will rise because less contribution margin will be available per unit to cover the fixed costs.

Exercise 5-4.   Baker Company will have a higher contribution margin ratio (and contribution margin per unit) due to its lower variable costs. Thus, the company's contribution margin (and net operating income) will increase more rapidly than Able Company's as sales increase. Therefore, Baker Company will realize the most rapid increase in net operating income. The impact on net operating income can also be viewed in terms of operating leverage. Baker Company will have a higher degree of operating leverage than Able Company because of its higher contribution margin. Therefore, as sales increase, Baker's net operating income will rise more rapidly than will Able's.

Chapter 6

Variable Costing and Segment Reporting: Tools for Management

Chapter Study Suggestions

This chapter covers an alternative method of determining unit product costs called variable costing. Throughout the chapter we compare variable costing with absorption costing, which was covered in an earlier chapter.

Note that the difference between the variable and absorption costing centers on how they handle fixed manufacturing overhead costs. This point is emphasized in Exhibit 6-1. Exhibits 6-2 through 6-4 are the heart of the chapter. These exhibits show how to compute unit product costs and they show the impact of the two methods on net operating income. You must thoroughly understand the computations in these exhibits to complete homework assignments.

In the second part of the chapter that covers segment reporting, make sure that you carefully study Exhibit 6-8. Notice particularly that on a segmented report the company is divided into progressively smaller parts. Make sure you fully understand the difference between traceable and common costs, and the difference between segment margin and contribution margin.

CHAPTER HIGHLIGHTS

A. Two different methods can be used to determine unit product costs—*absorption costing* and *variable costing.*

1. Under *absorption costing*, all manufacturing costs, both variable and fixed, are included in unit product costs.

Direct materials	$XXX
Direct labor..	XXX
Variable manufacturing overhead	XXX
Fixed manufacturing overhead	XXX
Absorption costing unit product cost..	$XXX

2. Under *variable costing*, only variable manufacturing costs—which usually consist of direct materials, direct labor, and variable manufacturing overhead—are included in unit product costs.

Direct materials	$XXX
Direct labor..	XXX
Variable manufacturing overhead	XXX
Variable costing unit product cost	$XXX

    a. Variable costing focuses on cost behavior. The contribution approach and cost-volume-profit analysis discussed in prior chapters assumed that variable costing rather than absorption costing is used. Absorption costing data should not be used in cost-volume-profit calculations—the results are unreliable.

    b. Under the variable costing method, fixed manufacturing costs are treated as period costs and are expensed in the period in which they are incurred, just like selling and administrative expenses.

B. Under absorption costing, fixed manufacturing costs may be shifted from one period to another due to changes in inventories.

1. A portion of the period's fixed manufacturing overhead costs is assigned to each unit that is produced. If the unit is not sold during the period, the fixed manufacturing overhead assigned to the unit is part of the inventories on the balance sheet rather than cost of goods sold on the income statement. This is referred to as *deferral of fixed manufacturing overhead in inventory.*

C. Exhibit 6-5 is a key exhibit that summarizes the relations between variable and absorption costing. Any difference in net operating income between the two methods can be traced to changes in the level of inventories.

1. When production and sales (in units) are equal, inventories don't change. When this occurs, variable and absorption costing yield the same net operating income.

2. When production exceeds sales (in units) and hence inventories increase, greater net operating income will be reported under absorption costing than under variable costing.

    a. When inventories increase, some of the current period's *fixed manufacturing overhead costs are deferred in inventory.*

    b. The amount of fixed manufacturing overhead cost deferred is equal to the increase in units in inventory multiplied by the fixed manufacturing overhead cost per unit.

3. When production is less than sales (in units) and hence inventories decrease, less net operating income will be reported under absorption costing than under variable costing.

    a. Fixed manufacturing overhead costs are released from inventory when the units are sold.

    b. The amount of fixed manufacturing overhead cost released is equal to the decrease in units in inventory multiplied by the fixed manufacturing overhead cost per unit.

D. The following form, which is illustrated in Exhibit 6-4, can be used to reconcile variable costing and absorption costing net operating incomes.

Variable costing net operating income...	$XXX
Add (deduct) fixed manufacturing overhead costs deferred in (released from) inventory under absorption costing..................................	XXX
Absorption costing net operating income..	$XXX

E. A number of factors should be considered when choosing between variable and absorption costing.

1. Advantages of variable costing and the contribution approach are as follows:

    a. The contribution approach works well with cost-volume-profit analysis. The data for the analysis can be taken directly from the contribution format income statement because it categorizes costs by how they behave.

b. Unlike absorption costing, variable cost-ing profits are unaffected by changes in production (and inventories).

c. Under variable costing, unit product costs are variable costs. Under absorption costing, unit product costs are a mixture of variable and fixed costs. This can be confusing to managers who tend to think of unit product costs as variable costs.

d. Under variable costing, fixed costs are highlighted rather than buried in cost of goods sold and in inventories.

e. As discussed in later chapters, variable costing data make it easier to estimate the profitability of products.

f. Also as discussed in later chapters, varia-ble costing works well with cost control methods such as standard cost variance analysis and flexible budgets.

g. Variable costing net operating income is closer to net cash flows than absorption costing net operating income. This can be important for organiza-tions that need to closely monitor their cash resources.

2. Nevertheless, absorption costing is the gener-ally accepted method for preparing external financial reports and for preparing income tax returns. Variable costing is usually limited to internal use within a com-pany. And because of the cost and possible confusion of maintaining two separate costing systems, most companies use absorption costing for internal as well as for external reports.

F. When companies adopt lean production, differenc-es in net operating income between variable costing and absorption costing are reduced or eliminated.

1. The sometimes erratic movement of net operat-ing income under absorption costing, and the differences in net operating income between absorption and variable costing, arise because of changing levels of inventory.

2. Under lean production, inventories are largely eliminated. Consequently, there is little opportunity for fixed manufacturing overhead costs to be shifted between periods under absorption costing. Thus, under lean production, net operating income is essentially the same whether variable and absorption costing is used, and the sometimes erratic movement of net operating income under absorption costing is largely eliminated.

G. To operate effectively, management needs more information than is provided by a single income statement for the entire organization. Management needs information about segments of the organization.

1. A *segment* is any part or activity of an organi-zation about which the manager seeks cost or revenue data. Examples of segments include sales territories, manufacturing divisions, departments, and groups or lines of products.

2. Segmented reports for the use of managers should be prepared in the contribution format devel-oped in earlier chapters.

3. Exhibit 6-8 illustrates a series of segmented reports. Notice that as you go from one segmented re-port to another in the exhibit, the reports focus on smaller and smaller parts of the company.

H. Two general guidelines should be used in assigning costs to the various segments when the contribution approach is used.

1. Only *traceable costs* should be charged to segments. The traceable costs of a segment consist of those costs—including fixed costs—that arise because of the existence of the segment. Only those costs that would disappear over time if the segment were elimi-nated are truly traceable costs.

2. *Common costs* should not be charged to the segments. Common costs are costs that support more than one segment, but are not traceable, in whole or in part, to any one of those segments. Common costs would not disappear over time if a segment were elim-inated, and therefore, should not be allocated to seg-ments for decision-making purposes. For example, the cost of the company's executive jet is a common cost of the products the company sells. Even if a product were dropped entirely, it is unlikely that there would be any significant change in the costs of owning and operating the executive jet.

I. The format of a segmented income statement is:

	Total	Segment A	Segment B
Sales	$XXX	$XXX	$XXX
Variable expenses	XXX	XXX	XXX
Contribution margin	XXX	XXX	XXX
Less traceable fixed expenses	XXX	XXX	XXX
Segment margin	XXX	$XXX	$XXX
Less common fixed expenses not traceable to individual segments	XXX		
Net operating income	$XXX		

1. A segmented income statement emphasizes the distinctions between variable and fixed costs and between traceable and common costs.

2. As an organization is segmented into smaller and smaller pieces, some costs that were previously traceable become common to the smaller segments. There are limits to how finely a cost can be divided.

3. The *segment margin* shows the profitability of a segment after it has covered all of the costs that can be traced to it.

4. Common costs should not be allocated to segments because such an allocation would convey the misleading impression that the cost can be avoided by eliminating the segment.

REVIEW AND SELF-TEST
Questions and Exercises

True or False

Enter a T or an F in the blank to indicate whether the statement is true or false.

___ 1. Under absorption costing, product costs consist of direct materials, direct labor, and both variable and fixed manufacturing overhead.

___ 2. Selling and administrative expenses are treated as period costs under both variable costing and absorption costing.

___ 3. Fixed manufacturing overhead costs are treated the same way under both the variable costing and absorption costing methods.

___ 4. Under absorption costing, it is possible to defer some of the fixed manufacturing overhead costs of the current period to future periods.

___ 5. Variable costing net operating income will always be higher than absorption costing net operating income.

___ 6. When production and sales are equal, the same net operating income will be reported regardless of whether variable costing or absorption costing is used.

___ 7. When production exceeds sales, the net operating income reported under absorption costing will generally be greater than the net operating income reported under variable costing.

___ 8. Changes in the level of production do not affect net operating income under the variable costing method.

___ 9. Absorption costing data are generally better suited for cost-volume-profit analysis than variable costing data.

___ 10. Common costs should be allocated to segments on the basis of sales dollars.

___ 11. The terms "traceable cost" and "variable cost" mean the same thing.

___ 12. As an organization is broken down into smaller segments, costs that were traceable to the larger segments may become common to the smaller segments.

Multiple Choice

Choose the best answer or response by placing the identifying letter in the space provided.

___ 1. White Company manufactures a single product and has the following cost structure:

Variable costs per unit:
Direct materials	$	3
Direct labor..	$	4
Variable manufacturing overhead.......	$	1
Variable selling and admin. expense ..	$	2

Fixed costs per month:
Fixed manufacturing overhead	$100,000
Fixed selling and admin. expense.......	$ 60,000

The company produces 20,000 units each month. The unit product cost under absorption costing is: a) $10; b) $13; c) $15; d) $12.

___ 2. Refer to the data in question 1 above. The unit product cost under variable costing is: a) $8; b) $10; c) $13; d) $11.

___ 3. Refer to the data in question 1 above. Assume beginning inventories are zero, 20,000 units are produced, and 19,000 units are sold in a month. If the unit selling price is $20, what is the net operating income under absorption costing for the month? a) $30,000; b) $38,000; c) $35,000; d) $42,000.

___ 4. Refer to the data in question 1 above. Assume beginning inventories are zero, and 20,000 units are produced, and 19,000 units are sold in a month. If the unit selling price is $20, what is the net operating income under variable costing for the month? a) $30,000; b) $38,000; c) $35,000; d) $42,000.

___ 5. Refer to your answers to parts 3 and 4 above. The net operating income differs between variable and absorption costing in this situation because: a) variable costs are $5,000 higher under variable costing; b) $5,000 in fixed manufacturing overhead has been deferred in inventories under absorption costing; c) $5,000 in fixed manufacturing overhead has been released from inventories under absorption costing; d) none of the above.

___ 6. Which of the following costs are treated as period costs under the variable costing method? a) fixed manufacturing overhead and both variable and fixed selling and administrative expenses; b) both variable and fixed manufacturing overhead; c) only fixed manufacturing overhead and fixed selling and administrative expenses.

_____ 7. When production exceeds sales, fixed manufacturing overhead costs: a) are released from inventory under absorption costing; b) are deferred in inventory under absorption costing; c) are released from inventory under variable costing; d) are deferred in inventory under variable costing.

_____ 8. When sales are constant but production fluctuates: a) net operating income will be erratic under variable costing; b) absorption costing will always show a net loss; c) variable costing will always show a positive net operating income; d) net operating income will be erratic under absorption costing.

_____ 9. Last year, Peck Company produced 10,000 units and sold 9,000 units. Fixed manufacturing overhead costs were $20,000, and variable manufacturing overhead costs were $3 per unit. For the year, one would expect net operating income under absorption costing to be: a) $2,000 more than net operating income under variable costing; b) $5,000 more than net operating income under variable costing; c) $2,000 less than net operating income under variable costing; d) $5,000 less than net operating income under variable costing.

_____ 10. Armco, Inc., produces and sells five products. Which of the following costs would typically be a traceable fixed cost of a product? a) advertising costs of the product; b) the salary of the company's president; c) depreciation of facilities jointly used to produce several products; d) responses a, b, and c, are all correct.

_____ 11. If a segment has a negative segment margin: a) the segment should be dropped; b) the segment should be retained only if it has a positive contribution margin; c) the segment is not covering its own traceable costs, but it still may be of benefit to the company; d) none of these.

_____ 12. Rumberger, Inc. sells two products: X and Y. Data concerning the company for July follow:

	Product X	Product Y
Sales	$200,000	$300,000
Variable expenses.............	$ 50,000	$100,000
Traceable fixed expenses..	$ 80,000	$150,000

In addition, common fixed expenses of $70,000 were incurred in July. What is the segment margin for Product X? a) $70,000; b) $120,000; c) $150,000; d) $38,000.

_____ 13. Refer to the data for Rumberger, Inc. in question 12 above. What is the net operating income for the entire company? a) $120,000; b) $(4,000); c) $70,000; d) $50,000.

_____ 14. Refer to the data for Rumberger, Inc. in question 12 above. Suppose advertising for Product Y is increased by $20,000 per month, which results in increased sales of $90,000 per month. This should have the following effect on Product Y's monthly segment margin: a) increase by $70,000; b) increase by $40,000; c) increase by $60,000; d) decrease by $20,000.

_____ 15. Refer to the data for Rumberger, Inc. in question 14 above. What would be the effect of the increase in advertising and sales of Product Y on the company's overall net operating income? a) increase by $70,000; b) increase by $40,000; c) increase by $60,000; d) decrease by $20,000.

Exercises

Exercise 6-1.   Selected data relating to the operations of Dover Company for last year are given below:

Units in beginning inventory	0
Units produced....................................	40,000
Units sold...	35,000
Units in ending inventory...................	5,000

Selling price per unit..........................	$	27
Variable costs per unit:		
Direct materials	$	7
Direct labor....................................	$	6
Variable manufacturing overhead ...	$	3
Variable selling and administrative .	$	2
Fixed costs:		
Fixed manufacturing overhead........	$160,000	
Fixed selling and administrative......	$140,000	

a. Assume that the company uses absorption costing.

Compute the absorption costing unit product cost. $_____

Determine the value of the ending inventory. $_____

Complete the following absorption costing income statement:

Sales		$_____
Cost of goods sold...		_____
Gross margin		_____
Selling and administrative expenses:		
Variable selling and administrative............................	_____	
Fixed selling and administrative................................	_____	_____
Net operating income		$_____

b. Assume that the company uses variable costing.

Compute the variable costing unit product cost. $_____

Determine the value of the ending inventory. $_____

Complete the following contribution format income statement using variable costing:

Sales.. $_____

Variable expenses:

   Variable cost of goods sold....................   _____

   Variable selling and administrative........   _____   _____

Contribution margin.................................   _____

Fixed expenses:

   Fixed manufacturing overhead...............   _____

   Fixed selling and administrative.............   _____   _____

Net operating income............................... $_____

c. Reconcile the two net operating incomes by filling in the following form:

Variable costing net operating income .... $_____

Add (deduct) fixed manufacturing overhead cost

   deferred in (released from) inventory under ab-

   sorption costing...   _____

Absorption costing net operating income .... $_____

Exercise 6-2.   Hodex Corporation manufactures and sells a unique product that has enjoyed brisk sales. The results of last month's operations are shown below (absorption costing basis):

Sales (10,000 units @ $20 per unit)............................	$200,000
Cost of goods sold (10,000 units @ $14 per unit)......	140,000
Gross margin..	60,000
Selling and administrative expenses	45,000
Net operating income..	$ 15,000

Variable selling and administrative expenses are $2 per unit. Variable manufacturing costs are $10 per unit and fixed manufacturing overhead costs are $48,000 per month. There was no beginning inventory. The company produced 12,000 units during the month.

a. Redo the company's income statement in the contribution format, using variable costing.

Sales .... $_____

Variable expenses:

   Variable cost of goods sold...................   _____

   Variable selling and administrative ....   _____   _____

Contribution margin ....   _____

Fixed expenses:

   Fixed manufacturing overhead ....   _____

   Fixed selling and administrative............   _____   _____

Net operating income .... $_____

b. Reconcile the variable costing and absorption costing net operating incomes:

Variable costing net operating income .... $_____

_____

_____

_____...   _____

Absorption costing net operating income............................. $_____

Exercise 6-3.   **Critical thought writing exercise:** Lake Corporation uses absorption costing to prepare the financial statements for its annual report to stockholders. Last year, the company had $10,000,000 in sales and reported a $400,000 loss in its annual report. According to a CVP analysis prepared for management's use using variable costing, $10,000,000 in sales is the break-even point for the company. Based on these data, was the company's ending inventory greater than, less than, or equal to its beginning inventory? Explain your answer.

_____

_____

_____

_____

_____

_____

_____

_____

_____

_____

_____

_____

_____

_____

_____

_____

Exercise 6-4.   The following data pertain to Bylund Company's operations for July.

	Total	Product X	Product Y
Number of units sold................		10,000	12,000
Selling price per unit................		$20.00	$25.00
Variable cost per unit:			
Production		$ 9.00	$10.00
Selling and administrative		$ 3.00	$ 3.75
Fixed costs:			
Production	$155,000		
Selling and administrative	$ 20,000		

Only $50,000 of the fixed production costs is traceable to the production of Product X and $75,000 is traceable to Product Y. All of the selling and administrative costs are common costs that cannot be traced to either product.

a.   Prepare a segmented income statement for Bylund Company using the following form:

Bylund Company
Income Statement
For the Month Ended July 31

	Total	Product X	Product Y
Sales...	$_____	$_____	$_____
Variable expenses:			
Production	_____	_____	_____
Selling and administrative	_____	_____	_____
Total variable expenses	_____	_____	_____
Contribution margin	_____	_____	_____
Traceable fixed expenses..	_____	_____	_____
Product line segment margin	_____	$_____	$_____
Common fixed expenses not traceable to individual products:			
Production	_____		
Selling and administrative	_____		
Total common fixed expenses	_____		
Net operating income..	$_____		

b. Should either Product X or Product Y be dropped? Why?

_____

_____

_____

_____

c. Product X can be enhanced by incurring an additional $25,000 in fixed production costs. The company would not increase the product's selling price, but the enhancement should result in increased unit sales. If sales increase by $80,000, should the product be enhanced?

_____

_____

_____

_____

_____

_____

_____

_____

Answers to Questions and Exercises

True or False

1. T   All manufacturing costs are included as product costs under absorption costing.

2. T   Selling and administrative expenses are never treated as product costs under either costing method.

3. F   Under variable costing, fixed manufacturing overhead costs are treated as period costs; under absorption costing, fixed manufacturing overhead costs are treated as product costs.

4. T   Fixed manufacturing overhead costs are deferred to the future under absorption costing when production exceeds sales.

5. F   Variable costing will produce higher net operating income than absorption costing only when sales exceed production.

6. T   When sales and production are equal, fixed manufacturing overhead cost is neither deferred in nor released from inventory under absorption costing.

7. T   When production exceeds sales, fixed manufacturing overhead cost is deferred in inventory under absorption costing. Consequently, net operating income is higher under absorption costing than under variable costing.

8. T   Changes in the number of units sold—not produced—affect net operating income under the variable costing method.

9. F   The reverse is true—variable costing data are better suited for CVP analysis than absorption costing data.

10. F   Common costs should never be allocated to segments. If they are allocated, managers may believe that these costs could be avoided by dropping the segment.

11. F   A traceable cost can be variable or fixed.

12. T   As an organization is divided into smaller and smaller segments, some costs that were previously traceable become common.

Multiple Choice

1. b

Variable manufacturing costs (3 + $4 + $1)	$ 8
Fixed manufacturing costs ($100,000 ÷ 20,000 units).......	5
Absorption costing unit product cost...	$13

2. a   Only the variable manufacturing costs are treated as product costs under variable costing. Thus, the unit product cost is $3 + $4 + $1 = $8.

3. c   The absorption costing net operating income is computed as follows:

Sales (19,000 units × $20 per unit)......................................	$380,000
Cost of goods sold (19,000 units × $13 per unit)...............	247,000
Gross margin................................	133,000
Selling and admin. expenses:	
Variable selling and admin. (19,000 units × $2 per unit)	38,000
Fixed selling and admin...........	60,000
Total selling and admin.............	98,000
Net operating income.................	$ 35,000

4. a   The variable costing net operating income is computed as follows:

Sales (19,000 units × $20 per unit)......................................	$380,000
Variable expenses:	
Variable cost of goods sold (19,000 units × $8 per unit)	152,000
Variable selling and admin. (19,000 units × $2 per unit)	38,000
Total variable expenses..............	190,000
Contribution margin...................	190,000
Fixed expenses:	
Fixed manuf. overhead...........	100,000
Fixed selling and admin..........	60,000
Total fixed expenses	160,000
Net operating income.................	$ 30,000

5. b Inventories increased by 1,000 units. Under absorption costing, $5 (=$100,000 ÷ 20,000 units) of fixed manufacturing overhead cost is applied to each unit that is produced. Thus, $5,000 in fixed manufacturing overhead costs are deferred in inventories and do not appear on the income statement as part of cost of goods sold.

6. a Fixed manufacturing overhead cost is expensed as incurred under variable costing. Also, both variable and fixed selling and administrative expenses are always treated as period costs under both variable and absorption costing.

7. b When production exceeds sales, units are added to inventory. Thus, fixed manufacturing overhead costs are deferred in inventory under absorption costing.

8. d When production fluctuates, net operating income will be erratic under absorption costing because fixed manufacturing overhead costs will be shifted into and out of inventory as production goes up and down.

9. a Under absorption costing, fixed manufacturing overhead cost per unit will be $2 (= $20,000 ÷ 10,000 units). If only 9,000 units are sold, then 1,000 units will go into inventory. Thus, under absorption costing, $2,000 in fixed manufacturing overhead cost will be deferred in inventory ($2 per unit × 1,000 units = $2,000). Net operating income will therefore be $2,000 higher under absorption costing than under variable costing.

10. a The cost of advertising a specific product could be eliminated if the product were dropped.

11. c A negative segment margin means that a segment is not covering its own traceable costs. However, the segment may still be of value to the company if it helps sell other products.

12. a The segment margin for Product X can be read directly from the segmented income statement that appears below:

	Total	Product X	Product Y
Sales...............	$500,000	$200,000	$300,000
Variable expenses	150,000	50,000	100,000
Contribution margin.........	350,000	150,000	200,000
Traceable fixed expenses	230,000	80,000	150,000
Segment margin...............	120,000	$ 70,000	$ 50,000
Common fixed expenses	70,000		
Net operating income	$ 50,000		

13. d See the segmented income statement above in the answer to question 12.

14. b

	Product Y	Percentage of Sales
Sales	$300,000	100 %
Variable expenses	100,000	$33 \frac{1}{3}$ %
Contribution margin.........	200,000	$66 \frac{2}{3}$ %
Traceable fixed expenses	150,000	50 %
Segment margin	$ 50,000	$16 \frac{2}{3}$ %

Using the contribution margin ratio method, the $90,000 increase in sales should lead to a $60,000 (= 66 2/3% × $90,000) increase in contribution margin. This would be offset by the $20,000 increase in advertising expenses, a traceable fixed expense, to yield a net $40,000 increase in segment margin.

15. b Because there is no mention of any change in common fixed expenses, the change in the company's overall net operating income should be the same as the change in Product Y's segment margin.

Exercises

Exercise 6-1.

a.

Direct materials	$	7
Direct labor...		6
Variable manufacturing overhead..		3
Fixed manufacturing overhead ($160,000 ÷ 40,000 units)..		4
Absorption costing unit product cost...................................	$	20

Ending inventory (5,000 units × $20 per unit)..................... $100,000

Absorption Costing Income Statement

Sales (35,000 units × $27 per unit)...		$945,000
Cost of goods sold (35,000 units × $20 per unit).............................		700,000
Gross margin		245,000
Selling and administrative expenses:		
Variable selling and administrative (35,000 units × $2 per unit)...	70,000	
Fixed selling and administrative..	140,000	210,000
Net operating income..		$ 35,000

b.

Direct materials	$	7
Direct labor...		6
Variable manufacturing overhead...........................		3
Variable costing unit product cost	$	16

Ending inventory (5,000 units × $16 per unit)....... $80,000

Variable Costing Income Statement

Sales (35,000 units × $27 per unit)...		$945,000
Variable expenses:		
Variable cost of goods sold (35,000 units × $16 per unit)	560,000	
Variable selling and administrative (35,000 units × $2 per unit)	70,000	630,000
Contribution margin		315,000
Fixed expenses:		
Fixed manufacturing overhead..	160,000	
Fixed selling and administrative	140,000	300,000
Net operating income..		$ 15,000

c. Reconciliation of variable costing and absorption costing net operating incomes:

Variable costing net operating income...	$15,000
Add fixed manufacturing overhead cost deferred in inventory	
under absorption costing (5,000 units × $4 per unit)...............	20,000
Absorption costing net operating income	$35,000

Exercise 6-2.

a.

Sales (10,000 units × $20 per unit)		$200,000
Variable expenses:		
Variable cost of goods sold		
(10,000 units × $10 per unit)	100,000	
Variable selling and administrative		
(10,000 units × $2 per unit)	20,000	120,000
Contribution margin...		80,000
Fixed expenses:		
Fixed manufacturing overhead......................	48,000	
Fixed selling and administrative		
($45,000 - (l0,000 units × $2 per unit))	25,000	73,000
Net operating income.......................................		$ 7,000

b.

Variable costing net operating income	$ 7,000
Add fixed manufacturing overhead cost deferred in inventory	
under absorption costing (2,000 units × $4 per unit*)	8,000
Absorption costing net operating income	$ 15,000

*$48,000 ÷ 12,000 units produced = $4 per unit.

Exercise 6-3.   Because Lake Company reported a loss when its sales were at the break-even level, fixed manufacturing overhead costs must have been released from inventory under the absorption costing approach. (The break-even point is computed assuming either that variable costing is used or that there is no change in inventory.) Therefore, the company's inventory level for the year decreased. When inventory levels decrease, fixed manufacturing overhead costs are released from inventory under absorption costing. Thus, the fixed manufacturing overhead costs released from inventory would have resulted in a loss for the year, even though from a variable costing point of view the company would have broken even.

Exercise 6-4.

a.

	Total	Product X	Product Y
Sales	$500,000	$200,000	$300,000
Variable expenses:			
Production	210,000	90,000	120,000
Selling and administrative	75,000	30,000	45,000
Total variable expenses	285,000	120,000	165,000
Contribution margin	215,000	80,000	135,000
Traceable fixed expenses	125,000	50,000	75,000
Product line segment margin	90,000	$ 30,000	$ 60,000
Common fixed expenses not traceable to individual products:			
Production	30,000		
Selling and administrative	20,000		
Total common fixed expenses	50,000		
Net operating income	$ 40,000		

b. Neither product should be dropped. They are both covering all of their own traceable costs and are contributing to covering the fixed common costs and to overall profits of the company.

c. Product X's contribution margin ratio is 40% (= $80,000 ÷ $200,000).

Increase in sales	$ 80,000
Contribution margin ratio	× 40%
Increase in contribution margin	$ 32,000
Less increase in fixed production costs...	25,000
Increase in net operating income	$ 7,000

Yes, the product should be enhanced.

Chapter 7

Activity-Based Costing: A Tool to Aid Decision Making

Chapter Study Suggestions

Activity-based costing is very similar to the methods you learned in Chapter 3. The biggest change is the use of many overhead cost pools, rather than a single overhead cost pool. However, within each overhead cost pool, the procedures are the same as they were in Chapter 3.

Your instructor may assign Appendix 7A, which is concerned with the construction of action analyses. Exhibit 7A-6 provides a roadmap to the appendix. The procedures are somewhat complex, so it is a good idea to frequently revisit Exhibit 7A-6 as you work through the appendix.

CHAPTER HIGHLIGHTS

A. Traditional costing systems in manufacturing companies, such as those discussed in Chapters 2 and 3, are primarily designed to provide product cost data for external financial reports rather than for internal decision-making.

1. For external financial reports, all manufacturing costs must be assigned to products—even manufacturing costs that are not actually caused by any particular product. For example, the rent on the factory building is the same (within limits) regardless of which products are produced and how much is produced, and yet this cost must be assigned to products for external financial reports.

2. For external financial reports, selling and administrative costs are not assigned to products, even if the products directly cause the costs. For example, sales commissions are not included in product costs in traditional costing systems even though sales commissions are directly caused by selling specific products.

3. Because all manufacturing costs must be assigned to products for external financial reports, the costs of idle capacity must also be assigned to products. As a consequence, products are charged for the costs of resources they don't use as well as for the costs of resources they do use.

4. In traditional costing systems, overhead costs are usually allocated to products using a single measure of activity such as direct labor-hours. This approach assumes that overhead costs are highly correlated with direct labor-hours; that is, it assumes that overhead costs and direct labor-hours tend to move together. If this assumption is not valid, product costs will be distorted.

B. *Activity-based costing (ABC)* attempts to remedy these deficiencies of traditional costing systems. The key concept in activity-based costing is that products (and customers) cause activities. These activities result in the consumption of resources, which in turn result in costs. Consequently, if we want to accurately assign costs to products and customers, we must identify and measure the activities that link products and customers to costs.

C. The distinction between manufacturing and non-manufacturing costs is critical in traditional costing systems. This distinction is much less important in activity-based costing. Like variable costing, activity-based costing is concerned with how costs behave. And like variable costing, activity-based costing is primarily used in internal reports and is intended to help managers make decisions.

D. Activity-based costing differs from traditional costing in a number of ways:

1. Non-manufacturing costs, as well as manufacturing costs, may be assigned to products.

2. Some manufacturing costs—the costs of idle capacity and organization-sustaining costs—may be excluded from products.

3. A number of activity cost pools are used in activity-based costing. Each cost pool has its own unique measure of activity that is used as the basis for allocating its costs to products, customers, and other cost objects.

   a. An *activity* is an event that causes consumption of overhead resources such as processing a purchase order.

   b. An *activity cost pool* is a "bucket" in which costs are accumulated that relate to a single activity such as processing purchase orders.

4. The allocation bases in activity-based costing (i.e., measures of activity) often differ from those used in traditional costing systems.

5. The overhead rates in activity-based costing (which are called *activity rates*), may be based on the level of activity at capacity rather than on the budgeted level of activity.

E. Implementing activity-based costing involves five steps:

1. Define activities, activity cost pools, and activity measures.

2. Assign overhead costs to activity cost pools.

3. Calculate activity rates, which function like predetermined overhead rates in a traditional costing system.

4. Assign overhead costs to cost objects using the activity rates and measures of activity.

5. Prepare management reports.

F. To more fully understand activity-based costing, it is useful to think in terms of a hierarchy of costs:

1. *Unit-level activities* are performed each time a unit is produced. An example is testing a completed unit.

2. *Batch-level activities* are performed each time a batch is handled or processed. For example, tasks such as placing purchase orders and setting up equipment are batch-level activities. These activities occur no matter how many units are produced in a batch.

3. *Product-level activities* are required to have a product at all. An example is maintaining an up-to-date parts list and instruction manual for the product. These activities must be performed regardless of how many batches are run or units produced.

4. *Customer-level activities* relate to specific customers and include sales calls and catalog mailings that are not tied to a specific product.

5. *Organization-sustaining activities* are carried out regardless of which customers are served, which products are produced, how many batches are run, or how many units are produced. Examples include providing a computer network for employees, preparing financial reports, providing legal advice to the board of directors, and so on. Organization-sustaining costs should not be allocated to products or customers for purposes of making decisions.

G. To understand the mechanics of activity-based costing, there is no good substitute for working through the example in the book step-by-step. Nevertheless, the process can be briefly summarized as follows:

1. Prepare the *first-stage allocation* of costs to the activity cost pools.

    a. Begin with a listing of the costs that will be included in the activity-based costing system and the results of interviews with employees that indicate how these costs are to be distributed across the activity cost pools. The interview results indicate what percentage of a specific cost such as indirect factory wages should be allocated to the first activity cost pool, the second activity cost pool, and so on.

    b. For example, the results of the interviews might indicate that 20% of the resources associated with office staff wages are consumed in processing purchase orders. If office staff wages are $200,000, then 20% of $200,000, or $40,000, would be allocated to the "processing purchase orders" activity cost pool.

2. Calculate the activity rates.

    a. An *activity rate* is a cost per unit of activity. For example, the activity rate for machine set-ups might be $14 per machine set-up.

    b. Suppose that 2,000 purchase orders are processed per year. If the total cost of processing purchase orders is $60,000 per year, then the average cost would be $30 per purchase order ($60,000 ÷ 2,000 = $30). This is the activity rate for the "processing purchase orders" activity cost pool.

    c. Activity rates are important in *activity-based management*. Activity rates can be compared across organizations or across different locations in the same organization. For example, the cost of $30 for processing a purchase order may be higher at some locations in a company and lower at others. The higher cost locations may learn how to better process purchase orders by studying the techniques used at the lower cost locations.

3. Prepare the *second-stage allocation of costs to products*, customers, and other cost objects. For example, if a product requires two purchase orders and the activity rate is $30 per purchase order, the product would be allocated $60 (2 purchase orders × $30 per purchase order). Sum the costs of all of the activities associated with the product to determine the total cost of the product.

H. Product costs computed under activity-based costing and traditional costing systems differ for a number of reasons. They differ in *what* costs are allocated to products as well as in *how* they are allocated. Focusing just on *how* the costs are allocated, some general patterns emerge.

1. An activity-based costing system typically shifts costs from high-volume products that are produced in large batches to low-volume products that are produced in small batches. Traditional costing systems apply batch-level and product-level costs uniformly to all products and the high-volume products absorb the bulk of such costs. In an activity-based costing system, such costs are assigned to the products that cause the costs, rather than spreading them uniformly over all products on the basis of volume.

2. The unit costs of the low-volume products usually increase more than the unit costs of the high-volume products decrease. The reason is that if X dollars are shifted from high-volume products to low-volume products, the cost savings for the high-volume products is spread over many units, whereas the increase in costs for the low-volume products is spread over few units.

REVIEW AND SELF-TEST
Questions and Exercises

True or False

Enter a T or an F in the blank to indicate whether the statement is true or false.

___ 1. If direct labor is used as the base for overhead cost assignment and direct labor is not highly correlated with the overhead cost, the result will be distorted product costs.

___ 2. In activity-based costing, some manufacturing costs may not be assigned to products.

___ 3. In activity-based costing, nonmanufacturing costs are not assigned to products.

___ 4. In designing an activity-based costing system, managers should keep in mind that the system must conform to Generally Accepted Accounting Principles (GAAP).

___ 5. In activity-based costing, activity rates should be based on budgeted or estimated activity rather than activity at capacity.

___ 6. In activity-based costing, the first-stage allocation of costs to activity cost pools is often based on the results of interviews with employees.

___ 7. In activity-based costing, the overhead costs of the entire company are distributed to products and other cost objects on the basis of a single well-chosen measure of activity.

___ 8. Direct labor-hours should never be used as an allocation base in activity-based costing.

Multiple Choice

Choose the best answer or response by placing the identifying letter in the space provided.

___ 1. Advertising a product would be considered a: a) unit-level activity; b) batch-level activity; c) product-level activity; d) customer-level activity; e) organization-sustaining activity.

___ 2. Providing legal advice to the president concerning a possible merger with another company would be considered a: a) unit-level activity; b) batch-level activity; c) product-level activity; d) customer-level activity; e) organization-sustaining activity.

___ 3. Writing software for a new computer game at a software company that produces and sells computer games would be considered a: a) unit-level activity; b) batch-level activity; c) product-level activity; d) customer-level activity; e) organization-sustaining activity.

___ 4. A software company orders 100,000 copies of a DVD from a supplier. This DVD contains a computer game designed and published by the software company and will be sold to customers in a special box. Ordering the DVDs would be considered a: a) unit-level activity; b) batch-level activity; c) product-level activity; d) customer-level activity; e) organization-sustaining activity.

___ 5. A company that provides photocopying services has an activity-based costing system with three activity cost pools—making photocopies, serving customers, and setting up machines. The activity rates are $0.02 per photocopy, $2.15 per customer, and $0.75 per machine-setup. If a customer requires setups on two different machines and makes 200 copies in total, how much cost would be assigned by the activity-based costing system for this transaction? a) $4.00; b) $2.15; c) $1.50; d) $7.65.

Exercises

Exercise 7-1.   Lambert Fabrication, Inc., uses activity-based costing data for internal decisions. The company has the following four activity cost pools:

Activity Cost Pool	Annual Activity
Producing units..............	5,000 machine-hours
Processing orders..........	1,000 orders
Customer support..........	200 customers
Other.............................	Not applicable

The "Other" activity cost pool consists of the costs of idle capacity and organization-sustaining costs.

    The company traces the costs of direct materials and direct labor to jobs (i.e., orders). Overhead costs—both manufacturing and non-manufacturing—are allocated to jobs using the activity-based costing system. These overhead costs are listed below:

Indirect factory wages.................................	$100,000
Other manufacturing overhead	$200,000
Selling and administrative expense..............	$400,000

To develop the company's activity-based costing system, employees were asked how they distributed their time and resources across the four activity cost pools. The results of those interviews appear below:

Results of Interviews of Employees

Distribution of Resource Consumption Across Activities

	Producing Units	Processing Orders	Customer Support	Other	Totals
Indirect factory wages...........................	40%	30%	10%	20%	100%
Other manufacturing overhead..............	30%	10%	0%	60%	100%
Selling and administrative expense.......	0%	25%	40%	35%	100%

a. Using the results of the interviews, carry out the first-stage allocation of costs to the activity cost pools.

	Producing Units	Processing Orders	Customer Support	Other	Totals
Indirect factory wages......................	$_____	$_____	$_____	$_____	$_____
Other manufacturing overhead.........	_____	_____	_____	_____	_____
Selling and administrative expense ..	_____	_____	_____	_____	_____
Total overhead cost..........................	$_____	$_____	$_____	$_____	$_____

b. Using the results of the first-stage allocation, compute the activity rates for each of the activity cost pools. (Activity rates are not computed for the "Other" activity cost pool because these costs will not be allocated to products or customers.)

Computation of Activity Rates

Activity Cost Pools	Total Cost	Total Activity	Activity Rate
Producing units	$_____	_____ machine-hours	$_____ per machine-hour
Processing orders	$_____	_____ orders	$_____ per order
Customer support	$_____	_____ customers	$_____ per customer

c. Data concerning one of the company's products are listed below:

Product W562

Selling price	$ 100
Annual sales (units)	1,000
Direct materials per unit.......	$ 24
Direct labor per unit.............	$ 6
Machine-hours per unit........	1.5
Orders processed..................	80

Using the activity rates you derived in part (b) above and the above data, compute the total amount of overhead cost that would be allocated to product W562.

Overhead Cost of Product W562

Activity Cost Pools	Activity Rate	Activity	ABC Cost
Producing units	$_____ per machine-hour	_____ machine-hours	$_____
Processing orders	$_____ per order	_____ orders	_____
Customer support	$_____ per customer	Not applicable	_____
Total..........................			$_____

d. Using the data developed above for product W562, complete the following report.

Product Margin—Product W562

Sales.....................................		$_____
Costs:		
Direct materials	$_____	
Direct labor	_____	
Producing units	_____	
Processing orders	_____	_____
Product margin....................		$_____

Answers to Questions and Exercises

True or False

1. T   It is implicitly assumed that overhead cost is proportional to whatever allocation base is used. If this assumption is not valid, overhead costs will be incorrectly assigned to products and other cost objects.

2. T   Organization-sustaining costs and the costs of idle capacity should not be assigned to products in activity-based costing.

3. F   In activity-based costing, some non-manufacturing costs may be assigned to products. What matters is whether a cost is caused by the product, not whether it is a manufacturing or non-manufacturing cost.

4. F   An activity-based costing system should be designed to aid decision making, not to conform to GAAP. Under GAAP, manufacturing costs that are not caused by any specific products must be assigned to products anyway and non-manufacturing costs that are caused by products cannot be assigned to them.

5. F   The practice of basing overhead rates on estimated or budgeted activity results in assigning the costs of idle capacity to products that are made during the period.

6. T   Because employee time is a resource, the activity-based costing system requires information about how people spend their time. There may be no better way to get this information than to ask people how they spend their time at work.

7. F   One of the characteristics of activity-based costing is the use of multiple measures of activity.

8. F   Direct labor-hours can be used as an allocation base if it provides a valid measure of activity for an activity cost pool. Direct labor-hours might, for example, be an appropriate measure of activity for an activity cost pool in which the costs of miscellaneous production supplies are accumulated.

Multiple Choice

1. c   The advertising is incurred on behalf of the product and is not caused by running any particular batch or making any particular unit of that product.

2. e   Providing legal advice, unless it is about a specific product or customer, would be considered an organization-sustaining activity.

3. c   Writing software for a new computer game is a product-level activity. It only has to be done once for the product and does not have to be repeated to make more units of the software.

4. b   This is a batch-level activity because the process of writing an order is the same whether 1 or 1 million copies of the DVD are ordered.

5. d   The costs would be assigned as follows:

Making photocopies (200 copies @ $0.02)	$4.00
Setting up machines (2 set-ups @ $0.75)	1.50
Serving customers (1 customer @ $2.15)	2.15
Total cost	$7.65

Exercises

Exercise 7-1.

a.

	Producing Units	Processing Orders	Customer Support	Other	Totals
Indirect factory wages......................	$ 40,000	$ 30,000	$ 10,000	$ 20,000	$100,000
Other manufacturing overhead.........	60,000	20,000	0	120,000	200,000
Selling and administrative expense..	0	100,000	160,000	140,000	400,000
Total overhead cost.........................	$100,000	$150,000	$170,000	$280,000	$700,000

Example: 30% of $100,000 = $30,000

↑

Percentage of indirect factory wages attributable to
processing orders according to the interview results.

b.

Computation of Activity Rates

Activity Cost Pools	Total Cost	Total Activity	Activity Rate
Producing units	$100,000	5,000 machine-hours	$ 20 per machine-hour
Processing orders	$150,000	1,000 orders	$150 per order
Customer support......	$170,000	200 customers	$850 per customer

c.

Overhead Cost of Product W562

Activity Cost Pools	Activity Rate	Activity	ABC Cost
Producing units	$ 20 per machine-hour	1,500 machine-hours	$30,000
Processing orders	$150 per order	80 orders	12,000
Customer support......	$850 per customer	Not applicable	
Total.........................			$42,000

d.

Product Margin—Product W562

Sales.....................................		$100,000
Costs:		
Direct materials................	$24,000	
Direct labor	6,000	
Producing units	30,000	
Processing orders	12,000	72,000
Product margin....................		$ 28,000

Appendix 7A

ABC Action Analysis

APPENDIX HIGHLIGHTS

A. It is difficult or impossible to determine from a conventional ABC report, such as those illustrated in the main body of the chapter, what costs are relevant and what costs are not relevant in a particular decision. One should not assume that costs assigned to a product or customer in an ABC analysis will necessarily disappear even if the product or customer were dropped. The action analysis report in Appendix 7A is designed to remedy this deficiency of conventional ABC reports.

B. *Action analysis report.* Before taking an action such as dropping a product or a customer, managers should prepare an action analysis report. The action analysis report does two things. First, it identifies where in the organization any cost savings would have to come from. Second, it provides a simple coding scheme—red, yellow, and green—that can be used to highlight how easy or difficult it would be to adjust a cost if there is a change in activity.

1. *Green costs* adjust automatically to changes in activity without any action by managers. For example, the power to run production equipment would automatically decrease if fewer units were made.

2. *Yellow costs* could be adjusted in response to changes in activity, but such adjustments require management action. The adjustment is not automatic. Many wages would be classified as yellow costs because managers would have to explicitly lay off workers or redeploy them to more profitable uses to actually save any money.

3. *Red costs* could be adjusted to changes in activity only with a great deal of difficulty and the adjustment would require management action. For example, staff salaries are often a red cost.

REVIEW AND SELF-TEST
Questions and Exercises

Exercise

Exercise 7A-1. This exercise is a continuation of Exercise 7-1. Lambert Fabrication's managers would like action analysis reports in addition to the reports you have already completed. For the purpose of this report, management classifies the company's costs as follows:

> **Green:** *Costs that adjust automatically to changes in activity without management action.*
> Direct materials
> **Yellow:** *Costs that could, in principle, be adjusted to changes in activity, but management action would be required.*
> Direct labor
> Indirect factory wages
> **Red:** *Costs that would be very difficult to adjust to changes in activity and management action would be required.*
> Other manufacturing overhead
> Selling and administrative expense

a. Using the results of the first-stage allocation, compute the activity rates for each of the activity cost pools as in Exhibit 7A-2. (Activity rates are not computed for the "Other" activity cost pool. These costs will not be allocated to products or customers.)

Computation of Activity Rates

	Producing Units	Processing Orders	Customer Support
Total activity..	_____ machine-hours	_____ orders	_____ customers
Indirect factory wages............................	$_____	$_____	$_____
Other manufacturing overhead...............	_____	_____	_____
Selling and administrative expense........	_____	_____	_____
Total overhead cost.................................	$_____	$_____	$_____

b. Using the activity rates you derived in part (a) above, compute the total amount of overhead cost that would be allocated to product W562 as in Exhibit 7A-3.

Action Analysis Cost Matrix for Product W562

	Producing Units	Processing Orders	Total
Total activity..	_____ machine-hours	_____ orders	
Indirect factory wages............................	$_____	$_____	$_____
Other manufacturing overhead.............	_____	_____	_____
Selling and administrative expense......	_____	_____	_____
Total overhead cost.................................	$_____	$_____	$_____

c. Prepare an action analysis report for product W562 as in Exhibit 7A-5.

Action Analysis of Product W562

Sales.. $_____

Green costs:

   Direct materials.................................... $_____   _____

Green margin ....   _____

Yellow costs:

   Direct labor ....   _____

   Indirect factory wages..........................   _____   _____

Yellow margin ....   _____

Red costs:

   Other manufacturing overhead..............   _____

   Selling and administrative expense.......   _____   _____

Red margin .... $_____

Answers to Questions and Exercises

Exercise

Exercise 7A-1.

a.

Computation of Activity Rates

	Producing Units	Processing Orders	Customer Support
Total activity	5,000 machine-hours	1,000 orders	200 customers
Indirect factory wages............................	$ 8	$ 30	$ 50
Other manufacturing overhead...............	12	20	0
Selling and administrative expense........	0	100	800
Total overhead cost................................	$20	$150	$850

Example: $30,000 ÷ 1,000 orders = $30 per order

Indirect factory wages allocated to the processing orders
activity cost pool in the first-stage allocation above.

b.

Action Analysis Cost Matrix for Product W562

	Producing Units	Processing Orders	Total
Total activity	1,500 machine-hours	80 orders	
Indirect factory wages..........................	$12,000	$ 2,400	$14,400
Other manufacturing overhead.............	18,000	1,600	19,600
Selling and administrative expense......	0	8,000	8,000
Total overhead cost..............................	$30,000	$12,000	$42,000

Example: $30 per order × 80 orders = $2,400

Cost per order from part (b) above.

c. The overhead costs for the action analysis can be taken directly from the row totals in the overhead cost analysis in part (b) above.

Action Analysis of Product W562

Sales...		$100,000
Green costs:		
Direct materials......................................	$24,000	24,000
Green margin		76,000
Yellow costs:		
Direct labor	6,000	
Indirect factory wages............................	14,400	20,400
Yellow margin		55,600
Red costs:		
Other manufacturing overhead..............	19,600	
Selling and administrative expense........	8,000	27,600
Red margin...		$ 28,000

Appendix 7B

Using a Modified Form of Activity-Based Costing to Determine Product Costs for External Reports

APPENDIX HIGHLIGHTS

A. A variation of activity-based costing can be used to determine product costs for external reports. In this variation, all manufacturing costs—including organization-sustaining costs—are allocated to products and all selling and administration costs—including those actually caused by products—are excluded from product costs.

B. This form of activity-based costing is identical to the job-order costing system illustrated in Chapter 3, with the exception that there is more than one overhead cost pool in activity-based costing. Within each cost pool, however, the techniques for assigning costs to products are the same as those described in Chapter 3.

C. While the product costs produced by such an activity-based costing system would be acceptable for external financial reports, they should not be used for making decisions. These product costs include organization-sustaining costs, which would be irrelevant in any decision that involves the product, and exclude selling and administrative costs such as sales commissions that would be relevant in many decisions concerning the product.

REVIEW AND SELF-TEST
Questions and Exercises

Exercise

Exercise 7B-1. Xrow Corporation manufactures two industrial products—R590 and R500. the company uses a modified form of activity-based costing to compute product costs for external financial reports. Data concerning those products and the company's activity-based costing system appear below:

	R590	R500
Units produced.................	50,000	75,000
Direct materials per unit ...	$53.73	$46.87
Direct labor per unit..........	$12.10	$24.20

Activities and Activity Measures	Estimated Overhead Cost	R590	R500	Total
Supporting direct labor (DLHs).........	$250,000	50,000	150,000	200,000
Setting up machines (setups)	80,000	150	50	200
Updating products (product updates).	35,000	20	5	25
Total manufacturing overhead cost....	$365,000			

a. Compute the activity rates for the company's activity-based costing system using the form below:

Computation of Activity Rates

Activities	(a) Estimated Overhead Cost	(b) Total Expected Activity	(a) ÷ (b) Activity Rate
Supporting direct labor ...	$_____	_____ DLHs	$____ per DLH
Setting up machines........	$_____	_____ setups	$____ per setup
Updating products...........	$_____	_____ product updates	$____ per product update

b. Use the activity rates you computed above to apply overhead costs to the products using the forms below:

Assigning Overhead Costs to Products:

Overhead Cost for Product R590

Activity Cost Pools		(a) Activity Rate	(b) Activity	(a) × (b) ABC Cost
Supporting direct labor .	$____	per DLH	_____ DLHs	$_____
Setting up machines......	$____	per setup	_____ setups	_____
Updating products.........	$____	per product update	_____ product updates	_____
Total.............................				$_____

Overhead Cost for Product R500

Activity Cost Pools		(a) Activity Rate	(b) Activity	(a) × (b) ABC Cost
Supporting direct labor ...	$____	per DLH	_____ DLHs	$_____
Setting up machines........	$____	per setup	_____ setups	_____
Updating products...........	$____	per product update	_____ product updates	_____
Total...............................				$_____

c. Use the form below to determine unit product costs of the company's two products:

Activity-Based Costing Product Costs

	R590	R500
Direct materials...............................	$_____	$_____
Direct labor...................................	_____	_____
Manufacturing overhead		
$_____ ÷ _____ units;		
$_____ ÷ _____ units).....	_____	_____
Unit product cost............................	$_____	$_____

Answers to Questions and Exercises

Exercise

Exercise 7B-1.

a.

Computation of Activity Rates

Activities	(a) Estimated Overhead Cost	(b) Total Expected Activity		(a) ÷ (b) Activity Rate	
Supporting direct labor ...	$250,000	200,000	DLHs	$ 1.25	per DLH
Setting up machines........	$ 80,000	200	setups	$ 400	per setup
Updating products...........	$ 35,000	25	product updates	$ 1,400	per product update

b.

Assigning Overhead Costs to Products

Overhead Cost for Product R590

Activity Cost Pools	(a) Activity Rate		(b) Activity		(a) × (b) ABC Cost
Supporting direct labor .	$ 1.25	per DLH	50,000	DLHs	$ 62,500
Setting up machines......	$ 400	per setup	150	setups	60,000
Updating products.........	$ 1,400	per product update	20	product updates	28,000
Total..............................					$150,500

Overhead Cost for Product R500

Activity Cost Pools	(a) Activity Rate		(b) Activity		(a) × (b) ABC Cost
Supporting direct labor ...	$ 1.25	per DLH	150,000	DLHs	$187,500
Setting up machines........	$ 400	per setup	50	setups	20,000
Updating products...........	$ 1,400	per product update	5	product updates	7,000
Total..............................					$214,500

c.

Activity-Based Costing Product Costs

	R590	R500
Direct materials	$53.73	$46.87
Direct labor....................................	12.10	24.20
Manufacturing overhead ($150,500 ÷ 50,000 units; $214,500 ÷ 75,000 units)	3.01	2.86
Unit product cost	$68.84	$73.93

Chapter 8

Profit Planning

Chapter Study Suggestions

Study the flow of budget data in Exhibit 8-2. This exhibit provides a good overview of the chapter and the budgeting process. Notice particularly how all the budgets depend in some way on the sales budget and that nearly all budgets eventually impact the cash budget. As suggested by this exhibit, the cash budget is a key budget that serves to tie together much of the budget process. Schedule 8 in the text contains an example of a cash budget.

Schedules 1 and 2, containing the sales and production budgets, are also very important and your homework assignments are very likely to concentrate on these two budgets.

CHAPTER HIGHLIGHTS

A. Profit planning is accomplished in most organizations with budgets. A *budget* is a detailed plan for the acquisition and use of financial and other resources over a specified time period.

    1. The *master budget* consists of a series of separate but interdependent budgets that formally lay out the company's sales, production, and financial goals and that culminates in a cash budget, budgeted income statement, and budgeted balance sheet.

    2. The budgeting process is concerned with both planning and control.

        a. *Planning* involves developing objectives and preparing budgets to achieve these objectives.

        b. *Control* involves the steps taken by management to increase the likelihood that all parts of the organization are working together to achieve the goals set down at the planning stage.

    3. Budgeting provides a number of benefits:

        a. The budget *communicates* management's plans throughout the entire organization.

        b. The budgeting process forces managers to *think ahead* and to *formalize* their planning efforts.

        c. The budgeting process provides a means of *allocating resources* to those parts of the organization where they can be used most effectively.

        d. Budgeting uncovers potential *bottlenecks* before they occur.

        e. The budget *coordinates* the activities of the entire organization by *integrating* the plans and objectives of the various parts.

        f. The budget provides goals and objectives that serve as *benchmarks* for evaluating subsequent performance.

B. This chapter and the next several chapters are concerned with *responsibility accounting*. The basic idea behind responsibility accounting is that each manager's performance should be judged by how well he or she manages those items—and only those items—under his or her control. Each manager is assigned responsibility for those items of revenues and costs in the budget that the manager is able to control to a significant extent. The manager is then held responsible for differences between the budget and actual results.

C. Budget preparation is a complex task requiring the cooperative effort of many managers.

    1. Operating budgets (the budgets discussed in this chapter) ordinarily cover a one-year period divided into quarters and months.

    2. Rather than impose a budget on a manager, the manager should be involved in setting his or her own budget. There are two reasons for this. First, managers are likely to have the best information concerning their own operations. Second, a manager is more likely to be committed to attaining a budget if the manager is given a major role in developing the budget.

D. The master budget consists of a number of separate but interdependent budgets. Exhibit 8-2 provides an overview of the master budget and shows how the parts of the master budget are linked together. Study this exhibit carefully.

    1. The *sales budget* (Schedule 1 in the text) is the beginning point in the budgeting process. It details the expected sales, in both units and dollars, for the budget period. The sales budget is accompanied by a *Schedule of Expected Cash Collections* that shows the anticipated cash inflow from sales and collections of accounts receivable for the budget period.

    2. In a manufacturing company, the sales budget is followed by the *production budget* (Schedule 2 in the text) that shows what must be produced to meet sales forecasts and to provide for desired levels of inventory.

        a. The production budget has the following format:

Budgeted unit sales	XXX
Add desired ending inventory ..	<u>XXX</u>
Total needs..............................	XXX
Less beginning inventory.........	<u>XXX</u>
Required production	<u>XXX</u>

        b. Study Schedule 2 in the text carefully. Note that the "Year" column is not simply the sum of the figures for the Quarters in Schedule 2. The desired ending inventory for the year is the desired ending inventory for the 4th Quarter. And the beginning inventory for the year is the beginning inventory for the 1st Quarter. Warning: Students often overlook this important detail.

    3. In a merchandising company such as a clothing store, the sales budget is followed by a *merchandise purchases budget* instead of a production budget.

This budget details the amount of goods that must be purchased from suppliers to meet customer demand and to maintain adequate stocks of ending inventory.

    a.   The format for the merchandise purchases budget is (in units or dollars):

Budgeted unit sales	XXX
Add desired ending inventory ..	XXX
Total needs	XXX
Less beginning inventory	XXX
Required purchases	XXX

    b.   Note the similarity between the production budget in a manufacturing company and the merchandise purchases budget in a merchandising company.

4.   In a manufacturing company, the *direct materials budget* follows the production budget. It details the amount of raw materials that must be acquired to support production and to provide for adequate inventories.

    a.   The format for the direct materials budget is:

Required production in units of finished goods	XXX
Raw materials required per unit of finished goods...................................	XXX
Raw materials needed to meet the production schedule...........................	XXX
Add desired ending raw materials inventory......................................	XXX
Total raw materials needs......................	XXX
Less beginning raw materials inventory	XXX
Raw materials to be purchased..............	XXX
Unit cost of raw materials	XXX
Raw materials to be purchased..............	XXX

    b.   The direct materials budget should be accompanied by a *Schedule of Expected Cash Disbursements* for raw materials.

    c.   An example of the direct materials budget appears in Schedule 3 in the text. Note that the "Year" column is not simply the sum of the amounts for the Quarters.

5.   In a manufacturing company, a *direct labor budget* (Schedule 4 in the text) follows the production budget.

6.   In a manufacturing company, a *manufacturing overhead budget* (Schedule 5 in the text) also follows the production budget and details all of the production costs that will be required other than direct materials and direct labor.

7.   In a manufacturing company, the *ending finished goods inventory budget* (Schedule 6 in the text) provides computations of unit product costs and of the carrying value of the ending inventory.

8.   In all types of companies, a *selling and administrative expense* budget (Schedule 7 in the text) is prepared.

9.   The *cash budget* (Schedule 8 in the text) summarizes all of the cash inflows and cash outflows appearing on the various budgets. In many companies, the cash budget is the single most important result of the budgeting process because it can provide critical advance warnings of potential cash problems. The cash budget allows managers to arrange for financing *before* a crisis develops. Potential lenders are more likely to provide financing if managers appear to be in control and looking ahead rather than simply reacting to crises.

    a.   The cash budget has the following format:

Cash balance, beginning	$XXX
Add receipts.......................................	XXX
Total cash available	XXX
Less disbursements.............................	XXX
Excess (deficiency) of cash available over disbursements	XXX
Financing...	XXX
Cash balance, ending..........................	$XXX

    b.   Study Schedule 8 with care, noting particularly how the financing section is handled.

    c.   As with the production budget and the direct materials budget, the "Year" column in Schedule 8 is not simply the sum of the amounts for the Quarters. The beginning cash balance for the year is the beginning cash balance for the first month or quarter. And the ending cash balance for the year is the ending cash balance for the final month or quarter.

10.   The budgeting process culminates with the preparation of a *budgeted income statement* (Schedule 9 in the text) and a *budgeted balance sheet* (Schedule 10 in the text).

REVIEW AND SELF-TEST
Questions and Exercises

True or False

Enter a T or an F in the blank to indicate whether the statement is true or false.

____ 1. A forecast of sales is the usual starting point in budgeting.

____ 2. A self-imposed budget is one prepared by top management and imposed on subordinate managers.

____ 3. Budgets are planning devices rather than control devices.

____ 4. The basic idea behind responsibility accounting is that each manager's performance should be judged by how well he or she manages those items under his or her control.

____ 5. Ending inventories occur because an organization is unable to sell all that it had planned to sell during a period.

____ 6. The required production in units for a budget period is equal to the expected unit sales for the period.

____ 7. Because of the technical nature of budgeting, it is best to leave budgeting entirely in the capable hands of the accounting staff.

____ 8. The required raw materials purchases for a period equals the raw materials required for production.

Multiple Choice

Choose the best answer or response by placing the identifying letter in the space provided.

____ 1. Ward Corp.'s actual sales were $30,000 in June, $50,000 in July, and $70,000 in August. Sales in September are expected to be $60,000. Thirty percent of a month's sales are collected in the month of sale, 50% in the first month after sale, 15% in the second month after sale, and the remaining 5% is uncollectible. Budgeted cash receipts for September should be: a) $60,500; b) $62,000; c) $57,000; d) $70,000.

____ 2. Beecher Inc. is planning to purchase inventory for resale costing $90,000 in October, $70,000 in November, and $40,000 in December. The company pays for 40% of its purchases in the month of purchase and 60% in the month following purchase. What would be the budgeted cash disbursements for purchases of inventory in December? a) $40,000; b) $70,000; c) $58,000; d) $200,000.

____ 3. Archer Company has budgeted sales of 30,000 units in April, 40,000 units in May, and 60,000 units in June. The company has 6,000 units on hand on April 1. If the company requires an ending inventory equal to 20% of the following month's sales, production during May should be: a) 32,000 units; b) 44,000 units; c) 36,000 units; d) 40,000 units.

____ 4. Refer to the data for Archer Company in question 3. Each unit requires 3 pounds of a material. A total of 24,000 pounds of the material were on hand on April 1, and the company requires materials on hand at the end of each month equal to 25% of the following month's production needs. The company plans to produce 32,000 units of finished goods in April. How many pounds of the material should the company plan to purchase in April? a) 105,000; b) 19,000; c) 87,000; d) 6,000.

____ 5. If the beginning cash balance is $15,000, the required ending cash balance is $12,000, cash disbursements are $125,000, and cash collections from customers are $90,000, the company must borrow: a) $32,000; b) $20,000; c) $8,000; d) $38,000.

Exercises

Exercise 8-1. Billings Company produces and sells a single product. Expected sales for the next four months are given below:

	April	*May*	*June*	*July*
Sales in units	10,000	12,000	15,000	9,000

The company needs a production budget for the second quarter. Experience indicates that end-of-month inventories should equal 10% of the following month's sales in units. At the end of March, 1,000 units were on hand. Complete the following production budget for the quarter:

	April	*May*	*June*	*Quarter*
Budgeted unit sales				
Add desired ending inventory				
Total needs				
Less beginning inventory				
Required production				

Exercise 8-2. Dodero Company's production budget for the next four months is given below:

	July	*August*	*September*	*October*
Required production (units)	15,000	18,000	20,000	16,000

Each unit of product uses five ounces of raw materials. At the end of June, 11,250 ounces of material were on hand. The company wants to maintain an inventory of materials equal to 15% of the following month's production needs.

Complete the following materials purchases budget for the third quarter:

	July	*August*	*September*	*Quarter*
Required production (units)				
Raw material needs per unit (ounces)				
Production needs (ounces)				
Add desired ending inventory (ounces)*				
Total needs (ounces)				
Less beginning inventory (ounces)				
Raw materials to be purchased (ounces)				

Exercise 8-3.   Whitefish Company budgets its cash two months at a time. Budgeted cash disbursements for March and April, respectively, are: for inventory purchases, $90,000 and $82,000; for selling and administrative expenses (includes $5,000 depreciation each month), $75,000 and $70,000; for equipment purchases, $15,000 and $6,000; and for dividend payments, $5,000 and $0. Budgeted cash collections from customers are $150,000 and $185,000 for March and April, respectively. The company will begin March with a $10,000 cash balance on hand. The minimum cash balance at the end of each month should be $5,000. If needed, the company can borrow money at 1% per month. All borrowings are at the beginning of a month, and all repayments are at the end of a month. Interest is paid only when principal is being repaid.

Complete the following cash budget for March and April:

	March	April	Two Months
Cash balance, beginning	$_____	$_____	$_____
Add collections from customers..................	_____	_____	_____
Total cash available.....................................	_____	_____	_____
Less disbursements:			
_____ ...	_____	_____	_____
_____ ...	_____	_____	_____
_____ ...	_____	_____	_____
_____ ...	_____	_____	_____
Total disbursements	_____	_____	_____
Excess (deficiency) of cash available over cash disbursements...................................	_____	_____	_____
Financing:			
Borrowings (at beginning)........................	_____		_____
Repayments (at ending)............................		_____	_____
Interest...		_____	_____
Total financing..	_____	_____	_____
Cash balance, ending...................................	$_____	$_____	$_____

Answers to Questions and Exercises

True or False

1. T A sales forecast is the basis for the company's sales budget. The sales budget, in turn, is the basis for most of the other parts of the master budget.

2. F A self-imposed budget is one in which a manager prepares his or her own budget with review by higher-level managers.

3. F Budgeting involves both planning and control. Once a budget is set, it then becomes a control device. It is the benchmark for assessing actual results.

4. T This is a clear, straightforward statement of the purpose of responsibility accounting.

5. F Ending inventories are carefully planned if a company is following good budget procedures.

6. F Production requirements are determined by the level of beginning inventory and the desired level of ending inventory as well as by the expected unit sales.

7. F The accounting staff may provide help in preparing budgets, but the underlying estimates and data should come from operating managers. There are two reasons for this. First, the operating managers generally have better information about their own operations than the accounting staff. Second, the operating managers must be involved in preparing their own budgets or they will not be committed to them.

8. F Raw materials purchases do not simply equal the raw materials required for production because of inventories. Beginning inventories decrease the amount of raw materials that must be purchased; desired ending inventories increase the purchases.

Multiple Choice

1. a The computations are:

September sales ($60,000 × 30%)	$18,000
August sales ($70,000 × 50%)	35,000
July sales ($50,000 × 15%)	7,500
Total cash receipts	$60,500

2. c The computations are:

November purchases ($70,000 × 60%)	$42,000
December purchases ($40,000 × 40%)	16,000
Total cash disbursements	$58,000

3. b The computations are:

Budgeted sales	40,000
Desired ending inventory (20% × 60,000)	12,000
Total needs	52,000
Less beginning inventory (20% × 40,000)	8,000
Required production	44,000

4. a The computations are:

Required production (units)	32,000
Material per unit (pounds)	× 3
Production needs (pounds)	96,000
Desired ending inventory (25% × 44,000 × 3 pounds)	33,000
Total needs	129,000
Less beginning inventory (25% × 96,000 pounds)	24,000
Required purchases (pounds)	105,000

5. a The computations are:

Beginning cash balance	$ 15,000
Cash receipts	90,000
Cash available	105,000
Cash disbursements	125,000
Deficiency of cash	$(20,000)

Because the company desires an ending cash balance of $12,000, the company must borrow $32,000 to make up for the cash deficiency of $20,000.

Exercises

Exercise 8-1.

	April	May	June	Quarter
Budgeted sales	10,000	12,000	15,000	37,000
Add desired ending inventory	1,200	1,500	900	900
Total needs	11,200	13,500	15,900	37,900
Less beginning inventory	1,000	1,200	1,500	1,000
Required production	10,200	12,300	14,400	36,900

Exercise 8-2.

	July	August	September	Quarter
Required production (units)	15,000	18,000	20,000	53,000
Raw material needs per unit (ounces)	× 5	× 5	× 5	× 5
Production needs (ounces)	75,000	90,000	100,000	265,000
Add desired ending inventory (ounces)*	13,500	15,000	12,000	12,000
Total needs (ounces)	88,500	105,000	112,000	277,000
Less beginning inventory (ounces)	11,250	13,500	15,000	11,250
Raw materials to be purchased (ounces)	77,250	91,500	97,000	265,750

*September desired ending inventory: 16,000 units for October × 5 ounces per unit = 80,000 ounces; 80,000 ounces × 15% = 12,000 ounces

Exercise 8-3.

	March	April	Two Months
Cash balance, beginning	$ 10,000	$ 5,000	$ 10,000
Add collections from customers	150,000	185,000	335,000
Total cash available	160,000	190,000	345,000
Less disbursements:			
Inventory purchases	90,000	82,000	172,000
Selling and administrative expenses (net of depreciation)	70,000	65,000	135,000
Equipment purchases	15,000	6,000	21,000
Dividends	5,000	0	5,000
Total disbursements	180,000	153,000	333,000
Excess (deficiency) of cash available over cash disbursements	(20,000)	37,000	12,000
Financing:			
Borrowings (at beginning)	25,000		25,000
Repayments (at ending)		(25,000)	(25,000)
Interest*		(500)	(500)
Total financing	25,000	(25,500)	(500)
Cash balance, ending	$ 5,000	$ 11,500	$ 11,500

* $25,000 × 1% × 2 = $500

Chapter 9

Flexible Budgets and Performance Analysis

Chapter Study Suggestions

The key exhibit in the chapter is Exhibit 9-7, which shows a flexible budget performance report with both activity variances and revenue and spending variances. Make sure you understand how this report is constructed and what it means.

CHAPTER HIGHLIGHTS

A. The sales budgets, production budgets, and cash budgets in Chapter 8 are static planning budgets. They show what revenues and costs should be at the originally budgeted level of activity. However, the actual level of activity ordinarily differs from what was assumed when the budget was constructed. Consequently, some costs (i.e., variable and mixed costs) *should* be different from what is shown in the planning budget. Because of this, the planning budget should *not* be used to assess performance.

B. A *flexible budget* shows what revenues and costs should have been for the *actual* level of activity of the period. An example of a flexible budget is shown in Exhibit 9-4. Each cost item on a flexible budget has its own cost formula such as $10,000 + $5q, where $10,000 is the fixed component, $5 is the variable component, and q is the level of activity.

C. The flexible budget can be compared to the planning budget as shown in Exhibit 9-5. The differences between the flexible budget and the planning budget are called *activity variances*.

1. These variances are routinely labeled favorable (F) or unfavorable (U), although some caution is advised when interpreting these variances. For example, if the actual level of activity exceeds the planned level of activity, the flexible budget will show a higher cost than the planning budget and the variance will be labeled unfavorable. However, is this really unfavorable? The cost is higher than planned simply because the level of activity is higher than planned—which will usually result in higher revenues than planned.

2. Consequently, it is best to focus attention on the overall activity variance—the one for net operating income. If activity is higher than planned, this variance will ordinarily be favorable—reflecting the fact that higher activity usually results in higher profit.

D. Remember that the flexible budget represents what the revenues and costs should have been for the actual level of activity. Therefore it would be natural to compare the flexible budget to the actual results as shown in Exhibit 9-6. The differences between the actual results and the flexible budget are called *revenue and spending variances*.

1. A revenue variance is favorable if the actual revenue exceeds what the revenue should have been according to the flexible budget. A revenue variance is unfavorable if the actual revenue is less than what the revenue should have been according to the flexible budget.

2. A spending variance is favorable if the actual cost is less than what the cost should have been according to the flexible budget. A spending variance is unfavorable if the actual cost is greater than what the cost should have been according to the flexible budget.

3. Fixed costs can have spending variances because actual fixed costs can differ from budgeted fixed costs.

   a. A cost is fixed if it does not depend on the level of activity. However, that does not mean a fixed cost cannot change for other reasons or that it cannot be controlled.

   b. For example, the cost of heating and lighting an administrative office is fixed—it does not depend on how many goods or services the company sells. Nevertheless, this cost can change from period to period due to seasonal factors, how conscientious people are in turning off lights, the thermostat setting, and so on.

   c. It is often easier to control fixed costs than variable costs. Many fixed costs involve discretionary activities such as travel costs, entertainment, and executive seminars.

E. A *flexible budget performance report* such as the one shown in Exhibit 9-7 shows both activity variances and revenue and spending variances.

1. The activity variances are computed and interpreted as discussed above.

2. The revenue and spending variances are computed and interpreted as discussed above.

3. Note that the sum of the activity variance and the spending variance for any cost item is the difference between the amount that was originally budgeted for that item and the actual cost of that item. The activity variance represents how much of that difference is simply due to a change in the level of activity. The spending variance represents how well the cost was controlled.

F. As shown in Exhibit 9-8, more than one cost driver (i.e., measure of activity) can be used to construct a flexible budget. In that case, the cost formula for a cost item may be a function of a number of different variables. For example, the cost formula for electricity in Exhibit 9-8 is $390 + $0.10q_1 + $6.00q_2$, where q_1 is the number of client-visits and q_2 is the number of hours of operations of the hairstyling salon.

G. Perhaps the most common errors in performance evaluation are implicitly assuming that all revenues and costs are fixed or assuming that they are all strictly variable.

1. When the planning budget is directly compared to actual results as in Exhibit 9-9, it is implicitly assumed that none of the items are affected by a change in activity—in other words, they are fixed. This assumption is valid for a few items that really are fixed, such as rent, but is not valid for revenues or for costs that are variable or mixed.

2. Sometimes a crude adjustment is made to the planning budget before it is compared to the actual results. The adjustment consists of adjusting all items in the planning budget in proportion to the change in activity. For example, if the actual activity is 10% higher than budgeted, every item in the planning budget is increased by 10%. Such a crude adjustment is shown in Exhibit 9-10. This adjustment implicitly assumes that all items in the planning budget are strictly variable. This assumption may be true of sales revenues and some cost items, but not cost items that are mixed or fixed.

REVIEW AND SELF-TEST
Questions and Exercises

True or False

Enter a T or an F in the blank to indicate whether the statement is true or false.

____ 1. The planning budget is a static budget that is prepared for a single level of activity.

____ 2. Fixed costs are not controllable and therefore should be omitted from performance reports.

____ 3. Actual costs should be directly compared to the planning budget to effectively control costs.

____ 4. If a cost item has a favorable activity variance, it means that spending was under control.

____ 5. An unfavorable activity variance for revenue can happen because prices were discounted more than expected.

____ 6. An unfavorable spending variance could be due to paying higher prices than should have been paid.

____ 7. A favorable revenue variance could be due to selling more units than expected; that is, it could be due to having more activity than expected.

____ 8. The activity variance for a fixed cost should be zero.

Multiple Choice

Choose the best answer or response by placing the identifying letter in the space provided.

____ 1. A restaurant has a cost with the following cost formula: $1,000 + $5q$, where q is the number of meals served. The restaurant's planning budget is based on 1,000 meals. Its actual level of activity was 900 meals and the actual amount of the cost at that level of activity was $5,575. What is the amount of the cost on the planning budget? a) $5,580; b) $5,500; c) $6,000; d) $5,575.

____ 2. Refer to the data in question 1 above. What is the amount of the cost on the flexible budget? a) $5,580; b) $5,500; c) $6,000; d) $5,575.

____ 3. Refer to the data in question 1 above. What is the activity variance for this cost? a) $500 F; b) $500 U; c) $75 F; d) $75 U.

____ 4. Refer to the data in question 1 above. What is the spending variance for this cost? a) $500 F; b) $500 U; c) $75 F; d) $75 U.

____ 5. A restaurant's revenue formula is $25q$, where q is the number of meals served. The restaurant's planning budget is based on 400 meals. Its actual level of activity was 380 meals and the actual revenue at that level of activity was $9,325. What is the amount of the revenue on the planning budget? a) $10,000; b) $9,500; c) $500; d) $9,325.

____ 6. Refer to the data in part 5 above. What is the amount of the revenue on the flexible budget? a) $10,000; b) $9,500; c) $500; d) $9,325.

____ 7. Refer to the data in part 5 above. What is the activity variance for revenue? a) $175 F; b) $175 U; c) $500 F; d) $500 U.

____ 8. Refer to the data in part 5 above. What is the revenue variance from the flexible budget performance report? a) $175 F; b) $175 U; c) $500 F; d) $500 U.

Exercises

Exercise 9-1.   Great Hots is a mobile hot dog stand that is owned by an independent investor. The stand is operated as a franchise which must pay franchise fees to the franchising corporation in exchange for equipment and management services. Great Hots sells its hot dogs for $195 each. Cost data appear below:

Item	Cost Formula
Wieners, buns, condiment, supplies.......	$0.70 per hot dog
Butane for stove...............................	$200 per month
Wages	$2,800 per month
Franchise fees	$600 per month plus $0.10 per hot dog

Prepare the company's planning budget for March assuming that the owner expects to sell 4,000 hot dogs.

Great Hots
Planning Budget
For the Month Ended March 31

Budgeted hot dogs (q) ....   _____

Revenue (_____) .... $_____

Expenses:

   Wieners, buns, condiments, supplies (_____) ..   _____

   Butane for stove (_____)...............................   _____

   Wages (_____) ....   _____

   Franchise fees (_____) ....   _____

Total expense ....   _____

Net operating income .... $_____

Exercise 9-2.   Refer to the data for Great Hots in Exercise 9-1. In March, actual sales totaled 4,200 hot dogs. Prepare the flexible budget for the month.

Great Hots
Flexible Budget
For the Month Ended March 31

Budgeted hot dogs (q) ....   _____

Revenue (_____) .... $_____

Expenses:

   Wieners, buns, condiments, supplies (_____) ..   _____

   Butane for stove (_____)...............................   _____

   Wages (_____) ....   _____

   Franchise fees (_____) ....   _____

Total expense ....   _____

Net operating income .... $_____

Exercise 9-3.   Refer to the data for Great Hots in Exercises 9-1 and 9-2. Prepare the following report that shows the activity variances for March.

Great Hots
Activity Variances
For the Month Ended March 31

	Planning Budget	*Flexible Budget*	*Activity Variances*	
Hot dogs (q)...	_____	_____		
Revenue (_____)....................	_____	$_____	_____	____
Expenses:				
Wieners, buns, condiments, supplies				
(_____).........................	$_____	_____	$_____	____
Butane for stove (_____)		_____		
Wages (_____)....................	_____	_____	_____	____
Franchise fees (_____)........	_____	_____	_____	____
Total expense...	_____	_____	_____	____
Net operating income	_____	$_____	_____	____

Exercise 9-4.   The actual operating results for Great Hots for March appear below:

Great Hots
Income Statement
For the Month Ended March 31

Actual hot dogs	4,200
Revenue..	$8,060
Expenses:	
Wieners, buns, condiments, supplies	2,970
Butane for stove	180
Wages...	2,950
Franchise fees..	1,020
Total expense	7,120
Net operating income	$ 940

Refer to the data for Great Hots in Exercises 9-1 and 9-2. Prepare the following report that shows the revenue and spending variances for March:

Great Hots
Revenue and Spending Variances
For the Month Ended March 31

	Flexible Budget	Actual Results	Revenue and Spending Variances
Hot dogs (q)	_____	_____	
Revenue (_____)	_____	$_____	_____ ___
Expenses:			
Wieners, buns, condiments, supplies			
(_____)	$_____	_____	$_____ ___
Butane for stove (_____)....		_____	
Wages (_____)	_____	_____	_____ ___
Franchise fees (_____)	_____	_____	_____ ___
Total expense	_____	_____	_____ ___
Net operating income	_____	$_____	_____ ___

Answers to Questions and Exercises

True or False

1. T   The planning budget is a static budget that is prepared for the expected level of activity.

2. F   Many fixed costs are controllable and must be on someone's performance report or no one will control them.

3. F   Costs will be higher or lower than budgeted simply due to changes in activity. It is unreasonable to expect, for example, that a production manager will be able to make 10% more units than budgeted (if requested by marketing) without spending more than was originally budgeted.

4. F   A favorable activity variance for a cost item simply means that the cost contains some variable element and the actual level of activity was less than budgeted. The variance has nothing to do with actual spending.

5. F   An unfavorable activity variance for revenue occurs only if the actual level of activity is less than budgeted. This variance is unaffected by price discounts.

6. T   An unfavorable spending variance happens because more was spent on the item than should have been spent according to the flexible budget. This could happen because prices for things the company purchases were higher than they should have been.

7. F   A favorable activity variance for revenue would be due to selling more units than expected. A favorable revenue variance has entirely different causes.

8. T   A fixed cost would not be adjusted for a change in the level of activity.

Multiple Choice

1. c $6,000 = \$1,000 + \$5 \times 1,000$

2. c $5,500 = \$1,000 + \$5 \times 900$

3. a   Activity variance = Planning budget − Flexible budget = $(\$1,000 + \$5 \times 1,000) - (\$1,000 + \$5 \times 900) = \$6,000 - \$5,500 = \$500$ F

4. d   Spending variance = Flexible budget − Actual cost = $(\$1,000 + \$5 \times 900) - \$5,575 = \$5,500 - \$5,575 = \$75$ U

5. a $10,000 = \$25 \times 400$

6. b $9,500 = \$25 \times 380$

7. d   Activity variance = Planning budget − Flexible budget = $(\$25 \times 400) - (\$25 \times 380) = \$10,000 - \$9,500 = \$500$ U

8. b   Revenue variance = Flexible budget − Actual revenue = $(\$25 \times 380) - \$9,325 = \$9,500 - \$9,325 = \$175$ U

Exercises

Exercise 9-1.

Great Hots
Planning Budget
For the Month Ended March 31

Budgeted hot dogs (q)	4,000
Revenue ($1.95q)	$7,800
Expenses:	
Wieners, buns, condiments, supplies ($0.70q).....	2,800
Butane for stove ($200)......................................	200
Wages ($2,800)	2,800
Franchise fees ($600 + $0.10q)............................	1,000
Total expense	6,800
Net operating income	$1,000

Exercise 9-2.

Great Hots
Flexible Budget
For the Month Ended March 31

Budgeted hot dogs (q)	4,200
Revenue ($1.95q)	$8,190
Expenses:	
Wieners, buns, condiments, supplies ($0.70q).....	2,940
Butane for stove ($200)......................................	200
Wages ($2,800)	2,800
Franchise fees ($600 + $0.10q)............................	1,020
Total expense	6,960
Net operating income	$1,230

Exercise 9-3.

Great Hots
Activity Variances
For the Month Ended March 31

	Planning Budget	Flexible Budget	Activity Variances	
Hot dogs (q)	4,000	4,200		
Revenue ($1.95q)	$7,800	$8,190	$390	F
Expenses:				
Wieners, buns, condiments, supplies ($0.70q).....	2,800	2,940	140	U
Butane for stove ($200)......................................	200	200	0	
Wages ($2,800)	2,800	2,800	0	
Franchise fees ($600 + $0.10q)............................	1,000	1,020	20	U
Total expense	6,800	6,960	160	U
Net operating income	$1,000	$1,230	$230	F

Exercise 9-4.

Great Hots
Revenue and Spending Variances
For the Month Ended March 31

	Flexible Budget	Actual Results	Revenue and Spending Variances	
Hot dogs (q)	4,200	4,200		
Revenue ($1.95q)	$8,190	$8,060	$130	U
Expenses:				
Wieners, buns, condiments, supplies ($0.70q)	2,940	2,970	30	U
Butane for stove ($200)	200	180	20	F
Wages ($2,800)	2,800	2,950	150	U
Franchise fees ($600 + $0.10q)	1,020	1,020	0	
Total expense	6,960	7,120	160	U
Net operating income	$1,230	$ 940	$290	U

Chapter 10

Standard Costs and Variances

Chapter Study Suggestions

Exhibit 10-4 provides a general model for variance analysis, and Exhibits 10-5 through 10-7 give detailed examples of the analysis of materials, labor, and variable manufacturing overhead. Note that the data from the standard cost card in Exhibit 10-2 are used in Exhibits 10-5, 10-6, and 10-7. As you study, follow the data from Exhibit 10-2 into the following exhibits. This will help you tie together the various parts of the chapter.

Exhibit 10-5 illustrates direct materials variances when all of the materials purchased in the current period are also used in the current period. Exhibit 10-8 covers the more general case in which purchases need not equal the amount of the material used in production.

CHAPTER HIGHLIGHTS

A. A *standard* is a benchmark or norm for evaluating performance. Manufacturing companies commonly set exacting standards for materials, labor, and overhead for each product. Some service companies, such as auto repair shops and fast food outlets, also set standards.

   1.   Standards are set for both the quantity and price of inputs.

   2.   Actual quantities and prices of inputs are compared to the standards. Differences are called variances. Under *management by exception,* only the significant variances are brought to the attention of management.

B. Setting accurate quantity and price standards is an important step in the control process.

   1.   Many persons should be involved in setting standards: accountants, purchasing agents, industrial engineers, production supervisors, and line managers.

   2.   Standards are either ideal or practical.

      a.   *Ideal standards* can only be attained by the best employees working at top efficiency 100% of the time. Ideal standards allow for no machine breakdowns, rest breaks or other lost time.

      b.   *Practical standards*, by contrast, allow for breakdowns and normal lost time (such as for rest breaks). Practical standards are tight, but attainable.

      c.   The use of ideal standards can easily lead to frustration, so practical standards probably provide better motivation than ideal standards.

   3.   Direct material standards are set for both the price and quantity of inputs.

      a.   The standard price per unit of the input is the amount that should be paid for the input.

      b.   The quantity standard should reflect the amount of material that is required to make one unit of product, including allowances for unavoidable waste and spoilage.

   4.   Direct labor price and quantity standards are expressed in terms of a labor rate and the labor-hours that are required to make a unit of product.

      a.   The standard direct labor rate per hour should include wages, fringe benefits, and employment taxes.

      b.   The standard labor-hours per unit should include allowances for rest breaks, personal needs of employees, clean-up, and machine down time.

   5.   As with direct labor, the price and quantity standards for variable overhead are generally expressed in terms of a rate and hours. The rate is the variable portion of the predetermined overhead rate. The quantity standard is expressed in terms of whatever basis is used for applying variable overhead to products. Most frequently, this is direct labor-hours.

   6.   The price and quantity standards for materials, labor, and overhead for a product are summarized on the product's *standard cost card* such as the one shown in Exhibit 10-2.

C. A *variance* is a difference between standard and actual prices or standard and actual quantities. The general model in Exhibit 10-4 shows how variances are computed. Study this model with care.

   1.   A price variance and a quantity variance can be computed for each of the three variable cost categories—materials, labor, and variable manufacturing overhead.

   2.   The *standard quantity allowed for the output* is the amount of an input that *should have been used* to complete the output of the period. This is a key concept in the chapter!

D. Direct Materials Variances. Exhibit 10-5 illustrates the variance analysis of direct materials in the special case in which purchases equal usage. Note that the center column (Actual Quantity of Inputs, at Standard Price) plays a part in the computation of both the price and quantity variances.

   1.   The *materials quantity variance* can be expressed in formula form as:

Materials quantity variance = $(AQ \times SP) - (SQ \times SP)$

or

   Materials quantity variance = $(AQ - SQ)\,SP$
where:

   AQ = Actual quantity of the input used
   SQ = Standard quantity of the input allowed for the actual output
   SP = Standard price of the input

Possible causes of an unfavorable materials quantity variance include untrained workers, faulty machines, low quality materials, and inaccurate standards.

2.   The *materials price variance* can be expressed in formula form as:

$$\text{Materials price variance} = (AQ \times AP) - (AQ \times SP)$$
or
$$\text{Materials price variance} = AQ (AP - SP)$$

where:
AQ = Actual quantity of the input purchased
AP = Actual price of the input purchased
SP = Standard price of the input

An unfavorable materials price variance has many possible causes, including excessive freight costs, loss of quantity discounts, the wrong grade or type of materials, rush orders, and inaccurate standards.

E. Direct Labor Variances. Exhibit 10-6 shows the variance analysis of direct labor. Notice that the format is the same as for direct materials, but the terms "rate" and "hours" are used in place of the terms "price" and "quantity".

1.   The quantity variance for labor is called the *labor efficiency variance*. The formula is:

$$\text{Labor efficiency variance} = (AH \times SR) - (SH \times SR)$$
or
$$\text{Labor efficiency variance} = (AH - SH) SR$$

where:
AH = Actual labor-hours
SH = Standard labor-hours allowed for the actual output
SR = Standard labor rate

Possible causes of an unfavorable labor efficiency variance include poorly trained workers, low quality materials, faulty equipment, poor supervision, insufficient work to keep everyone busy, and inaccurate standards.

2.   The price variance for labor is called the *labor rate variance*. The formula is:

$$\text{Labor rate variance} = (AH \times AR) - (AH \times SR)$$
or
$$\text{Labor rate variance} = AH (AR - SR)$$

where:
AH = Actual labor-hours
AR = Actual labor rate
SR = Standard labor rate

Possible causes of an unfavorable labor rate variance include poor assignment of workers to jobs, unplanned overtime, pay increases, and inaccurate standards.

F.   Variable Manufacturing Overhead Variances. Exhibit 10-7 illustrates the variance analysis of variable manufacturing overhead. Note that the format is the same as for direct labor.

1.   The *variable overhead efficiency variance* is computed as follows:

$$\text{Variable overhead efficiency variance} = (AH \times SR) - (SH \times SR)$$
or
$$\text{Variable overhead efficiency variance} = (AH - SH) SR$$

where:
AH = Actual hours (usually labor-hours)
SH = Standard hours allowed for the actual output
SR = Standard variable manufacturing overhead rate

2.   The *variable overhead rate variance* is computed as follows:

$$\text{Variable overhead rate variance} = (AH \times AR) - (AH \times SR)$$
or
$$\text{Variable overhead rate variance} = AH (AR - SR)$$

where:
AH = Actual hours (usually labor-hours)
AR = Actual variable manufacturing overhead rate
SR = Standard variable manufacturing overhead rate

G. The materials price variance is usually computed when materials are purchased, whereas the materials quantity variance is usually computed when materials are used in production. Consequently, the price variance is computed based on the amount of material purchased whereas the quantity variance is computed based on the amount of material used in production. This gives rise to the modification of the general model for direct materials variances that is illustrated in Exhibit 10-8.H.   Not all variances are worth investigating. Managers should be interested only in the variances that are significant and out of the norm. Statistical control charts, such as the one in Exhibit 10-9, can be used to identify the variances that are worth investigating.

H. There are some potential problems with the use of standard costs. Most of these problems result from improper use of standard costs or from using standard costs in situations in which they are not appropriate.

1.   Standard cost variance reports are usually prepared on a monthly basis and may be released to managers too late to be really useful. Some companies are now reporting variances and other key operating data daily or even more frequently.

2.   Managers should avoid using variance reports as a way to find someone to blame. Management by exception, by its nature, tends to focus on the negative.

3.   If labor is fixed, the only way to avoid an unfavorable labor efficiency variance may be to keep workers busy all the time producing output—even if there is no demand. This can lead to excess work in process and finished goods inventories.

4.   A favorable variance may not be good. For example, Pizza Haven has a standard for the amount of mozzarella cheese in a pizza. A favorable variance means that less cheese was used than the standard specifies. The result is a substandard pizza.

5.   A standard cost reporting system may lead to an emphasis on meeting standards to the exclusion of other important objectives, such as maintaining and improving quality, on-time delivery, and customer satisfaction.

6.   Just meeting standards may not be sufficient; continual improvement may be necessary.

REVIEW AND SELF-TEST
Questions and Exercises

True or False

Enter a T or an F in the blank to indicate whether the statement is true or false.

____ 1. Practical standards are generally viewed as better than ideal standards for motivating employees.

____ 2. Ideal standards allow for machine breakdown time and other normal inefficiencies.

____ 3. Raw materials price variances should be computed and reported only when materials are placed into production.

____ 4. Waste on the production line will result in a materials price variance.

____ 5. If the actual price or quantity exceeds the standard price or quantity, the variance is unfavorable.

____ 6. Labor rate variances are generally out of the control of management.

____ 7. Managers should thoroughly investigate all differences (variances) between standard cost and actual cost.

____ 8. In a company with fixed labor, an undue focus on labor efficiency variances may result in the production of excess inventories.

Multiple Choice

Choose the best answer or response by placing the identifying letter in the space provided.

____ 1. The labor rate variance is determined by multiplying the difference between the actual labor rate and the standard labor rate by: a) the standard hours allowed; b) the actual hours worked; c) the budgeted hours allowed; d) none of these.

____ 2. If inferior-grade materials are purchased, the result may be: a) an unfavorable materials price variance; b) a favorable materials price variance; c) an unfavorable labor efficiency variance; d) a favorable labor efficiency variance; e) responses b and c are both correct; f) responses a and d are both correct.

____ 3. During June, Bradley Company produced 4,000 units of product. The standard cost card indicates the following labor standards per unit of output: 3.5 hours at $6 per hour = $21. During the month, the company worked 15,000 hours. The standard hours allowed for the month were: a) 14,000 hours; b) 15,000 hours; c) 24,000 hours; d) 18,000 hours.

____ 4. Refer to the data in question 3 above. What was the labor efficiency variance for June? (F indicates a Favorable variance and U indicates an Unfavorable variance.) a) $1,000 F; b) $1,000 U; c) $6,000 F; d) $6,000 U.

____ 5. Refer to the data in question 3 above. The total labor cost during June was $88,000 for the 15,000 hours that were worked. What was the labor rate variance for June? a) $6,000 F; b) $6,000 U; c) $2,000 F; d) $2,000 U.

____ 6. During July, Bradley Company produced 3,000 units. The standard cost card indicates the following materials standards per unit of output: 2 pounds @ $0.50 per pound = $1. During July, 8,000 pounds of material were purchased at a cost of $3,900. The materials price variance for July was: a) $100 F; b) $100 U; c) $4,100 F; d) $4,100 U.

____ 7. Refer to the data in question 6 above. 6,100 pounds of material were used in July to produce the output of 3,000 units. The materials quantity variance for July was: a) $1,550 F; b) $1,550 U; c) $50 F; d) $50 U.

___ 8. During August, Bradley Company produced 3,500 units of product using 12,750 labor-hours. The standard cost card indicates the following variable manufacturing overhead standards per unit of output: 3.5 labor-hours at $2 per labor-hour = $7. During the month, the actual variable manufacturing overhead cost incurred was $25,000. The variable overhead rate variance was: a) $500 U; b) $500 F; c) $24,500 U; d) $24,500 F.

___ 9. Refer to the data in question 8 above. The variable overhead efficiency variance was: a) $7,000 F; b) $7,000 U; c) $1,000 F; d) $1,000 U.

Exercises

Exercise 10-1.   Selected data relating to Miller Company's operations for April are given below:

Number of units produced...................................	500	units
Number of actual direct labor-hours worked......	1,400	hours
Total actual direct labor cost	$10,850	

The standard cost card indicates that 2.5 hours of direct labor time is allowed per unit, at a rate of $8 per hour.

a. Complete the following analysis of direct labor cost for the month:

Standard Hours Allowed for Actual Output, at Standard Rate (SH × SR)	Actual Hours of Input, at Standard Rate (AH × SR)	Actual Hours of Input, at Actual Rate (AH × AR)

Labor efficiency variance	Labor rate variance
= _____	= _____

Spending variance = _____

_____

b. Redo the above analysis of direct labor cost for the month, using the following formulas:

Labor efficiency variance = (AH – SH) SR

Labor rate variance = AH (AR – SR)

Exercise 10-2.   The following activity took place in Solo Company during May:

Number of units produced......................	450 units
Material purchased...............................	1,500 feet
Material used in production....................	720 feet
Cost per foot for material purchased......	$3

The standard cost card indicates that 1.5 feet of materials are allowed for each unit of product. The standard cost of the materials is $4 per foot.

a. Complete the following analysis of direct materials cost for the month:

Standard Quantity Allowed for Actual Output, at Standard Price $(SQ \times SP)$	Actual Quantity of Input, at Standard Price $(AQ \times SP)$	Actual Quantity of Input, at Actual Price $(AQ \times AP)$

Materials quantity variance

= _____

Materials price variance

= _____

b. Redo the above analysis of direct materials cost for the month, using the following formulas:

Materials quantity variance $= (AQ - SQ)\ SP$

Materials price variance $= AQ\ (AP - SP)$

Answers to Questions and Exercises

True or False

1. **T** Practical standards are considered to provide better motivation than ideal standards because they are attainable by workers.

2. **F** Ideal standards do not allow for either machine breakdowns or other normal inefficiencies.

3. **F** The purchasing manager is responsible for the materials price variance. This variance should be computed when the purchasing manager does his or her work—not when the materials are put into production.

4. **F** Waste will result in a materials quantity variance.

5. **T** This statement is true by definition.

6. **F** Labor rate variances can arise from overtime and other causes that are within the control of management.

7. **F** Managers should not waste time investigating insignificant variances.

8. **T** When labor is fixed, the only way to generate a more favorable labor efficiency variance may be to keep everyone busy producing output—even if there is no demand.

Multiple Choice

1. **b** This point is illustrated in Exhibit 10-7.

2. **e** The materials price variance will probably be favorable because the inferior grade materials probably will cost less. The labor efficiency variance will probably be unfavorable because the inferior grade materials will probably require more work.

3. **a** 4,000 units $\times$ 3.5 hours per unit = 14,000 hours.

4. **d** Efficiency variance = (AH − SH) SR
$$= (15,000 - 14,000)\ \$6$$
$$= \$6,000\ U$$

5. **c** Rate variance = (AH $\times$ AR) −(AH $\times$ SR)
$$= (\$88,000) - (15,000 \times \$6)$$
$$= \$2,000\ F$$

6. **a** Price variance = (AQ $\times$ AP) − (AQ $\times$ SP)
$$= (\$3,900) - (8,000 \times \$0.50)$$
$$= \$100\ F$$

7. **d** Quantity variance = (AQ − SQ) SP
$$= (6,100 - 2 \times 3,000)\ \$0.50$$
$$= \$50\ U$$

8. **b** Rate variance = (AH $\times$ AR) − (AH $\times$ SR)
$$= (\$25,000) - (12,750 \times \$2)$$
$$= \$500\ F$$

9. **d** Efficiency variance = (AH − SH) SR
$$= (12,750 - 3.5 \times 3,500)\ \$2$$
$$= \$1,000\ U$$

Exercises

Exercise 10-1.

a.

Standard Hours Allowed for Actual Output, at Standard Rate (SH × SR)	Actual Hours of Input, at Standard Rate (AH × SR)	Actual Hours of Input, at Actual Rate (AH × AR)
1,250 hours* × $8.00 per hour = $10,000	1,400 hours × $8.00 per hour = $11,200	$10,850

Labor efficiency variance = $1,200 U | Labor rate variance = $350 F

Spending variance = $850 U

*500 units × 2.5 hours per unit = 1,250 hours

b. AR = $10,850 ÷ 1,400 hours = $7.75 per hour
Labor efficiency variance = (AH − SH) SR = (1,400 hours − 1,250 hours) $8.00 per hour = $1,200 U
Labor rate variance = AH (AR − SR) = 1,400 hours ($7.75 per hour − $8.00 per hour) = $350 F

Exercise 10-2.

a.

Standard Quantity Allowed for Actual Output, at Standard Price (SQ × SP)	Actual Quantity of Input, at Standard Price (AQ × SP)	Actual Quantity of Input, at Actual Price (AQ × AP)
675 foot* × $4.00 per foot = $2,700	720 feet × $4.00 per foot = $2,880	1,500 foot × $3.00 per foot = $4,500

Materials quantity variance = $180 U

1,500 foot × $4.00 per foot = $6,000

Materials price variance = $15,00 F

*450 units × 1.5 feet per unit = 675 feet

b. Materials quantity variance = (AQ − SQ) SP
= (720 feet − 675 feet) $4.00 per foot = $180 U
Materials price variance = AQ (AP − SP)
= 1,500 feet ($3.00 per foot − $4.00 per foot) = $1,500 F

Note that more materials were purchased (1,500 feet) than were used in production (720 feet). When computing the price variance, use the quantity of materials purchased. When computing the quantity variance, use the quantity of materials used in production.

Appendix 10A

Predetermined Overhead Rates and Overhead Analysis in a Standard Costing System

APPENDIX HIGHLIGHTS

A. The predetermined overhead rate is computed as follows:

$$\text{Predetermined overhead rate} = \frac{\text{Estimated total manufacturing overhead cost}}{\text{Estimated total amount of the allocation base}}$$

1. The estimated total amount of the allocation base is also known as the *denominator level of activity*. The numerator in the predetermined overhead rate is the estimated manufacturing overhead at that level of activity.

2. The predetermined overhead rate can be divided into two parts, one for the variable overhead costs and the other for the fixed overhead costs.

    a. The fixed component of the predetermined overhead rate depends on the level of the denominator activity that is chosen. The larger the denominator activity, the lower the rate will be.

    b. The variable component of the predetermined overhead rate does not depend on the level of the denominator activity; it is constant.

B. Exhibit 10A-2 shows that overhead is applied to work in process differently under a *standard cost system* than it is under a *normal cost system.*

1. In a normal cost system, overhead is applied by multiplying the predetermined overhead rate by the actual hours of activity for a period.

2. In contrast, under a standard cost system overhead is applied to work in process by multiplying the predetermined overhead rate by the *standard hours allowed for the output of the period.* The standard hours allowed for the output are computed by multiplying the standard hours per unit of output by the actual output of the period.

C. The last part of the appendix is concerned with the two fixed manufacturing overhead variances—the budget variance and the volume variance. The *fixed overhead budget variance*, or simply "budget variance," is the difference between actual fixed overhead costs and budgeted fixed overhead costs.

$$\text{Budget variance} = \text{Actual fixed overhead cost} - \text{Budgeted fixed overhead cost}$$

2. The formula for the fixed overhead volume variance is:

$$\text{Volume variance} = \begin{array}{c}\text{Fixed component of} \\ \text{the predetermined} \\ \text{overhead rate}\end{array} \times \left(\begin{array}{c}\text{Denominator} \\ \text{hours}\end{array} - \begin{array}{c}\text{Standard} \\ \text{hours} \\ \text{allowed}\end{array}\right)$$

D. The volume variance does not measure how well spending was controlled. It is completely determined by the relation between the denominator hours and the standard hours allowed for the actual output.

    a. If the denominator hours exceed the standard hours allowed for the output of the period, the volume variance is unfavorable.

    b. If the denominator hours are less than the standard hours allowed for the output of the period, the volume variance is favorable.

E. In a standard cost system, the amount of overhead applied to products is determined by the standard hours allowed for the actual output.

1. If the actual overhead cost exceeds the amount of overhead cost applied to units of product, then the overhead is underapplied. If the actual overhead cost incurred is less than the amount of overhead cost applied to units, then the overhead is overapplied.

2. In a standard cost system, the sum of the overhead variances equals the amount of underapplied or overapplied overhead.

	Variable overhead rate variance
+	Variable overhead efficiency variance
+	Fixed overhead budget variance
+	Fixed overhead volume variance
=	Overhead underapplied or overapplied

If the sum of the variances is unfavorable, the overhead is underapplied. If the sum of the variances is favorable, the overhead is overapplied.

REVIEW AND SELF-TEST
Questions and Exercises

True or False

Enter a T or an F in the blank to indicate whether the statement is true or false.

___ 1. The fixed overhead volume variance measures how well fixed overhead spending was controlled.

___ 2. If the denominator activity level exceeds the standard hours allowed for the output, the volume variance will be favorable.

___ 3. In a standard cost system, if overhead is overapplied, then the sum of the four manufacturing overhead variances will be favorable.

Multiple Choice

Choose the best answer or response by placing the identifying letter in the space provided.

___ 1. In a standard cost system, overhead is applied to production on the basis of: a) the actual hours required to complete the output of the period; b) the standard hours allowed to complete the output of the period; c) the denominator hours chosen for the period; d) none of these.

___ 2. If the standard hours allowed for the output of a period exceed the denominator hours used in setting overhead rates, there will be: a) a favorable budget variance; b) an unfavorable budget variance; c) a favorable volume variance; d) an unfavorable volume variance.

___ 3. Baxter Company's flexible budget for manufacturing overhead indicates that the fixed overhead should be $30,000 at the denominator level of 3,000 standard direct labor-hours. In March, the actual fixed overhead cost incurred was $33,000. Baxter Company standards call for 2 direct labor-hours per unit of output. In March, the company produced 2,000 units using 4,100 direct labor-hours (DLHs). What is the fixed portion of the predetermined overhead rate? a) $10 per DLH; b) $11 per DLH; c) $30 per DLH; d) $2 per DLH.

___ 4. Refer to the data in part (5) above concerning Baxter Company. What was the fixed overhead budget variance for March? a) $10,000 F; b) $10,000 U; c) $3,000 U; d) $3,000 F.

___ 5. Refer to the data in part (5) above concerning Baxter Company. What was the fixed overhead volume variance for March? a) $10,000 F; b) $10,000 U; c) $3,000 U; d) $3,000 F.

Exercises

Exercise 10A-1. Marina Company uses a standard cost system in which manufacturing overhead is applied to units of product on the basis of standard direct labor-hours (DLHs). Marina Company's standards call for variable manufacturing overhead of $0.90 per direct labor-hour and fixed manufacturing overhead of $24,000 per year.

The denominator activity level used in setting predetermined overhead rates is 12,000 direct labor-hours. The standard time to complete one unit of product is 1.5 direct labor-hours.

For the company's most recent year, the following actual operating data are available:

Units produced	9,000 units
Actual direct labor-hours worked....	14,000 hours
Actual variable overhead cost	$12,880
Actual fixed overhead cost..............	$23,750

a. Compute the predetermined overhead rate that would be used by the company, and break it down into variable and fixed components:

Predetermined overhead rate ... _____

Variable component .... _____

Fixed component..................... _____

b. How much overhead would have been applied to work in process during the year? _____

c. Complete the following variance analysis of fixed overhead cost for the company's most recent year:

Fixed Overhead Applied to Work in Process	*Budgeted Fixed Overhead*	*Actual Fixed Overhead*
Volume variance	Budget variance	
= _____	= _____	
Total Variance = _____		

144

Answers to Questions and Exercises

True or False

1. F   The fixed overhead volume variance results from a difference between the denominator level of activity and the standard hours allowed for the actual output of the period. It has nothing to do with spending.

2. F   The reverse is true—the volume variance would be unfavorable.

3. T   Overapplied overhead is equivalent to favorable variances and underapplied overhead is equivalent to unfavorable variances.

Multiple Choice

1. b   This point is illustrated in Exhibit 10A-2.

2. c   The volume variance is favorable any time the standard hours allowed for the actual output of the period exceeds the denominator level of activity.

3. a

$$\text{Fixed component of the predetermined overhead rate} = \frac{\$30,000}{3,000 \text{ DLHs}} = \$10 \text{ per DLH}$$

4. c

$$\text{Budget variance} = \text{Actual fixed overhead cost} - \text{Budgeted fixed overhead cost}$$
$$= \$33,000 - \$30,000$$
$$= \$3,000 \text{ U}$$

5. a

$$\text{Volume variance} = \text{Fixed overhead rate} \times \left(\text{Denominator hours} - \text{Standard hours allowed} \right)$$
$$= \$10 \times (3,000 - 4,000) = \$10,000 \text{ F}$$

Appendix 10A

Exercises

Exercise 10A-1.

a. The total estimated manufacturing overhead at the denominator level of activity is $34,800 (=$0.90 per DLH × 12,000 DLHs + $24,000).

Predetermined overhead rate ($34,800 ÷ 12,000 DLHs) .... $2.90 per DLH
Variable component ($10,800 ÷ 12,000 DLHs) .... $0.90 per DLH
Fixed component ($24,000 ÷ 12,000 DLHs)........................ $2.00 per DLH

b. Overhead applied:
   9,000 units × 1.5 DLHs per unit = 13,500 DLHs allowed
   13,500 DLHs × $2.90 per DLH = $39,150 overhead applied

c. Fixed overhead variance analysis:

Fixed Overhead Applied to Work in Process	*Budgeted Fixed Overhead*	*Actual Fixed Overhead*
13,500 DLHs × $2.00 per DLH = $27,000	$24,000	$23,750

Volume variance = $3,000 F | Budget variance = $250 F

Total Variance = $3,250 F

146

Appendix 10B

Journal Entries to Record Variances

APPENDIX HIGHLIGHTS

A. Many companies carry inventories at standard cost and record standard cost variances in the company's formal accounting records. This simplifies bookkeeping.

B. Favorable variances are recorded as credits, and unfavorable variances are recorded as debits.

   1. The entry to record an unfavorable material price variance upon purchase of materials on account would be:

Raw Materials	XXX	
Materials Price Variance (U)	XXX	
Accounts Payable		XXX

   2. The entry to record a favorable material quantity variance would be:

Work in Process	XXX	
Materials Quantity Variance (F)		XXX
Raw Materials		XXX

   3. The entry to record an unfavorable labor efficiency variance and a favorable labor rate variance would be:

Work in Process	XXX	
Labor Efficiency Variance (U)	XXX	
Labor Rate Variance (F)		XXX
Wages Payable		XXX

REVIEW AND SELF-TEST
Questions and Exercises

Exercise

Exercise 10B-1. Refer to the data for Solo Company in Exercise 10-2. Prepare journal entries to record all activity relating to direct materials for the month:

	Debit	*Credit*

Answers to Questions and Exercises

Exercise

Exercise 10B-1.

Raw Materials	6,000	
Materials Price Variance		1,500
Accounts Payable		4,500
Work in Process	2,700	
Materials Quantity Variance	180	
Raw Materials		2,880

Chapter 11

Performance Measurement in Decentralized Organizations

Chapter Study Suggestions

The chapter contains three major parts. The first part of the chapter covers return on investment (ROI) and residual income. You should memorize the formulas for ROI and residual income which are used extensively in homework.

The second part of the chapter deals with some nonfinancial performance measures that are used in manufacturing. You should memorize the formulas for delivery cycle time, throughput time, and manufacturing cycle efficiency.

The third part of the chapter covers the balanced scorecard. This section is much more conceptual than the other parts of the chapter. There are no formulas to memorize, but make sure you understand how a balanced scorecard is organized and how to interpret the connections between the various performance measures on a balanced scorecard.

The first appendix to the chapter covers transfer pricing. The key ideas in the appendix are the lower limits and the upper limits for a negotiated transfer price. Make sure you understand how these limits are determined.

The second appendix to the chapter covers service department charges. Pay careful attention to the fact that budgeted, rather than actual, service department costs should be charged to using departments.

CHAPTER HIGHLIGHTS

A. A *decentralized organization* is one in which decision making is spread throughout the organization, with managers at all levels making decisions. Managers in a decentralized organization are held responsible for those areas over which they have control.

    1.   The manager of a *cost center* has control over cost but not over revenues or investments. A cost center manager is usually held responsible for minimizing cost while providing quality goods and services in response to demand from customers inside and outside the organization.

    2.   The manager of a *profit center* has control over both cost and revenue. A profit center manager is usually held responsible for maximizing profit.

    3.   The manager of an *investment center* has control over cost, revenue, and investments in operating assets. An investment center manager is ordinarily evaluated on the basis of return on investment or residual income, as explained below.

B. *Return on investment (ROI)* is defined as:

$$ROI = \frac{\text{Net operating income}}{\text{Average operating assets}}$$

ROI can also be expressed in terms of margin and turnover:

$$ROI = Margin \times Turnover$$

where:

$$Margin = \frac{\text{Net operating income}}{\text{Sales}}$$

$$Turnover = \frac{\text{Sales}}{\text{Average operating assets}}$$

    1.   *Net operating income* is income before interest and taxes.

    2.   *Operating assets* include cash, accounts receivable, inventory, and all other assets held for productive use within the organization. Operating assets do *not* include investments in other companies and investments in undeveloped land.

    3.   Unfortunately, a division manager who is evaluated based on ROI will tend to reject a project whose ROI is less than the division's current ROI but greater than the company's minimum rate of return. However, from the standpoint of the entire company such a project should be accepted.

C. Residual income is another approach that is used to measure performance in an investment center.

    1.   *Residual income* is the net operating income that an investment center earns above the minimum required rate of return on operating assets and is defined as follows:

$$\begin{matrix}\text{Residual} \\ \text{income}\end{matrix} = \begin{matrix}\text{Net} \\ \text{operating} \\ \text{income}\end{matrix} - \left(\begin{matrix}\text{Required} \\ \text{rate of} \\ \text{return}\end{matrix} \times \begin{matrix}\text{Average} \\ \text{operating} \\ \text{assets}\end{matrix}\right)$$

    2.   The residual income approach to performance evaluation encourages investment in worthwhile projects—overcoming the major difficulty with ROI. Any project whose rate of return exceeds the company's required rate of return will be favored by managers—even a project whose rate of return is less than the division's current ROI.

    3.   A major disadvantage of the residual income approach is that it can't be easily used to compare divisions of different sizes. Larger divisions naturally tend to have larger residual incomes.

D. Operating Performance Measures. Exhibit 11-2 defines the operating measures *Wait Time, Through-put Time, Process Time, Inspection Time, Move Time*, and *Queue Time.*

    1.   *Throughput time* is the amount of time required to make a product. It is also known as the manufacturing cycle time. Throughput time is the sum of process time, inspection time, move time, and queue time as shown below:

Throughput Time = Process Time + Inspection Time + Move Time + Queue Time

    2.   *Delivery cycle time* is the amount of time that elapses between the time when a customer submits an order and when the order is shipped.

Delivery Cycle Time = Wait Time + Throughput Time

    3.   *Manufacturing cycle efficiency (MCE)* is a measure of the efficiency of the production process. It is computed as follows:

$$MCE = \frac{\text{Value-added (Process) Time}}{\text{Throughput (Manufacturing Cycle) Time}}$$

Inspection Time, Move Time, and Queue Time are all non-value-added activities; they do not add anything of value to the product. Ideally, MCE would be 1, indicating all of the throughput time is value-added time.

E. The Balanced Scorecard. A *balanced scorecard* is an integrated set of performance measures that are derived from and support the company's strategy.

    1.   Each company's balanced scorecard should be different because each company's strategy is different.

    2.   The balanced scorecard emphasizes continual improvement and trends rather than meeting preset targets or standards.

    3.   The performance measures on a balanced scorecard should be linked on a cause-and-effect basis. The cause-and-effect links are essentially hypotheses of the form "If there is an improvement in this performance measure, then there will be improvement in that performance measure."

        a.   For example, the manager of a fast-food restaurant might reason that if the amount of time hamburgers sit on the warming rack before being served is reduced, then customers will like the hamburgers better. And if customers like the hamburgers better, then more hamburgers will be sold. The performance measures on the balanced scorecard would be "time on the warming rack", "customer satisfaction with hamburgers," and "sales of hamburgers."

        b.   Most performance measures fall into four categories: financial, customer, internal business processes, and learning and growth. "Time on the warming rack" is a measure of internal business process performance. "Customer satisfaction" is a customer-oriented performance measure. And "sales of hamburgers" is a financial measure of performance.

        c.   The performance measures and the hypotheses underlying them should tell a story about how improvements in internal business processes will ultimately lead to improvements in meeting the company's objectives.

        d.   If real, sustained improvement in one performance measure does not lead to the predicted improvement in another performance measure, then the company's strategy should be reconsidered. The assumptions underlying the strategy may be false.

    4.   The entire company should have a comprehensive balanced scorecard. In addition, individuals should have scorecards that contain only those performance measures they can actually influence.

REVIEW AND SELF-TEST
Questions and Exercises

True or False

Enter a T or an F in the blank to indicate whether the statement is true or false.

___ 1. Residual income is equal to the difference between total revenues and total operating expenses.

___ 2. A manager who is evaluated based on ROI may reject investment opportunities that would be beneficial to the company as a whole.

___ 3. Under the residual income approach, the objective is to maximize the rate of return on operating assets.

___ 4. ROI equals margin divided by turnover.

___ 5. Throughput time equals delivery cycle time less wait time.

___ 6. If the MCE is less than 1, the production process includes non-value-added time.

___ 7. Any two companies should have basically the same balanced scorecard.

___ 8. If non-financial performance measures in a balanced scorecard improve, but financial performance does not improve, then the company should probably reconsider its strategy.

Multiple Choice

Choose the best answer or response by placing the identifying letter in the space provided.

___ 1. A company reported the following results:

Average operating assets ..	$ 45,000
Sales.................................	$180,000
Contribution margin	$ 21,600
Net operating income........	$ 9,000

The company's ROI is: a) 48%; b) 12%; c) 20%; d) 30%.

___ 2. A company reported the following results:

Average operating assets	$ 300,000
Stockholders' equity	$ 50,000
Sales...	$ 900,000
Net operating income....................	$ 75,000
Minimum required rate of return ..	18%

The company's residual income is: a) $25,000; b) $15,000; c) $21,000; d) 475,000.

___ 3. The delivery cycle time consists of: a) the time required to get a product to a customer after production is complete; b) the time required to get delivery of raw materials; c) the velocity of production plus the throughput time; d) the time required from receipt of an order from a customer to shipment of the completed goods.

___ 4. The following data are average times per order over the last month.

Wait time to start production .	15.0 days
Inspection time	0.6 days
Process time...........................	3.0 days
Move time..............................	1.4 days
Queue time.............................	7.0 days

The throughput time would be: a) 12.0 days; b) 7.0 days; c) 5.0 days; d) 20.0 days.

___ 5. Refer to the data in question (4) above. The MCE would be: a) 75%; b) 30%; c) 25%; d) 42%.

___ 6. Refer again to the data in question (4) above. What percentage of the throughput time is spent in non-value-added activities: a) 25%; b) 70%; c) 75%; d) 58%.

Exercises

Exercise 11-1. Frankel Company has provided the following data for its Connectors Division for last year:

Sales....................................	$2,000,000
Net operating income...........	$ 160,000
Average operating assets......	$ 800,000
Minimum rate of return........	16%

a. Compute the return on investment (ROI) for the Connectors Division, using margin and turnover.

b. Compute the residual income for the Connectors Division.

Exercise 11-2. During the last quarter, Scott Company recorded the following average times per order received and processed:

Wait time to start production............	9.0 days
Inspection time................................	0.8 days
Process time	3.0 days
Move time	0.2 days
Queue time	6.0 days

a. Compute the throughput time.

Throughput time =

b. Compute the manufacturing cycle efficiency (MCE).

MCE =

c. What percentage of the production time is spent in non-value-added activities?

d. Compute the delivery cycle time.

Delivery cycle time =

153

Answers to Questions and Exercises

True or False

1. **F** Residual income is the difference between net operating income and the minimum return that must be generated on operating assets.

2. **T** This is a major criticism of the ROI method.

3. **F** Under the residual income approach, the objective is to maximize residual income, not return on investment.

4. **F** ROI equals margin multiplied by turnover.

5. **T** Delivery cycle time equals wait time plus throughput time. Therefore, throughput time equals delivery cycle time less wait time.

6. **T** Because the MCE is measured by value-added time divided by throughput time, an MCE of less than 1 means that the throughput time contains some amount of non-value-added time.

7. **F** Because companies have different strategies, their balanced scorecards should be different.

8. **T** A balanced scorecard reflects the company's strategy—showing how actions taken by lower level managers to improve their non-financial performance measures should result in improved financial performance. If improved financial performance does not result from improvements in the nonfinancial performance measures, the company should rethink its strategy.

Multiple Choice

1. **c** The computations are:

$$ROI = \frac{\$9,000}{\$180,000} \times \frac{\$180,000}{\$45,000} = 5\% \times 4 = 20\%$$

2. **c** The computations are:

Average operating assets	$300,000
Net operating income...........	$ 75,000
Minimum required return (18% × $300,000)	54,000
Residual income	$ 21,000

3. **d** This point is illustrated in Exhibit 11-2.

4. **a** Throughput time = Process time + Inspection time + Move time + Queue time
= 3.0 days + 0.6 days + 1.4 days + 7.0 days
= 12.0 days

5. **c**

$$MCE = \frac{\text{Value-added time}}{\text{Throughput time}} = \frac{3.0 \text{ days}}{12.0 \text{ days}} = 25\%$$

6. **c** If the MCE is less than one, non-value-added time is present in the production process. In this case because the MCE is 25%, 75% of the time is spent in non-value-added activities (1.00- 0.25 = 0.75 or 75%).

Exercises

Exercise 11-1.

a.

$$\text{Margin} = \frac{\text{Net operating income}}{\text{Sales}} = \frac{\$160,000}{\$2,000,000} = 8\%$$

$$\text{Turnover} = \frac{\text{Sales}}{\text{Average operating assets}} = \frac{\$2,000,000}{\$800,000} = 2.5$$

ROI = Margin × Turnover
    = 8% × 2.5 = 20%

b.

Average operating assets	$ 800,000
Net operating income	$ 160,000
Minimum required return (16% × $800,000)..	128,000
Residual income...	$ 32,000

Exercise 11-2.

a. Throughput time = Process time + Inspection time + Move time + Queue time
        = 3.0 days + 0.8 days + 0.2 days + 6.0 days = 10.0 days

b. $$\text{MCE} = \frac{\text{Value-added time}}{\text{Throughput time}} = \frac{3.0 \text{ days}}{10.0 \text{ days}} = 30\%$$

c. Because 30% of throughput time is value-added time, 70% represents non-value-added time.

d. Delivery cycle time = Wait time + Throughput time
        = 9.0 days + 10.0 days = 19.0 days

Appendix 11A

Transfer Pricing

APPENDIX HIGHLIGHTS

A. One part of a company often provides goods or services to another part of the company. For example, the General Motors truck division sells delivery trucks to the Chevrolet Division. The price charged for such a sale inside a company is called a *transfer price.*

   1.   The selling division would like the transfer price to be high and the buying division would like the transfer price to be low.

   2.   Three general approaches are used to set transfer prices: (1) allow the involved managers to negotiate their own transfer price; (2) set the transfer price equal to cost; or (3) set the transfer price equal to the outside market price.

B. With negotiated transfer prices, the managers can choose whether to agree to a transfer or not. If they do agree to the transfer, they must agree on the transfer price. Presumably, neither manager would agree to a transfer price unless it increases his or her division's profit.

   1.   From the viewpoint of the selling division, the transfer price must cover at least variable costs plus any opportunity costs. This sets a limit on how low the transfer price can go in negotiations.

$$\frac{\text{Transfer}}{\text{price}} \geq \frac{\text{Variable}}{\text{cost}} + \frac{\text{Opportunity}}{\text{cost}}$$

      a.   There is an opportunity cost if there is a constraint. In that case, filling the buying division's order would result in lost sales to other customers.

      b.   The opportunity cost per unit transferred internally is computed as follows:

$$\frac{\text{Opportunity}}{\text{cost}} = \frac{\substack{\text{Total contribution margin} \\ \text{on lost sales}}}{\text{Number of units transferred}}$$

   2.   If the buying division can purchase what it needs from an outside supplier, the manager of the buying division would not want to pay a higher price within the company. From the viewpoint of the buying division, the upper limit on the transfer price is given by:

$$\frac{\text{Transfer}}{\text{price}} \leq \frac{\text{Cost of buying from}}{\text{an outside supplier}}$$

   3.   In principle, negotiated transfer prices should work. If it is in the best interests of the company for the transfer to be made, it will always be possible for the managers to find a transfer price between the lower and upper limits that would make them both better off.

   4.   However, managers may not understand what is in their own best interests or they may be uncooperative. In either case, negotiations my drag on and even fail. Perhaps for that reason, most companies use rules to set transfer prices that are based on either cost or market price.

C. Cost-based transfer prices are convenient to use, but may lead to bad decisions.

   1.   Variable cost understates the real cost to the company of the transfer when there are opportunity costs. In essence, the manager of the buying division will be getting the transferred good or service at a discounted price below true cost to the company. This can lead to unwise decisions such as pricing products too low.

   2.   Full absorption cost rarely reflects the true cost to the company of a transfer. If the transfer has no effect on total fixed costs, then the true cost to the company of the transfer is variable cost plus, possibly, opportunity cost. This very rarely equals full absorption cost.

   3.   When the transfer price is set equal to cost, the only division that shows any profit on the transaction is the one that makes a final sale to an outside party. Other divisions will show no profit for their efforts.

   4.   When transfers are priced at the selling division's actual cost, there is no incentive to control costs. The selling division simply passes its costs on to the next division. For this reason, if transfer prices are based on cost, standard costs rather than actual costs should be used.

D. Market prices are often used as transfer prices. This solution works very well when the selling division has no idle capacity. However, when the selling division has idle capacity, the market price overstates the real cost of the transfer.

REVIEW AND SELF-TEST
Questions and Exercises

True or False

Enter a T or an F in the blank to indicate whether the statement is true or false.

___ 1. When a division is operating at capacity, the cost of transferring a product or service to another division includes opportunity cost.

___ 2. Transfer prices based on actual cost are superior in that they provide incentive for the control of costs between transferring divisions.

Multiple Choice

Choose the best answer or response by placing the identifying letter in the space provided.

___ 1. Division A produces a part that it sells to outside customers. Data concerning this part appear below:

Selling price to outside customers..	$	60
Variable cost per unit	$	40
Total fixed cost...............................	$100,000	
Capacity in units..............................	20,000	

Division B of the same company now purchases 5,000 units of a similar part from an outside supplier at a price of $58 per unit. Division B wants to purchase these 5,000 units from Division A instead, but Division A has no idle capacity. Division A should insist on a transfer price of at least: a) $60; b) $58; c) $40; d) $45.

___ 2. Refer to the data in question (1) above. If Division A has idle capacity, the manager of Division A should insist that the transfer price be at least: a) $60; b) $40; c) between $45 and $58; d) between $40 and $58.

Exercise

Exercise 11A-1. Perchon Company's Regulator Division produces a small valve used by other companies as a key part in their products. Cost and sales data relating to the valve are given below:

Selling price per unit.........	$50
Variable costs per unit	$30
Fixed costs per unit*.........	$12

*Based on the Regulator Division's capacity of 40,000 valves per year.

Perchon Company's Boiler Division is introducing a new product that will use a valve such as the one produced in the Regulator Division. An outside supplier has quoted the Boiler Division a price of $48 per valve for the 10,000 valves the Boiler Division needs every year. The Boiler Division would like to purchase the valves from the Regulator Division instead if an acceptable transfer price can be worked out.

a. Assume that the Regulator Division is presently selling all the valves it can produce to outside customers. What is the lowest acceptable transfer price from the viewpoint of the selling division?

b. From the standpoint of the entire company, should the Boiler Division purchase the valves from the Regulator Division or from the outside supplier? Explain.

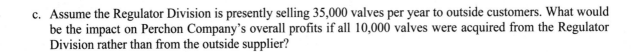

c. Assume the Regulator Division is presently selling 35,000 valves per year to outside customers. What would be the impact on Perchon Company's overall profits if all 10,000 valves were acquired from the Regulator Division rather than from the outside supplier?

d. Assume that the Regulator Division has ample idle capacity to handle all the Boiler Division's needs. What is the lowest acceptable transfer price from the viewpoint of the selling division?

Answers to Questions and Exercises

True or False

1. T The opportunity cost is the contribution margin lost from giving up outside sales.

2. F The opposite is true. When actual cost is used as a transfer price there is little or no incentive to control costs because whatever cost is incurred can simply be passed on to the next division.

Multiple Choice

1. a Transfer price = Variable costs + Opportunity cost
   Transfer price = $40 + ($60 − $40)
   Transfer price = $60

2. b Transfer price = Variable costs + Opportunity cost
   Transfer price = $40 + $0
   Transfer price = $40

Exercise

Exercise 11A-1.

a. If the Regulator Division transfers a valve to the Boiler Division, it cannot be sold on the outside market. Therefore, the Regulator Division loses $50 in revenue. Thus, the lowest transfer price the Regulator Division could accept is $50. This is verified by using the formula approach as follows:

$$\frac{\text{Transfer}}{\text{price}} \geq \frac{\text{Variable}}{\text{cost}} + \frac{\text{Total contribution margin on lost sales}}{\text{Number of units transferred}}$$

$$\frac{\text{Transfer}}{\text{price}} \geq \$30 + \frac{(\$50\text{-}\$30)\times 10,000}{10,000} = \$30 + (\$50 - \$30) = \$50$$

b. The valves should be purchased from the outside supplier because the price will be only $48 per valve. In contrast, the company will give up $50 in revenue for each valve transferred internally rather than sold on the outside market.

c.

Regulator Division capacity.....................................	40,000 valves
Less Boiler Division's requirements......................	10,000 valves
Valves available for sale to outsiders....................	30,000 valves
Potential sales to outsiders....................................	35,000 valves
Valves available for sale to outsiders....................	30,000 valves
Lost sales	5,000 valves
Cost of transferring internally:	
Variable cost $30 × 10,000................................	$300,000
Lost contribution margin ($50 − $30) × 5,000 ...	100,000
Total cost of transferring internally	$400,000
Cost of purchasing from an outside supplier	$480,000

Profits will be $80,000 higher if the valves are acquired internally rather than purchased outside.

d. Transfer Price = $30 + $0 = $30
   There is no lost contribution margin because the Regulator Division has idle capacity.

Appendix 11B

Service Department Charges

APPENDIX HIGHLIGHTS

A. The costs of service departments are charged to the operating departments for a variety of reasons, including:

1. To encourage managers of operating departments to make wise use of services provided by service departments.

2. To provide more complete cost data for making decisions in operating departments.

3. To help measure profitability in operating departments.

4. To put pressure on service departments to operate efficiently.

B. Operating departments should be charged for budgeted, not actual, service department costs. Charging for actual costs would allow the service department to pass on any excess costs to the operating departments. This would have the effect of making the operating departments responsible for how well costs are controlled in the service departments.

C. Service department costs should be separated into fixed and variable components and separately charged to the operating departments.

1. Variable service department costs:

a. Charges for variable service department costs should be based on whatever causes those costs. For example, if variable maintenance costs increase and decrease in proportion to machine-hours, then machine-hours should be used as the base for variable maintenance charges.

b. Charges for variable service department costs should be determined by multiplying the *budgeted* rate by the *actual* level of activity in the using department. For example, variable maintenance costs would be charged to operating departments by multiplying the budgeted rate (for example, $2.50 per machine-hour) by the actual activity in each department (for example, 850 machine-hours in the Assembly Department).

2. Fixed service department costs:

a. The fixed costs of service departments are incurred in order to have the *capacity* to provide service during a period. This capacity may or may not be fully utilized. The fixed costs of service departments should be charged to consuming departments in proportion to the capacity they require, not the capacity they use. Thus, the fixed costs should be charged in *predetermined, lump-sum* amounts.

b. When charging fixed costs, the *budgeted* (not actual) costs should be charged on the basis of either *long-run average* activity or *peak period* requirements (not budgeted or actual activity). The reason for this is that the level of the fixed costs is determined by management's planning for the long run average or for peak period activity. Management wants to make sure that there is enough capacity to handle peak period or long run average needs.

D. A variable base such as sales dollars should not be used for charging service department costs. If a variable base is used, the amount of fixed cost charged to a department will be affected by what happens in other departments. A decrease in activity in other departments will result in an increase in the amount of the fixed cost charged to the department.

E. Any difference between the actual service department costs and the costs charged to the operating departments at the end of the period should be retained in the service department as a spending variance. This variance should be the responsibility of the manager of the service department.

REVIEW AND SELF-TEST
Questions and Exercises

True or False

Enter a T or an F in the blank to indicate whether the statement is true or false.

___ 1. Variable costs of service departments should be charged to operating departments in predetermined, lump-sum amounts.

___ 2. Operating departments should be charged for the budgeted, not actual, costs of service departments.

Multiple Choice

Choose the best answer or response by placing the identifying letter in the space provided.

The following data are used in multiple choice questions 1 through 3:

Data for Wasatch Company's two operating departments follow:

	Budgeted Machine Hours	Peak Period Requirement
Operating Department #1	15,000	40%
Operating Department #2	25,000	60%
Total machine-hours	40,000	100%

The Wasatch Company has a Repair Department that serves these two operating departments. The variable repair costs are budgeted at $0.20 per machine-hour. Fixed costs are budgeted at $12,000 per year. Fixed Repair Department costs are charged to operating departments on the basis of peak period requirements.

At the end of the year, the actual machine-hours worked by the operating departments were 16,000 hours for Department #1 and 24,000 hours for Department #2. The actual Repair Department costs were $8,600 variable and $13,000 fixed.

___ 1. The amount of variable repair cost charged to Department #1 at the end of the year should be: a) $4,800; b) $5,200; c) $3,200; d) $7,200.

___ 2. The amount of fixed repair cost charged to Department #2 at the end of the year should be: a) $4,800; b) $7,800; c) $3,200; d) $7,200.

___ 3. The amount of actual repair costs not charged to the operating departments and retained in the Repair Department at the end of the year as a spending variance should be: a) $600; b) $1,600; c) $1,000; d) $1,400.

Exercise

Exercise 11B-1. The municipal motor pool provides cars on loan to city employees who must travel on official business. The city has three departments that use this service—Public Safety, General Administration, and Sanitation. Data concerning these departments' annual use of the motor pool (in thousands of miles driven) appear below:

	Public Safety	General Administration	Sanitation
Budgeted use (thousands of miles).......	600	800	200
Actual use (thousands of miles)	500	900	250
Peak period requirements	35%	50%	15%

The motor pool's budgeted annual fixed costs are $330,000. Peak period requirements determine the level of the fixed costs. Budgeted variable costs are $80 per thousand miles driven.

Suppose the motor pool's actual costs for the year were $345,000 for fixed costs and $138,000 for variable costs. How much of this actual cost should be allocated to Public Safety at the end of the year for performance evaluation purposes?

Answers to Questions and Exercises

True or False

1. F Fixed costs—not variable costs—should be charged out in predetermined, lump-sums.

2. T Operating departments should be charged for budgeted, rather than actual, service department costs. The service departments should be held responsible for their own cost control. Charging actual costs to other departments implicitly holds those other departments responsible for how well the service department controls costs.

Multiple Choice

1. c 16,000 hours × $0.20 per hour = $3,200.

2. d $12,000 × 60% = $7,200.

3. b The computations are:

Actual costs ($8,600 + $13,000) ...		$21,600
Allocated costs:		
Variable*	$8,000	
Fixed**	12,000	20,000
Unallocated		$ 1,600

*(16,000 + 24,000) × $0.20 = $8,000
** The budgeted amount.

Exercise

Exercise 11B-1.

Variable cost allocation:	
Budgeted rate × Actual activity	
$80 per thousand miles × 500 thousand miles	$ 40,000
Fixed cost allocation:	
Budgeted fixed cost × Percentage of peak period needs	
$330,000 × 35%	115,500
Total	$155,500

Chapter 12

Differential Analysis: The Key to Decision Making

Chapter Study Suggestions

The concept of relevant costs and benefits, the costs and benefits that differ between alternatives, is covered in the first few pages of the chapter. Study these pages carefully because this idea underpins almost everything in the chapter. A number of specific decision-making situations are covered in the chapter, but the relevant cost concept is the key to the solution in every case.

CHAPTER HIGHLIGHTS

A. Every decision involves a choice from among at least two alternatives. A *relevant cost* or benefit is a cost or benefit that differs between alternatives. If a cost or benefit does not differ between alternatives, it is not relevant in the decision and can be ignored. *Avoidable cost*, *differential cost,* and *incremental cost* are synonyms for relevant cost.

1. Two broad classifications of costs are irrelevant in decisions: (a) sunk costs; and (b) future costs that do not differ between alternatives. *Sunk costs* are costs that have already been incurred and are irrevocable. Thus, they cannot differ between alternatives and are always irrelevant.

2. To make a decision, you should:

    a. Eliminate the costs and benefits that do not differ between alternatives. As stated above, irrelevant costs consist of sunk costs and future costs that do not differ between alternatives.

    b. Make a decision based on the remaining costs and benefits–those that differ between alternatives.

3. Costs that are relevant in one situation may not be relevant in another. There are no rules for identifying what costs are relevant and what costs are irrelevant except that costs that do not differ between alternatives are irrelevant.

B. You should disregard irrelevant costs and benefits in decisions for three reasons:

    a. In any given situation, the irrelevant costs greatly outnumber the relevant costs. Focusing just on the relevant costs takes less time and effort.

    b. Intermingling irrelevant with relevant costs may draw attention away from the really critical data—the relevant costs.

    c. Including irrelevant costs in a decision analysis often leads to mistakes.

C. *Adding or dropping a segment* such as a product line is one of the decision-making situations covered in the chapter. In making this decision, compare the contribution margin of the segment to the fixed costs that could be avoided by dropping the segment. If the contribution margin lost by dropping a segment is greater than the fixed costs that can be avoided, then the segment should be retained. If the contribution margin lost by dropping a segment is less than the fixed costs that can be avoided, then the segment should be dropped.

1. Exhibit 12-3 illustrates an alternative approach in which two income statements are prepared—one for each alternative. This approach will yield the same result as incremental analysis if both are done correctly.

2. The decision to keep or drop a product line or other segment of a company is often clouded by the allocation of common fixed costs as discussed in an earlier chapter.

    a. Allocations of common costs can make a profitable product line or other segment *appear* to be unprofitable.

    b. Common fixed costs should never be allocated to segments of a company; segments should be charged only with those costs that would be eliminated if the segment were eliminated.

D. A decision to produce a part (or a service) internally rather than to buy it from a supplier is called a *make or buy decision*. The relevant costs in such a decision, as always, are the costs that differ between the alternatives.

1. Exhibit 12-5 contains an example of a make or buy decision. Notice from the exhibit that the costs that are relevant in a make or buy decision are the costs that *differ* between the make or buy alternatives.

2. Opportunity cost may be a key factor in a make or buy decision as well as in other decisions.

    a. If the resources that are currently being used to make a part or a product all have excess capacity, then the opportunity cost is zero.

    b. On the other hand, if there is no excess capacity, then there is an opportunity cost. This opportunity cost is the incremental profit that could be obtained from the best alternative use of the capacity. Opportunity cost is a relevant cost that should be included in the decision analysis.

E. Another decision concerns *special orders*—one-time orders that don't affect regular sales. Such an order should be accepted if the incremental revenue from the special order exceeds the incremental (i.e., avoidable) costs of the order. Any opportunity costs should be taken into account.

F. A *constraint* is anything that limits the organization's ability to further its goals. When the constraint is a machine or a workstation, it is called a *bottleneck*. For example, a company may be able to sell 1,000 units of a product per week, but the product may require a machine that is capable of only producing 800 units a week. The machine would be a bottleneck.

1. When demand exceeds capacity, the company has a production constraint. In that case, managers must decide what the company *will* and *will not* do because the company cannot do everything. The problem is how to best utilize a constrained resource.

2. Fixed costs are likely to be unaffected by the decision of how best to utilize the constrained resource. If the fixed costs are unaffected by the decision, and hence irrelevant, maximizing the company's total contribution margin is equivalent to maximizing the company's profit. Given capacity and the company's fixed costs, the problem is how to best use that capacity to maximize total contribution margin and profit.

3. The key to the efficient utilization of a scarce resource is *the contribution margin per unit of the constrained resource*. The products with the greatest contribution margin per unit of the constrained resource are the most profitable; they generate the greatest profit from a given amount of the constrained resource. These products should be emphasized over products with a lower contribution margin per unit of the constrained resource.

4. Because the constraint limits the output of the entire organization, increasing the amount of the constrained resource can yield a huge payoff. This is called "elevating the constraint" and can be accomplished in a variety of ways including working overtime on the bottleneck, buying another machine, subcontracting work, and so on.

5. The contribution margin per unit of the constrained resource is also a measure of opportunity cost. For example, when considering whether to accept an order for a product that uses the constrained resource, the opportunity cost of using the constrained resource should be considered. That opportunity cost is the lost contribution margin for the job that would be displaced if the order were accepted.

G. In some industries, such as petroleum refining, a number of end products are produced from a single raw material input. Such end products are known as *joint products*. The *split-off point* is that point in the manufacturing process at which the joint products can be recognized as separate products.

1. Decisions as to whether a joint product should be sold at the split-off point or processed further and then sold are known as *sell or process further* decisions.

2. Costs incurred up to the split-off point are called *joint costs*. These costs are irrelevant in decisions concerning whether a product should be processed further after the split-off point because they will be incurred regardless of what is done after the split-off point.

3. It is profitable to continue processing joint products after the split-off point so long as the incremental revenue from such processing exceeds the incremental processing costs.

REVIEW AND SELF-TEST
Questions and Exercises

True or False

Enter a T or an F in the blank to indicate whether the statement is true or false.

___ 1. All costs are relevant in a decision except costs that do not differ between alternatives.

___ 2. In a decision, variable costs are relevant costs and fixed costs are irrelevant.

___ 3. Sunk costs may be relevant in a decision.

___ 4. Future costs are always relevant in a decision.

___ 5. Costs that are relevant in one decision are not necessarily relevant in another decision.

___ 6. If a company is able to avoid more in fixed costs than it loses in contribution margin by dropping a product, then it will be better off financially if the product is eliminated.

___ 7. Allocation of common fixed costs to product lines and to other segments of a company helps the manager determine if the product line or segment is profitable.

___ 8. Opportunity cost may be a key factor in a make or buy decision.

___ 9. If there is a constrained resource, the product that has the highest contribution margin per unit should be emphasized.

___ 10. A joint product should continue to be processed after the split-off point so long as the incremental revenue from such processing exceeds the incremental processing costs.

___ 11. Joint product costs are irrelevant in decisions regarding what to do with joint products after the split-off point.

Multiple Choice

Choose the best answer or response by placing the identifying letter in the space provided.

___ 1. All of the following costs are relevant in a make or buy decision except: a) the opportunity cost of space; b) costs that are avoidable by buying rather than making; c) variable costs of producing the item; d) costs that are differential between the make and buy alternatives; e) all of the above costs are relevant.

___ 2. One of Simplex Company's products has a contribution margin of $50,000 and fixed costs totaling $60,000. If the product is dropped, $40,000 of the fixed costs will continue unchanged. As a result of dropping the product, the company's net operating income should: a) decrease by $50,000; b) increase by $30,000; c) decrease by $30,000; d) increase by $10,000.

___ 3. Halley Company produces 2,000 parts each year that are used in one of its products. The unit product cost of this part is:

Variable manufacturing cost..	$ 7.50
Fixed manufacturing cost	6.00
Unit product cost	$13.50

The part can be purchased from an outside supplier for $10 per unit. If the part is purchased from the outside supplier, two-thirds of the fixed manufacturing costs can be eliminated. The effect on net operating income as a result of purchasing the part would be a: a) $3,000 increase; b) $1,000 decrease; c) $7,000 increase; d) $5,000 decrease.

___ 4. Product A has a contribution margin of $8 per unit, a contribution margin ratio of 50%, and requires 4 machine-hours to produce. Product B has a contribution margin of $12 per unit, a contribution margin ratio of 40%, and requires 5 machine-hours to produce. If the constraint is machine-hours, then the company should emphasize: a) Product A; b) Product B.

5. Sunderson Products, Inc. has received a special order for 1,000 units of a sport-fighting kite. The customer has offered a price of $9.95 for each kite. The unit costs of the kite, at its normal sales level of 30,000 units per year, are detailed below:

Variable production costs	$5.25
Fixed production costs...........................	$2.35
Variable selling costs............................	$0.75
Fixed selling and administrative costs ...	$3.45

There is ample idle capacity to produce the special order without any increase in total fixed costs. The variable selling costs on the special order would be $0.15 per unit instead of $0.75 per unit. The special order would have no impact on the company's other sales. What effect would accepting this special order have on the company's net operating income? a) $1,850 increase; b) $1,850 decrease; c) $4,550 increase; d) $4,550 decrease.

6. Products A and B are joint products. Product A can be sold for $1,200 at the split-off point, or processed further at a cost of $600 and then sold for $1,700. Product B can be sold for $3,000 at the split-off point, or processed further at a cost of $800 and then sold for $4,000. The company should process further: a) Product A; b) Product B; c) both products; d) neither of the products.

Exercises

Exercise 12-1. The most recent income statement for the men's formal wear department of Merrill's Department Store is given below:

Sales.....................................		$500,000
Variable expenses		200,000
Contribution margin...............		300,000
Fixed expenses:		
Salaries and wages..............	$150,000	
Insurance on inventories.....	10,000	
Depreciation of fixtures*....	65,000	
Advertising	100,000	325,000
Net operating income (loss) ...		$ (25,000)

*Six year remaining useful life, with little or no current resale value.

Management is thinking about dropping the men's formal wear department. If the department is dropped, a make-work position will be found for one long-time employee who is due to retire in several years. That employee's salary is $30,000. The fixtures in the department would have no resale value and would be hauled to the county dump.

Prepare an analysis, using the following form, to determine whether the department should be dropped.

Contribution margin lost if the department is dropped ..... $_____

Less avoidable fixed costs:

_____ .... $_____

_____ ....   _____

_____ ....   _____   _____

Increase (decrease) in net operating income .... $_____

Based on this analysis, should the men's formal wear department be dropped?

Redo the analysis, using the alternate format shown below:

	Keep Department	Drop Department	Difference: Income Increase or (Decrease)
Sales..	$ 500,000	$_____	$_____
Variable expenses	200,000	_____	_____
Contribution margin....................	300,000	_____	_____
Fixed expenses:			
Salaries and wages....................	150,000	_____	_____
Insurance on inventories..........	10,000	_____	_____
Depreciation of fixtures*.........	65,000	_____	_____
Advertising	100,000	_____	_____
Total fixed expenses	325,000	_____	_____
Net operating income (loss)........	$ (25,000)	$_____	$_____

Exercise 12-2. Watson Company produces two products from a common input. Data relating to the two products are given below:

	Product A	Product B
Sales value at the split-off point	$60,000	$120,000
Allocated joint product costs	$45,000	$ 90,000
Sales value after further processing..	$90,000	$200,000
Cost of further processing.................	$20,000	$ 85,000

Determine which of the products should be sold at the split-off point, and which should be processed further before sale. Use the form that appears below.

	Product A	Product B
Sales value after further processing......................	$_____	$_____
Sales value at the split-off point	_____	_____
Incremental revenue from further processing.......	_____	_____
Less cost of further processing	_____	_____
Profit (loss) from further processing....................	$_____	$_____

Exercise 12-3.   Petre Company is now making a small part that is used in one of its products. The company's accounting department reports the following costs of producing the part internally:

	Per Part
Direct materials	$15
Direct labor	10
Variable manufacturing overhead	2
Fixed manufacturing overhead, traceable	4
Fixed manufacturing overhead, allocated common	5
Unit product cost	$36

A total of 75% of the traceable fixed manufacturing overhead cost consists of depreciation of special equipment, and 25% consists of supervisory salaries. The special equipment has no resale value and does not wear out through use. The supervisory salaries could be avoided if production of the part were discontinued.

An outside supplier has offered to sell the parts to Petre Company for $30 each, based on an order of 5,000 parts per year. Should Petre Company accept this offer, or continue to make the parts internally? Assume that direct labor is a variable cost. Use the following form in your answer:

	Relevant Costs for 5,000 Parts	
	Make	*Buy*
Outside purchase price		$_____
Cost of making internally:		
_____	$_____	
_____	_____	
_____	_____	
_____	_____	
_____	_____	
Total cost	$_____	$_____

Exercise 12-4. Kuski Corporation makes two models of its hair dryer at a facility in Lexington. The copper-winding machine has been the constraint in the factory in the past. The capacity of this machine is 9,600 minutes per month. Data concerning these two products appear below:

	Standard	Premium
Unit selling price	$14.00	$20.00
Variable cost per unit	$5.00	$8.00
Copper-winding machine time per unit	0.5 minute	0.6 minute
Monthly demand	12,000 units	8,000 units

a. Determine if the copper-winding machine is currently a constraint. In other words, does demand exceed capacity? Use the form below to answer this question

	Standard	Premium	Total
_____	_____	_____	
_____	_____	_____	
Copper-winding time required to satisfy demand	_____	_____	_____

b. Compute the contribution margin per copper-winding minute for the two products using the following form:

	Standard	Premium
Unit selling price	_____	_____
Variable cost per unit	_____	_____
Contribution margin per unit	_____	_____
Copper-winding machine time per unit	_____	_____
Contribution margin per minute	_____	_____

c. Assuming that the copper-winding machine is the company's constraint, how many units of each product should be made in order to maximize net operating income?

Answers to Questions and Exercises

True or False

1. T   Costs that differ between alternatives are relevant. Costs that do not differ between alternatives are not relevant.

2. F   Fixed costs can be relevant and variable costs can be irrelevant. What is relevant and what is irrelevant depends on the particular decision.

3. F   Sunk costs are never relevant because they have already been incurred and thus can't be avoided by choosing one alternative over another.

4. F   Future costs are relevant only if they differ between alternatives; future costs that do not differ between alternatives are irrelevant.

5. T   For example, a product line manager's salary would be relevant in a decision to drop the product line, but would not be relevant in a decision about how much to spend on advertising.

6. T   If the avoidable fixed costs exceed the lost contribution margin, profits would increase if the product line were dropped.

7. F   Allocation of common fixed costs to product lines and to other segments of a company can easily result in misleading data and can make a product line appear to be unprofitable when in fact it may be one of a company's best products.

8. T   Opportunity cost can be a key factor in *any* decision involving a constrained resource.

9. F   The product with the highest contribution margin per unit of the constrained resource should be emphasized. A product might have a high contribution margin per unit but require a disproportionately large amount of the constrained resource.

10. T   Processing further under these conditions will increase profits.

11. T   At the split-off point, joint product costs have already been incurred and are not affected by what is done with the joint products from that point forward.

Multiple Choice

1. e   These costs are all relevant because they all differ between the alternatives.

2. c   The computations are:

Contribution margin lost..............	$(50,000)
Less avoidable fixed costs*........	20,000
Decrease in operating income......	$(30,000)

*$60,000 − $40,000 = $20,000

3. a   The computations are:

	Differential Cost Make	Buy
Variable manufacturing costs..........................	$ 7.50	
Avoidable fixed manufacturing cost............	4.00	
Outside purchase price .		$10.00
Total relevant cost........	$11.50	$10.00

2,000 units × $1.50 = $3,000

4. b   The computations are:

	A	B
Contribution margin per unit (a)	$8.00	$12.00
Machine-hours to produce (b).....................................	4.00	5.00
CM per machine-hour (a) ÷ (b)............................	$2.00	$ 2.40

5. c   The computations are:

Incremental revenue ($9.95 × 1,000)		$9,950
Incremental costs:		
Variable production ($5.25 × 1,000)........	$5,250	
Variable selling ($0.15 × 1,000)........	150	5,400
Increase in operating income		$4,550

6. b   The computations are:

	A	B
Sales value after further processing	$1,700	$4,000
Sales value at split-off.........	1,200	3,000
Incremental sales value........	500	1,000
Incremental processing cost.	600	800
Advantage (disadvantage) of further processing........	$(100)	$ 200

Exercises

Exercise 12-1.

Contribution margin lost if the department is dropped		$(300,000)
Less avoidable fixed costs:		
Salaries and wages ($150,000 - $30,000)......................	$120,000	
Insurance on inventories...	10,000	
Advertising	100,000	230,000
Decrease in overall company net operating income..........		$(70,000)

Based on the analysis above, the department should not be dropped. The solution using the alternate format appears below:

	Keep Department	Drop Department	Difference: Income Increase or (Decrease)
Sales..	$ 500,000	$ 0	$(500,000)
Variable expenses	200,000	0	200,000
Contribution margin....................	300,000	0	(300,000)
Fixed expenses:			
Salaries and wages....................	150,000	30,000	120,000
Insurance on inventories..........	10,000	0	10,000
Depreciation of fixtures*.........	65,000	65,000	0
Advertising	100,000	0	100,000
Total fixed expenses	325,000	95,000	230,000
Net operating income (loss)........	$ (25,000)	$ (95,000)	$ (70,000)

* If the department were dropped, the remaining book value of the fixtures would be written off immediately. If the department were not dropped, the remaining book value would be written off over a number of years in the form of depreciation charges. In either case, the entire remaining book value will eventually flow through the income statement as charges in one form or another.

Exercise 12-2.

	Product A	Product B
Sales value after further processing	$90,000	$200,000
Sales value at the split-off point	60,000	120,000
Incremental revenue from further processing	30,000	80,000
Less cost of further processing	20,000	85,000
Profit (loss) from further processing....................	$10,000	$ (5,000)

Exercise 12-3.

	Relevant Costs for 5,000 Parts	
	Make	*Buy*
Outside purchase price		$150,000
Cost of making internally:		
Direct materials..	$ 75,000	
Direct labor	50,000	
Variable manufacturing overhead...........................	10,000	
Fixed manufacturing overhead, traceable	5,000	
Fixed manufacturing overhead, allocated common .		
Total	$140,000	$150,000
Difference in favor of making	$10,000	

The depreciation on the equipment and the common fixed overhead are not avoidable costs.

Exercise 12-4.

a. Demand exceeds capacity for the copper-winding machine, as shown below:

	Standard	*Premium*	*Total*
Monthly demand (a).....................................	12,000 units	8,000 units	
Copper-winding machine time per unit (b).	0.5 min./unit	0.6 min./unit	
Copper-winding time required to satisfy			
demand (a) × (b)......................................	6,000 min.	4,800 min.	10,800 min.

b.

	Standard	*Premium*
Unit selling price...	$14.00	$20.00
Variable cost per unit	5.00	8.00
Contribution margin per unit (a)	$ 9.00	$12.00
Copper-winding machine time per unit (b).	0.5 min.	0.6 min.
Contribution margin per minute (a) ÷ (b)....	$18/min.	$20/min.

c. Because the contribution margin per copper-winding minute is higher for the premium model than for the standard model, the premium model should be emphasized. The optimal plan is to produce all 8,000 units of the premium model and use the remaining capacity to make 9,600 units of the standard model.

Total copper-winding time available..	9,600 minutes
Time required to produce 8,000 units of the premium model...	4,800 minutes
Time remaining with which to make the standard model (a)....	4,800 minutes
Time required to make one unit of the standard model (b).......	0.5 minute/unit
Number of units of the standard model produced (a) ÷ (b).......	9,600 units

Chapter 13

Capital Budgeting Decisions

Chapter Study Suggestions

You must have a solid understanding of present value to understand the material in this chapter. If you have not worked with present value before, study Appendix 13A, "The Concept of Present Value," before starting the chapter.

Once you understand present value, you will be ready to tackle the capital budgeting methods in the chapter. The first of these methods is called the net present value method. Follow through each number in Exhibits 13-1 and 13-4 and trace the present value factors back to the tables given at the end of the chapter.

The second capital budgeting method covered in the chapter is called the internal rate of return method. It is illustrated in Example D. Both the internal rate of return method and the net present value method are based on discounting future cash flows.

Two other methods of making capital budgeting decisions are presented in the chapter—the payback method and the simple rate of return method.

CHAPTER HIGHLIGHTS

A. *Capital budgeting* is the process of planning significant investments in projects that have long-term implications such as the purchase of new equipment or the introduction of a new product.

1. Capital budgeting decisions fall into two broad categories:

    a. *Screening decisions:* Potential projects are categorized as acceptable or unacceptable.

    b. *Preference decisions*: After screening out all of the unacceptable projects, more projects may remain than can be funded. Consequently, projects must be ranked in order of preference.

2. The time value of money is a central consideration in capital budgeting. A dollar in the future is worth less than a dollar today for the simple reason that a dollar today can be invested to yield more than a dollar in the future.

    a. *Discounted cash flow methods* give full recognition to the time value of money.

    b. Two methods that discount cash flows are the *net present value method* and the *internal rate of return method*.

    c. Two of the methods presented in the chapter do not discount cash flows—the *payback method* and *simple rate of return method*. For this reason, these methods are deficient.

B. The net present value method is illustrated in Exhibit 13-1, Exhibit 13-2, and Exhibit 13-4. The basic steps in this method are:

1. Determine the required investment and the future cash inflows and outflows that result from the investment.

2. Use the *present value tables* in Appendix 13B to find the appropriate *present value factors*.

    a. The values (or factors) in the present value tables depend on the discount rate and the number of periods.

    b. The *discount rate* in present value analysis is the company's required rate of return, which is often the company's cost of capital. The *cost of capital* is the average rate of return the company must pay its long-term creditors and stockholders for the use of their funds. The details of the cost of capital are covered in finance courses.

3. Multiply each cash flow by the appropriate present value factor and then sum the results. The end result (which is net of the initial investment) is called the *net present value* of the project.

4. In a screening decision, the investment is acceptable if the net present value is positive. If the net present value is negative, the investment should be rejected.

C. Discounted cash flow analysis is based on *cash flows*—not accounting net operating income.

1. Typical cash flows associated with an investment are:

    a. Outflows include initial investment, installation costs, increased working capital needs, repairs and maintenance, and incremental operating costs.

    b. Inflows include incremental revenues, reductions in costs, salvage value, and release of working capital at the end of the project.

2. Depreciation is not a cash flow and therefore is not included in net present value calculations. (However, depreciation can affect taxes, which *is* a cash flow. This aspect of depreciation is covered in Appendix 13C.)

3. Projects frequently require an infusion of cash (i.e., working capital) to finance inventories, receivables, and other working capital items. Typically, at the end of the project this working capital can be recovered. Thus, working capital is counted as a cash outflow at the beginning of a project and as a cash inflow at the end of the project.

4. We usually assume that all cash flows, other than the initial investment, occur at the *ends* of periods.

D. The internal rate of return method is another discounted cash flow method used in capital budgeting decisions.

1. The *internal rate of return* is the rate of return promised by an investment project over its useful life; it is the discount rate for which the net present value of the project is zero.

2. When the cash flows are the same every year, the following formula can be used to find the internal rate of return:

$$\frac{\text{Factor of the}}{\text{internal rate of return}} = \frac{\text{Investment required}}{\text{Annual net cash inflows}}$$

3.   For example, assume an investment of $3,791 is made in a project that will last five years and has no salvage value. Also assume that the annual net cash inflow from the project will be $1,000.

$$\text{Factor of the internal rate of return} = \frac{\$3,791}{\$1,000} = 3.791$$

The same net cash inflow is received at the end of every year beginning with the first year, so use Exhibit 13B-2 in Appendix 13B, which contains the present value factors for annuities. Because this is a project with a five-year life, use the 5-year row in the table. Scanning along the 5-year row, it can be seen that this factor represents a 10% rate of return. Therefore, the internal rate of return is 10%.

4.   If the net cash inflows are not the same every year, the internal rate of return is found using trial and error or a software application. The internal rate of return is whatever discount rate makes the net present value of the project equal zero.

5.   In a screening decision, the internal rate of return is compared to the required rate of return. If the internal rate of return is less than the required rate of return, the project is rejected. If it is greater than or equal to the required rate of return, the project is accepted.

E. The *total-cost* or the *incremental-cost* approach can be used in conjunction with the net present value method to compare projects.

1.   Exhibit 13-7 illustrates the total cost approach. Note in Exhibit 13-7 that *all* cash inflows and *all* cash outflows for each alternative are included in the solution.

2.   The incremental-cost approach ignores all cash flows that are the same under both alternatives. Exhibit 13-8 illustrates this approach.

3.   If done correctly, both the total-cost and incremental-cost approaches will lead to the same decision.

F. Sometimes no revenue or cash inflow is involved in a decision. In this situation, the *least cost* alternative should be selected. Exhibits 13-9 and 13-10 illustrate least-cost decisions.

G. It is often difficult to quantify all the costs and benefits involved in a decision. An investment in automation provides a good example.

1.   The reduction in direct labor cost from automation may be easy to quantify. Intangible benefits, such as greater throughput or greater flexibility in operations, are usually very difficult to quantify.

It would be a mistake to ignore these intangible benefits simply because they are difficult to quantify.

2.   The difficulty can often be resolved by computing how large the intangible benefits would have to be to make the investment attractive. The steps in this approach are:

a.   Compute the net present value of the tangible costs and benefits. If the result is positive, the investment is acceptable because the intangible benefits simply make it even more attractive.

b.   If the net present value of the tangible costs and benefits is negative, compute the additional annual net cash inflows that would make the net present value positive.

c.   If the intangible benefits are likely to be at least as large as the required additional annual net cash inflows, accept the project.

H. When more acceptable projects exist than can be funded, the projects must be ranked in order of preference.

1.   When using the internal rate of return to rank competing investment projects, the preference rule is: *The higher the internal rate of return, the more desirable the project.*

2.   If the net present value method is used to rank competing investment projects, the net present value of one project should not be compared directly to the net present value of another project, unless the investments in the projects are equal.

a.   To compare projects that require different investment amounts, the *project profitability index* is computed:

$$\text{Project profitability index} = \frac{\text{Net present value of the project}}{\text{Investment required}}$$

The project profitability index is basically the same idea as the contribution margin per unit of the constrained resource in Chapter 12. In this case, the constrained resource is investment funds.

b.   The higher the profitability index, the more desirable the project.

I. The present value method is generally superior to the internal rate of return method, although both are used in practice. The internal rate of return method assumes that any net cash inflows received during the life of the project can be reinvested at a rate of return equal to the internal rate of return. This assumption is questionable if the internal rate of return is high. In contrast, the net present value method assumes that any cash flows received during the life of the project are reinvested at a rate of return equal to the discount rate. Ordinarily, this is a more realistic assumption.

J. Two other capital budgeting methods are considered in the chapter. These methods do not involve discounting cash flows One of these is the payback method.

1.   The *payback period* is the number of years required for an investment project to recover its cost out of the cash receipts it generates.

  a.   When the cash inflows from the project are the same every year, the following formula can be used to compute the payback period:

$$\text{Payback period} = \frac{\text{Investment required}}{\text{Annual net cash inflows}}$$

  b.   If new equipment is replacing old equipment, the "investment required" should be reduced by any salvage value obtained from the disposal of old equipment. And in this case, in computing the "annual net cash inflows," only the incremental cash inflow provided by the new equipment over the old equipment should be used.

2.   The payback period is not a measure of profitability. Rather it is a measure of how long it takes for a project to recover its investment cost.

3.   The payback method ignores the time value of money and all cash flows that occur once the initial cost has been recovered. Therefore, this method is very crude and should be used only with a great deal of caution. Nevertheless, the payback method can be useful in industries where project lives are very short and uncertain.

K. The simple rate of return method is another capital budgeting method that does not involve discounted cash flows.

1.   The *simple rate of return* method focuses on accounting net operating income rather than on cash flows:

$$\frac{\text{Simple rate}}{\text{of retun}} = \frac{\begin{array}{c}\text{Annual incremental}\\ \text{net operating income}\end{array}}{\text{Initial investment}}$$

If new equipment is replacing old equipment, then the "initial investment" in the new equipment is the cost of the new equipment reduced by any salvage value obtained from the old equipment.

2.   Like the payback method, the simple rate of return method does not consider the time value of money. Therefore, the rate of return computed by this method is not an accurate guide to the profitability of an investment project.

REVIEW AND SELF-TEST
Questions and Exercises

True or False

Enter a T or an F in the blank to indicate whether the statement is true or false.

____ 1. Under the net present value method, the present value of all cash inflows associated with an investment project is compared to the present value of all cash outflows, with the difference, or net present value, determining whether or not the project is acceptable.

____ 2. One key shortcoming of discounted cash flow methods is that they do not provide for the recovery of the original investment.

____ 3. Cash outlays for noncurrent assets such as machines are considered in a capital budgeting analysis, but not cash outlays for current assets such as inventory.

____ 4. The internal rate of return is the discount rate for which a project's net present value is zero.

____ 5. The internal rate of return method makes more realistic assumptions about the rate of return that is earned on cash generated by an investment than the net present value method.

____ 6. In present value analysis, as the discount rate increases, the present value of a given future cash inflow also increases.

____ 7. When comparing two investment alternatives, the total-cost approach provides the same ultimate answer as the incremental-cost approach.

____ 8. When ranking investment projects, a project with a high net present value should be ranked above a project with a lower net present value.

____ 9. In preference decision situations, the net present value and internal rate of return methods may yield conflicting rankings of projects.

____ 10. The payback method does not consider the time value of money.

____ 11. The present value of a cash inflow to be received in 5 years is greater than the present value of the same sum to be received in 10 years.

Multiple Choice

Choose the best answer or response by placing the identifying letter in the space provided.

The following data relate to questions 1 and 2.

Peters Company is considering a machine to further automate its production line. The machine would cost $30,000, and have a ten-year life with no salvage value. It would save $8,000 per year in labor costs, but would increase power costs by $1,000 annually. The company's discount rate is 12%.

____ 1. The present value of the annual net cost savings is: a) $39,550; b) $45,200; c) $5,650; d) $70,000.

____ 2. The net present value of the entire project is: a) $(15,200); b) $5,650; c) $9,550; d) $30,000.

____ 3. Acme Company is considering investing in a new machine that costs $84,900 and that has a useful life of 12 years with no salvage value. The machine will generate $15,000 annually in net cash inflows. The internal rate of return on the investment is: a) 8%; b) 10%; c) 12%; d) 14 %.

____ 4. White Company's required rate of return and discount rate is 12%. The company is considering an investment that would yield a cash inflow of $10,000 in five years. What is the most that the company should be willing to invest in this project? a) $36,050; b) $5,670; c) $17,637; d) $2,774.

____ 5. An investment of $30,000 in working capital would provide cash inflows of $10,000 per year for six years. If the company's discount rate is 18%, and if the working capital is released at the end of the six years, then the project's net present value is: a) $4,980; b) $(4,980); c) $16,080; d) $(12,360).

____ 6. A project with a 10-year life has tangible costs and benefits with a $113,000 *negative* net present value. The company's discount rate is 12%. What amount of annual cash inflow would have to be provided by the project's intangible benefits in order for the project to be acceptable? a) $11,300; b) $13,560; c) $18,000; d) $20,000.

___ 7. A machine is under consideration that would cost $30,000, save $6,000 per year in cash operating costs, and have an expected life of 15 years with zero salvage value. The payback period on the machine is: a) 2 years; b) 7.5 years; c) 5 years; d) 0.2 years.

___ 8. Refer to the data in question (7) above. The simple rate of return is approximately: a) 20%; b) 13.3%; c) 18%; d) 10%.

Exercises

Exercise 13-1.   You have recently won $100,000 in a contest. You have been given the option of receiving $100,000 today or receiving $12,000 at the end of each year for the next 20 years.

a. If you can earn 8% on investments, which of these two options would you select? (Note: The net present value method assumes that any cash flows are reinvested at a rate of return equal to the discount rate. Therefore, to answer this question you can compare the net present values of the cash flows under the two alternatives using 8% as the discount rate.)

Item	*Year(s)*	*Amount of Cash Flows*	*8% Factor*	*Present Value of Cash Flows*
Receive the annuity...................................	_____	$_____	_____	$_____
Receive the lump sum..............................	_____	$_____	_____	_____
Net present value in favor of the				
_____.....................				$_____

b. If you can earn 12% on investments, which of these two options would you select?

Item	*Year(s)*	*Amount of Cash Flows*	*12% Factor*	*Present Value of Cash Flows*
Receive the annuity	_____	$_____	_____	$_____
Receive the lump sum.............................	_____	$_____	_____	_____
Net present value in favor of the				
_____.....................				$_____

Exercise 13-2.   Lynde Company has been offered a contract to provide a key replacement part for the Army's main attack helicopter. The contract would expire in eight years. The projected cash flows that result from the contract are given below:

Cost of new equipment................................	$300,000
Working capital needed.............................	$100,000
Annual net cash inflows	$ 85,000
Salvage value of equipment in eight years..	$ 50,000

The company's discount rate is 16%. The working capital would be released for use elsewhere at the end of the project.

Complete the analysis below to determine whether the contract should be accepted. (Ignore income taxes.)

Item	Year(s)	Amount of Cash Flows	16% Factor	Present Value of Cash Flows
Cost of new equipment	_____	$_____	_____	$_____
Working capital needed	_____	$_____	_____	_____
Annual net cash receipts	_____	$_____	_____	_____
Salvage value of equipment.....	_____	$_____	_____	_____
Working capital released	_____	$_____	_____	_____
Net present value				$_____

Exercise 13-3.   Swift Company is considering the purchase of a new machine that will cost $20,000. The machine will provide revenues of $9,000 per year. Out-of-pocket operating costs will be $6,000 per year. The new machine will have a useful life of 10 years and will have zero salvage value. The company's required rate of return is 12%. (Ignore income taxes.) What is the internal rate of return to the nearest whole percent?

Annual revenue	$_____
Annual operating costs......	_____
Incremental cash inflow....	$_____

$$\text{Factor of the internal rate of return} = \frac{\text{Investment required}}{\text{Annual net cash inflows}}$$

$$= \frac{\rule{3cm}{0.4pt}}{\rule{3cm}{0.4pt}} = \rule{1.5cm}{0.4pt}$$

Exercise 13-4. Harlan Company would like to purchase a new machine that makes wonderfully smooth fruit sorbet that the company can sell in the premium frozen dessert sections of supermarkets. The machine costs $450,000 and has a useful life of ten years with a salvage value of $50,000. Annual revenues and expenses resulting from the new machine are:

Sales revenue		$300,000
Selling and administrative expenses:		
Advertising	$100,000	
Salaries of operators	70,000	
Maintenance	30,000	
Depreciation	40,000	240,000
Net operating income		$ 60,000

a. Harlan Company will not invest in new equipment unless it promises a payback period of 4 years or less. Compute the payback period on the sorbet machine.

Computation of the annual net cash inflow:

Net operating income .... $_____

Add: Noncash deduction for depreciation... _____

Annual net cash inflow............................. $_____

Computation of the payback period:

$$\text{Payback period} = \frac{\text{Investment required}}{\text{Annual net cash inflows}}$$

$$= \frac{\rule{3cm}{0.4pt}}{\rule{3cm}{0.4pt}} = \text{\_\_\_\_years}$$

b. Compute the simple rate of return on the investment in the new machine.

$$\text{Simple rate of return} = \frac{\text{Annual incremental revenue} - \text{Annual incremental expenses}}{\text{Initial investment}}$$

$$= \frac{\rule{3cm}{0.4pt}}{\rule{3cm}{0.4pt}} = \text{\_\_\_\_}$$

Answers to Questions and Exercises

True or False

1. T   Exhibit 13-4 illustrates this point.

2. F   Discounted cash flow methods do provide for recovery of original investment, as illustrated in Exhibit 13-3.

3. F   All cash flows should be included in a capital budgeting analysis.

4. T   This statement is true by definition; the principle is illustrated in Exhibit 13-5.

5. F   The opposite is true.

6. F   The opposite is true—the higher the discount rate, the lower is the present value of a given future cash inflow.

7. T   The total-cost approach and the incremental-cost approach are just different ways of obtaining the same result.

8. F   Net present value shouldn't be used to rank projects when investment funds are limited because one project may have a higher net present value than another simply because it is larger. The project profitability index should be used to compare projects.

9. T   See the example in the text in the section "Comparing the Preference Rules."

10. T   A major defect of the payback method is that dollars are given the same weight regardless of when they are received.

11. T   When discounting, the shorter the time period, the greater the present value.

Multiple Choice

1. a   The computations are:

Savings in labor costs	$ 8,000
Less increased power costs	1,000
Net cost savings	$ 7,000
Present value factor for 12% for 10 years (Exhibit 13B-2).............	× 5.650
Present value of cost savings	$39,550

2. c   The computations are:

Investment in the machine	$(30,000)
Present value of cost savings	39,550
Net present value	$ 9,550

3. d   The computations are:

$$\frac{\text{Factor of the internal rate of return}}{} = \frac{\text{Investment required}}{\text{Annual net cash inflows}}$$

$$= \frac{\$84,900}{\$15,000} = 5.660$$

Looking at the 12-year row in the annuity Exhibit 13B-2, a factor of 5.660 equals a return of 14%.

4. b   The computations are:

Return in 5 years............................	$10,000
Present value factor for 12% for 5 years (Exhibit 13B-1)................	× 0.567
Present value................................	$ 5,670

This is the maximum amount the company should be willing to invest. If it were to invest more than $5,670, the net present value of the investment would be negative.

5. c   The computations are:

	Year(s)	Amount	18% Factor	Present Value
Working capital investment:				
	Now	$(30,000)	1.000	$(30,000)
Cash inflow:				
	1-6	10,000	3.498	34,980
Working capital released:				
	6	30,000	0.370	11,100
Net present value				$ 16,080

6. d   The computation is:

$$\frac{\text{Net present value, } \$113,000}{\text{Present value factor, } 5.650} = \$20,000$$

7. c The computation is:

$$\text{Payback period} = \frac{\text{Investment required}}{\text{Annual net cash inflows}}$$

$$= \frac{\$30,000}{\$6,000 \text{ per year}} = 5 \text{ years}$$

8. b The annual incremental net operating income is the difference between the cost savings of $6,000 per year and the annual depreciation charge of $2,000 = $30,000 ÷ 15 years.

$$\text{Simple rate of retun} = \frac{\text{Annual incremental net operating income}}{\text{Initial investment}}$$

$$= \frac{\$6,000 - \$2,000}{\$30,000} = 13.3\%$$

Exercises

Exercise 13-1.

a. The annuity is preferable if the discount rate is 8%:

Item	Year(s)	Amount of Cash Flows	8% Factor	Present Value of Cash Flows
Receive the annuity..................................	1-20	$ 12,000	9.818	$117,816
Receive the lump sum..............................	Now	$100,000	1.000	100,000
Net present value in favor of the annuity.				$ 17,816

b. The lump sum is preferable if the discount rate is 12%:

Item	Year(s)	Amount of Cash Flows	12% Factor	Present Value of Cash Flows
Receive the annuity	1-20	$ 12,000	7.469	$ 89,628
Receive the lump sum.....................................	Now	$100,000	1.000	100,000
Net present value in favor of the lump sum....				$ 10,372

Exercise 13-2.

Item	Year(s)	Amount of Cash Flows	16% Factor	Present Value of Cash Flows
Cost of new equipment	Now	($ 300,000)	1.000	($300,000)
Working capital needed	Now	($ 100,000)	1.000	(100,000)
Annual net cash receipts	1-8	$ 85,000	4.344	369,240
Salvage value of equipment	8	$ 50,000	0.305	15,250
Working capital released..........	8	$ 100,000	0.305	30,500
Net present value......................				$ 14,990

Yes, the contract should be accepted. The net present value is positive, which means that the contract will provide more than the company's 16% required rate of return.

Exercise 13-3.

Annual revenue	$9,000
Annual operating costs......	6,000
Incremental cash inflow	$3,000

$$\text{Factor of the internal rate of return} = \frac{\text{Investment required}}{\text{Annual net cash inflows}}$$

$$= \frac{\$20,000}{\$3,000} = 6.667$$

The 6.667 factor falls between the 8% and 9% rates of return in Exhibit 13B-2 and is closest to 8%, therefore the internal rate of return is about 8%.

Exercise 13-4.

a. The annual net cash inflow is:

Net operating income.................................	$ 60,000
Add: Noncash deduction for depreciation...	40,000
Annual net cash inflow	$100,000

The payback period is:

$$\text{Payback period} = \frac{\text{Investment required}}{\text{Annual net cash inflows}} = \frac{\$450,000}{\$100,000 \text{ per year}} = 4.5 \text{ years}$$

The machine would not be purchased because it will not provide the 4-year payback period required by the company.

b. The simple rate of return is:

$$\text{Simple rate of return} = \frac{\text{Annual incremental net operating income}}{\text{Initial investment}}$$

$$= \frac{\$60,000}{\$450,000} = 13.3\%$$

Appendix 13A

The Concept of Present Value

APPENDIX HIGHLIGHTS

A. A dollar received today is more valuable than a dollar received in the future for the simple reason that a dollar received today can be invested—yielding more than a dollar in the future.

B. Present value analysis recognizes the time value of money.

   1. Present value analysis involves expressing a future cash flow in terms of present dollars. When a future cash flow is expressed in terms of its present value, the process is called *discounting*.

   2. Use Exhibit 13B-1 in Appendix 13B to determine the present value of a single sum to be received in the future. This table contains factors for various rates of interest for various periods, which when multiplied by a future sum, will give the sum's present value.

   3. Use Exhibit 13B-2 in Appendix 13B to determine the present value of an *annuity*, or stream, of cash flows. This table contains factors that, when multiplied by the stream of cash flows, will give the stream's present value. Be careful to note that this annuity table is for a very specific type of annuity in which the first payment occurs at the end of the first year.

Appendix 13C

Income Taxes in Capital Budgeting

APPENDIX HIGHLIGHTS

A. Income taxes complicate capital budgeting. Both the costs and benefits of a project should be stated on an after-tax basis.

    1.   The true cost of a tax-deductible expenditure is the amount of the payment net of any reduction in income taxes due to the payment. The net after-tax cost for a tax-deductible expenditure can be computed as follows:

$$\text{After-tax cost} = (1\text{-Tax rate}) \times \begin{array}{c}\text{Tax deductible} \\ \text{cash expense}\end{array}$$

    2.   Not all cash outflows are tax deductible.

        a.   An investment in working capital is not tax deductible; it is not an expense.

        b.   The cost of a depreciable asset *is not* tax deductible in the period in which it is purchased. However, depreciation on the asset *is* tax deductible. (See section C below.)

        c.   Any gain or loss (i.e., difference between salvage value and book value) on disposal of an asset *is* taxable.

B. As with cash expenditures, taxable cash receipts should be placed on an after-tax basis.

    1.   A cash receipt net of its tax effect is known as an *after-tax benefit*. The net after-tax cash inflow from revenue or other taxable cash receipts can be computed as follows:

$$\text{After-tax benefits} = (1\text{-Tax rate}) \times \begin{array}{c}\text{Taxable cash} \\ \text{receipt}\end{array}$$

    2.   Not all cash receipts are taxable. For example, the release of working capital at the end of a project is not a taxable cash inflow.

C. Depreciation is not a cash outflow. However, depreciation deductions do affect the amount of taxes that a company will pay.

    1.   Depreciation deductions act as a *tax shield*. Depreciation deductions shield revenues from taxation and reduce income taxes.

    2.   The formula used to compute the tax savings from the depreciation tax shield is:

$$\begin{array}{c}\text{Tax savings from the} \\ \text{depreciation tax shield}\end{array} = \text{Tax rate} \times \begin{array}{c}\text{Depreciation} \\ \text{deduction}\end{array}$$

D. In the United States, the depreciation rules are complex.

    1.   To simplify matters, we assume in the text that for tax purposes the entire original cost of an asset (without any reduction for salvage value) is depreciated using the straight-line method.

    2.   If an asset is disposed of after it has been fully depreciated for tax purposes, any proceeds are fully taxable.

E. Exhibit 13C-4 contains a comprehensive example of income taxes and capital budgeting. Follow this example carefully step by step.

    1.   All cash flows involving tax-deductible expenses and taxable receipts are placed on an after-tax basis by multiplying the cash flow by one minus the tax rate.

    2.   Also notice that the depreciation deductions are multiplied *by the tax rate itself* to determine the tax savings (cash inflow) resulting from the tax shield.

    3.   These two above points should be studied with great care until both are thoroughly understood.

REVIEW AND SELF-TEST
Questions and Exercises

True or False

Enter a T or an F in the blank to indicate whether the statement is true or false.

___ 1. The after-tax cost of a tax-deductible item is computed by multiplying the amount of the tax deduction by the tax rate.

___ 2. Because salvage value is not considered when computing depreciation for tax purposes, any salvage value received on sale of an asset after it has been fully depreciated is taxed as income.

___ 3. The release of working capital at the end of an investment project is a taxable cash inflow.

Multiple Choice

Choose the best answer or response by placing the identifying letter in the space provided.

___ 1. A project is being considered for which the annual cash operating expenses are $20,000. If the company's tax rate is 30%, what is the after-tax cost of these operating expenses? a) $6,000; b) $14,000; c) $20,000; $60,000.

___ 2. A project is being considered for which the annual cash revenues are $80,000. If the company's tax rate is 30%, what is the after-tax benefit of the revenues? a) $0; b) $24,000; c) $56,000; d) $80,000.

___ 3. A company's depreciation deduction is $50,000 and its tax rate is 30%. The company's savings from the depreciation tax shield is: a) $15,000; b) $35,000; c) $50,000; d) $30,000.

___ 4. A company is considering a project that would require a $200,000 working capital investment. If the company's tax rate is 30%, then the initial investment in working capital should be shown in the capital budgeting analysis as a cash outflow of: a) $200,000; b) $140,000; c) $60,000; d) $0.

___ 5. Refer to the data in question 4 above. The working capital would be released for use elsewhere at the end of the project in four years. The company's discount rate is 10%. What is the approximate present value of the after-tax cash flows associated with the release of the working capital? a) $200,000; b) $95,600; c) $136,600; d) $0.

Exercise

Exercise 13C-1. Marvel Company has $60,000 to invest and is considering two alternatives:

	Investment X	Investment Y
Cost of equipment.................	$60,000	—
Working capital needed........	—	$60,000
Annual cash inflows	$20,000	$20,000
Salvage value.......................	$ 3,000	—
Life of the project	5 years	5 years

The company's after-tax cost of capital is 12%, and the tax rate is 30%.

Compute the net present value of each investment using the form that appears below. The company uses the straight-line method of depreciation for tax purposes, with zero salvage value assumed.

Items	Year(s)	(1) Amount	(2) Tax Effect	(1) × (2) After-Tax Cash Flow	12% Factor	Present Value
Investment X:						
Cost of equipment	_____	$_____	_____	$_____	_____	$_____
Annual cash inflows........	_____	$_____	_____	$_____	_____	_____
Depreciation deductions..	_____	$_____	_____	$_____	_____	_____
Salvage value	_____	$_____	_____	$_____	_____	_____
Net present value.............	_____					$_____
Investment Y:						
Working capital needed...	_____	$_____	_____	$_____	_____	$_____
Annual cash inflows........	_____	$_____	_____	$_____	_____	_____
Working capital released.	_____	$_____	_____	$_____	_____	_____
Net present value.............	_____					$_____

Answers to Questions and Exercises

True or False

1. F The after-tax cost of a tax deductible cash expense is determined by multiplying it by *one minus* the tax rate.

2. T The salvage value is fully taxable as income because the taxpayer will already have fully depreciated the asset.

3. F The release of working capital is a return of the taxpayer's original investment (which itself is not a tax deduction) and thus would not be taxable as income.

Multiple Choice

1. b $(1 - 0.30) \times \$20,000 = \$14,000$

2. c $(1 - 0.30) \times \$80,000 = \$56,000$

3. a $0.30 \times \$50,000 = \$15,000$

4. a Working capital represents an investment, not an expense, so there is no effect on taxes.

5. c The release of working capital does not affect taxes. Therefore, the entire $200,000 represents an after-tax cash flow. The present value factor for four periods at 10% per period is 0.683, so the present value of the $200,000 is $0.683 \times \$200,000$ or $136,600.

Exercise

Exercise 13C-1.

Items	Year(s)	(1) Amount	(2) Tax Effect	(1) × (2) After-Tax Cash Flow	12% Factor	Present Value
Investment X:						
Cost of equipment...........	Now	$(60,000)	—	$(60,000)	1.000	$(60,000)
Annual cash inflows	1-5	$ 20,000	1 − 0.30	$ 14,000	3.605	50,470
Depreciation deductions .	1-5	$ 12,000	0.30	$ 3,600	3.605	12,978
Salvage value.................	5	$ 3,000	1 − 0.30	$ 2,100	0.567	1,191
Net present value						$ 4,639
Investment Y:						
Working capital needed..	Now	$(60,000)	—	$(60,000)	1.000	$(60,000)
Annual cash inflows	1-5	$ 20,000	1 − 0.30	$ 14,000	3.605	50,470
Working capital released	5	$ 60,000	—	$ 60,000	0.567	34,020
Net present value						$ 24,490

Chapter 14

Statement of Cash Flows

Chapter Study Suggestions

The statement of cash flows is constructed by examining changes in balance sheet accounts. The chapter contains three key exhibits. The first, Exhibit 14-2, shows how changes in current balance sheet accounts affect net income on the operating section of the statement of cash flows. The second, Exhibit 14-3, shows how changes in noncurrent balance sheet accounts affect the investing and financing sections of the statement of cash flows. The third key exhibit is Exhibit 14-10, which shows the format for a statement of cash flows.

CHAPTER HIGHLIGHTS

A. The purpose of the statement of cash flows is to highlight the major activities that have provided and used cash during the period.

B. *Cash* on the statement of cash flows is broadly defined to include both cash and cash equivalents. Cash equivalents consist of short-term, highly liquid investments such as Treasury bills, commercial paper, and money market funds that are made solely for the purpose of generating a return on temporarily idle cash.

C. The net cash flow of a period is equal to the change in the cash account. The statement of cash flows is based on the fact that the change in cash during a period can be expressed in terms of the changes in all of the noncash balance sheet accounts. (See footnote 1 in the text for details.) The statement of cash flows is basically a listing of changes in the noncash balance sheet accounts.

D. Changes in noncash account balances have the following effects on the statement of cash flows.

   1. Changes in asset accounts:

      a. Increases are subtracted. (Think of the cash that must be used to buy inventory.)

      b. Decreases are added. (Think of the cash that comes from selling inventory.)

   2. Changes in contra-asset, liability, and equity accounts:

      a. Increases are added. (Think of the cash that comes from borrowing money.)

      b. Decreases are subtracted. (Think of the cash that must be used to pay back a debt.)

E. The statement of cash flows is divided into three sections—operating activities, investing activities, and financing activities.

   1. As a general rule, *operating activities* directly or indirectly affect net income. These activities include:

      a. Net income (or net loss).

      b. Changes in current assets.

      c. Changes in noncurrent assets that affect net income, such as depreciation and amortization.

      d. Changes in current liabilities (except for debts to lenders and dividends).

      e. Changes in noncurrent liabilities that affect net income, such as interest on debt.

   2. *Investing activities* consist of changes in noncurrent assets that are not included in net income.

   3. *Financing activities* consist of transactions that involve borrowing from creditors (other than the payment of interest), and transactions that involve the owners of the company. Specific financing activities include:

      a. Changes in current liabilities that are debts to lenders rather than obligations to suppliers, employees, or government.

      b. Changes in noncurrent liabilities that are not included in net income.

      c. Changes in capital stock accounts.

      d. Dividends paid to the company's stockholders.

F. In some cases, the net change in an account is shown on the statement of cash flows. In other cases, the increases and decreases are disclosed separately. The treatment depends on whether the change appears in the operating activities section or in the investing and financing activities sections.

   1. For operating activities, only the net change in an account is shown on the statement of cash flows.

   2. For financing and investing activities, items on the statement of cash flows must be presented in gross amounts rather than in net amounts. For example, if a company buys $100,000 of new equipment and sells $30,000 of used equipment, both amounts must be disclosed rather than the net effect of a $70,000 increase in the equipment account.

G. The net result of the cash inflows and outflows arising from operating activities is referred to as the *net cash provided by operating activities*. This figure can be determined using the *direct method* or the *indirect method*.

   1. Under the direct method, the income statement is reconstructed on a cash basis from top to bottom. This method is covered in Appendix 14A.

   2. Under the indirect method, the net cash provided by operations is computed by starting with net income and adjusting it to a cash basis. Key Concept #3 in Exhibit 14-4 shows the steps to follow in this adjustment process.

3. The direct and indirect methods yield exactly the same amount for the net cash provided by operating activities.

H. Exhibits 14-6 through 14-10 illustrate how to construct a statement of cash flows. Make sure you understand the details of this process.

I. *Free cash flow* is defined to be the net cash provided by operating activities less capital expenditures and dividends. Free cash flow measures the company's ability to fund capital expenditures and dividends from its operating cash flows.

REVIEW AND SELF-TEST
Questions and Exercises

True or False

Enter a T or an F in the blank to indicate whether the statement is true or false.

___ 1. Dividends received on stock held as an investment are included in the operating activities section of the statement of cash flows.

___ 2. Interest paid on amounts borrowed is included in the financing activities section of the statement of cash flows.

___ 3. Lending money to another entity (such as to a subsidiary) is classified as a financing activity.

___ 4. Paying cash dividends to the company's stockholders is classified as a financing activity.

___ 5. Transactions involving all forms of debt—including accounts payable, short-term borrowing, and long-term borrowing—are classified as financing activities on the statement of cash flows.

___ 6. For both financing and investing activities, items on the statement of cash flows should be presented gross rather than net.

___ 7. The direct and indirect methods can yield different amounts for the net cash provided by operating activities.

___ 8. Only changes in noncurrent accounts are analyzed for a statement of cash flows.

___ 9. If a company is profitable, the net cash flow must be positive.

___ 10. If free cash flows are negative, the company needed to find sources of funding other than operations to pay for its capital expenditures and dividends.

Multiple Choice

Choose the best answer or response by placing the identifying letter in the space provided.

___ 1. When constructing a statement of cash flows, an increase in inventory would be: a) added to net income in the operating activities section; b) subtracted from net income in the operating activities section; c) added in the investing activities section; d) subtracted in the investing activities section.

___ 2. When constructing a statement of cash flows, an increase in accounts payable would be: a) added to net income in the operating activities section; b) subtracted from net income in the operating activities section; c) added in the financing activities section; d) subtracted in the financing activities section.

___ 3. When constructing a statement of cash flows, an increase in bonds payable would be: a) added in the investing activities section; b) subtracted in the investing activities section; c) added in the financing activities section; d) subtracted in the financing activities section.

___ 4. When constructing a statement of cash flows, an increase in long-term investments would be: a) added in the investing activities section; b) subtracted in the investing activities section; c) added in the financing activities section; d) subtracted in the financing activities section.

___ 5. When constructing a statement of cash flows, cash dividends paid to the company's stockholders would be: a) added to net income in the operating activities section; b) subtracted from net income in the operating activities section; c) added in the financing activities section; d) subtracted in the financing activities section.

___ 6. When constructing a statement of cash flows, an increase in the company's common stock account would be: a) added in the investing activities section; b) subtracted in the investing activities section; c) added in the financing activities section; d) subtracted in the financing activities section.

___ 7. If a company's net cash provided by operating activities is $105 million, its capital expenditures amount to $36 million, its net borrowing is $32 million, and its dividends are $22 million, its free cash flow is: a) $15 million; b) $47 million; c) $37 million; d) $51 million.

Exercises

Exercise 14-1. Ingall Corporation's comparative balance sheet and income statement for the most recent year follow:

Ingall Corporation
Comparative Balance Sheet
(dollars in millions)

	Ending Balance	Beginning Balance
Assets		
Current assets:		
Cash and cash equivalents....................	$ 10	$ 14
Accounts receivable	21	15
Inventory..	50	43
Total current assets.....................................	81	72
Property, plant, and equipment....................	190	140
Less accumulated depreciation.............	65	54
Net property, plant, and equipment	125	86
Total assets...	$206	$158
Liabilities and Stockholders' Equity		
Current liabilities:		
Accounts payable	$ 26	$ 25
Accrued liabilities	10	12
Income taxes payable	13	18
Total current liabilities	49	55
Bonds payable	50	40
Total liabilities	99	95
Stockholders' equity:		
Common stock	80	60
Retained earnings................................	27	3
Total stockholders' equity..........................	107	63
Total liabilities and stockholders' equity	$206	$158

Ingall Corporation
Income Sheet
(dollars in millions)

Net sales	$230
Cost of goods sold...	120
Gross margin	110
Selling and administrative expenses......................	70
Net operating income	40
Non operating items: Gain on sale of equipment ..	10
Income before taxes	50
Income taxes..	14
Net income	$ 36

Notes: Dividends of $12 million were declared and paid during the year. Used equipment was sold for $25 million in cash. The equipment had an original cost of $20 million and accumulated depreciation of $5 million.

Using the form on the following page, determine the change in each balance sheet account.

Ingall Corporation
Comparative Balance Sheet
(dollars in millions)

	Ending Balance	Beginning Balance	Change
Assets			
Current assets:			
Cash and cash equivalents....................	$ 10	$ 14	_____
Accounts receivable	21	15	_____
Inventory	50	43	_____
Total current assets	81	72	
Property, plant, and equipment....................	190	140	_____
Less accumulated depreciation.............	65	54	_____
Net property, plant, and equipment	125	86	
Total assets	$206	$158	
Liabilities and Stockholders' Equity			
Current liabilities:			
Accounts payable	$ 26	$ 25	_____
Accrued liabilities.................................	10	12	_____
Income taxes payable	13	18	_____
Total current liabilities	49	55	
Bonds payable	50	40	_____
Total liabilities...	99	95	
Stockholders' equity:			
Common stock......................................	80	60	_____
Retained earnings	27	3	_____
Total stockholders' equity	107	63	
Total liabilities and stockholders' equity.....	$206	$158	

Exercise 14-2.   Determine the gross additions to the Property, Plant, and Equipment account and the total credits to the Accumulated Depreciation account during the year using the T-accounts below:

Property, Plant, and Equipment

Beginning Balance	_____		
Additions	_____	Sale of equipment	_____
Ending Balance	_____		

Accumulated Depreciation

		Beginning Balance	_____
Accumulated depreciation on equipment that was sold	_____	Credits	_____
		Ending Balance	_____

Exercise 14-3.   Determine Ingall Corporation's net cash provided by (used in) operating activities using the indirect method and the form below.

Net income		$_____
Adjustments to convert net income to a cash basis:		
Depreciation	$_____	
_____ in accounts receivable	_____	
_____ in inventory	_____	
_____ in accounts payable	_____	
_____ in accrued liabilities	_____	
_____ in income taxes payable	_____	
Gain on sale of equipment		_____
Net cash provided by (used in) operating activities ...		$_____

Exercise 14-4.   Prepare a statement of cash flows for Ingall Corporation using the form below.

Ingall Corporation
Statement of Cash Flows

Operating activities

Net cash provided by (used in) operating activities............... $_____

Investing activities

_____...... $_____

_____...... _____

Net cash provided by (used in) investing activities .... _____

Financing activities

_____...... _____

_____...... _____

_____...... _____

Net cash provided by (used in) financing activities............... _____

Net increase (decrease) in cash... _____

Cash balance, beginning .... _____

Cash balance, ending .... $_____

Answers to Questions and Exercises

True or False

1. T Dividends received are part of net income and therefore are included in operating rather than investing activities.

2. F Interest paid on amounts borrowed is included in operating activities because interest enters into net income.

3. F Lending money to another entity is classified as an investing activity.

4. T Dividends do not affect net income and therefore are not considered to be an operating activity.

5. F Transactions involving accounts payable are included among operating activities—not financing activities.

6. T Only transactions involving operating activities are presented in net amounts.

7. F The direct and indirect methods will always yield exactly the same amount for the net cash provided by operating activities.

8. F Changes in all noncash accounts, current as well as noncurrent, are analyzed when preparing a statement of cash flows.

9. F Net cash flow may be negative even if a company is profitable. For example, a profitable company may make a major investment using cash reserves it has accumulated in the past.

10. T By definition, free cash flow is net cash provided by operating activities less capital expenditures and dividends.

Multiple Choice

1. b Inventory is a current asset. Increases in current assets are subtracted from net income. Changes in current assets are considered to be the result of operating activities.

2. a Accounts payable is a current liability. Increases in current liabilities are added to net income. Changes in current liabilities are considered to be the result of operating activities.

3. c Bonds payable is a noncurrent liability. An increase in a noncurrent liability is added. A change in a noncurrent liability is considered to be a financing activity unless it enters into net income.

4. b Long-term investments is a noncurrent asset account. An increase in a noncurrent asset is subtracted. A change in a noncurrent asset is considered to be an investing activity unless it directly enters into the determination of net income.

5. d Dividends are subtracted and are classified as a financing activity because they do not enter into the determination of net income.

6. c An increase in the common stock account is added and is a financing activity.

7. b Free cash flow = Net cash provided by operating activities – Capital expenditures – Dividends = $105 million – $36 million – $22 million = $47 million.

Exercises

Exercise 14-1. The completed worksheet for Ingall Corporation appears below:

Ingall Corporation
Comparative Balance Sheet
(dollars in millions)

	Ending Balance	Beginning Balance	Change
Assets			
Current assets:			
Cash and cash equivalents....................	$ 10	$ 14	-4
Accounts receivable	21	15	+6
Inventory	50	43	+7
Total current assets....................................	81	72	
Property, plant, and equipment....................	190	140	+50
Less accumulated depreciation.............	65	54	+11
Net property, plant, and equipment	125	86	
Total assets	$206	$158	
Liabilities and Stockholders' Equity			
Current liabilities:			
Accounts payable	$ 26	$ 25	+1
Accrued liabilities................................	10	12	-2
Income taxes payable	13	18	-5
Total current liabilities	49	55	
Bonds payable	50	40	+10
Total liabilities..	99	95	
Stockholders' equity:			
Common stock......................................	80	60	+20
Retained earnings	27	3	+24
Total stockholders' equity	107	63	
Total liabilities and stockholders' equity.....	$206	$158	

Exercise 14-2.

Property, Plant, and Equipment			
Beginning balance	140		
Additions	70	Sale of equipment	20
Ending balance	190		

Accumulated Depreciation			
		Beginning balance	54
Accumulated depreciation on equipment that was sold	5	Credits	16
		Ending balance	65

Exercise 14-3.   The operating activities section of the statement of cash flows constructed using the indirect method appears below:

Net income		$36
Adjustments to convert net income to a cash basis:		
Depreciation (credits from Exercise 14-1 above) ...	$16	
Increase in accounts receivable	(6)	
Increase in inventory	(7)	
Increase in accounts payable	1	
Decrease in accrued liabilities	(2)	
Decrease in income taxes payable	(5)	
Gain on sale of equipment	(10)	(13)
Net cash provided by operating activities		$23

Exercise 14-4.

Ingall Corporation
Statement of Cash Flows

Operating activities		
Net cash provided by operating activities		$ 23
Investing activities		
Proceeds from sale of equipment	$25	
Increase in plant and equipment (from Exercise 14-2 above) ...	(70)	
Net cash used in investing activities		(45)
Financing activities		
Increase in bonds payable	10	
Increase in common stock	20	
Dividends	(12)	
Net cash provided by financing activities		18
Net decrease in cash		(4)
Cash balance, beginning		14
Cash balance, ending		$ 10

Appendix 14A

The Direct Method of Determining the Net Cash Provided by Operating Activities

APPENDIX HIGHLIGHTS

A. The direct method differs from the indirect method only in the operating activities section of the statement of cash flows. The investing and financing activities sections of the statement are identical for the direct and indirect methods.

B. In the indirect method, the income statement is reconstructed from the top down by converting it to a cash basis.

   1. To adjust revenue to a cash basis:

     • Subtract (add) any increase (decrease) in accounts receivable.

   2. To adjust cost of goods sold to a cash basis:

     • Add (subtract) any increase (decrease) in inventory.

     • Subtract (add) any increase (decrease) in accounts payable.

   3. To adjust selling and administrative expenses to a cash basis:

     • Add (subtract) any increase (decrease) in prepaid expenses.

     • Subtract (add) any increase (decrease) in accrued liabilities.

     • Subtract the period's depreciation and amortization charges.

   4. To adjust income tax expense to a cash basis:

     • Subtract (add) any increase (decrease) in taxes payable.

     • Subtract (add) any increase (decrease) in deferred taxes.

REVIEW AND SELF-TEST
Questions and Exercises

Exercise

Exercise 14A-1. Refer to the data in Exercise 14-1 for Ingall Corporation. Using the direct method, determine Ingall Corporation's net cash provided by operating activities.

Sales..	$_____	
Adjustments to a cash basis:		
_____ in accounts receivable...	_____	$_____
Cost of goods sold	_____	
Adjustments to a cash basis:		
_____ in inventory..	_____	
_____ in accounts payable..	_____	_____
Selling and administrative expenses...	_____	
Adjustments to a cash basis:		
_____ in accrued liabilities...	_____	
Depreciation	_____	_____
Income tax expense	_____	
Adjustments to a cash basis:		
_____ in income taxes payable...	_____	_____
Net cash provided by (used in) operating activities......................	$_____	

Answers to Questions and Exercises

Exercise

Exercise 14A-1. The direct method can be used to arrive at the same answer as in Exercise 14-3 above.

Sales...	$230	
Adjustments to a cash basis:		
Increase in accounts receivable...	−6	$224
Cost of goods sold..	120	
Adjustments to a cash basis:		
Increase in inventory..	+7	
Increase in accounts payable..	−1	126
Selling and administrative expenses..	70	
Adjustments to a cash basis:		
Decrease in accrued liabilities..	+2	
Depreciation (see Exercise 14-2 above)..	16	56
Income taxes..	14	
Adjustments to a cash basis:		
Decrease in income taxes payable...	+5	19
Net cash provided by operating activities...		$ 23

Chapter 15

Financial Statement Analysis

Chapter Study Suggestions

The chapter is divided into two parts. The first part discusses financial statements that are prepared in comparative and common-size form. This part of the chapter involves nothing more complicated than computing percentages.

The second part of the chapter deals with ratio analysis. Altogether, seventeen ratios are presented in this part of the chapter. You should memorize the formula for each ratio because it is likely that you will be expected to know these formulas on exams. At first this may seem like an overwhelming task, but most of the ratios are intuitive and easy to compute. You should also learn how to interpret each ratio. Exhibit 15-6 in the text provides a compact summary of the ratios.

CHAPTER HIGHLIGHTS

A. Financial statement analysis is concerned with assessing the financial condition of a company.

    1. To be most useful, comparisons should be made from one year to another, as well as with other companies within the same industry.

    2. An analyst should not rely on just financial statement analysis.

        a. The ratios should be viewed as a starting point rather than as an end in themselves. They indicate what should be pursued in greater depth.

        b. One problem is that companies may use different accounting methods such as LIFO or FIFO and these differences in accounting methods may make comparisons difficult.

        c. Another problem is that the ratios are based on accounting data that really only show what has happened in the past—not what is going to happen in the future.

B. Three common analytical techniques for financial statement analysis are: 1) dollar and percentage changes on statements (horizontal analysis); 2) common-size statements (vertical analysis); and 3) ratios.

    1. In horizontal analysis, two or more yearly statements are placed side by side and changes between years are analyzed. These comparisons are made both in terms of dollars and percentage changes from year to year.

        a. Showing changes in dollar form helps to identify the most significant changes.

        b. Showing changes in percentage form helps to identify the most unusual changes.

        c. Trend percentages are often computed. Each item, such as sales or net income, is stated as a percentage of the same item in a base year.

    2. In a common-size statement, amounts on the balance sheet are stated as a percentage of total assets and amounts on the income statement are stated as a percentage of sales. Showing the balance sheet and the income statement in common-size form helps show the relative importance of the various items and makes it easier to compare companies. Preparation of common-size statements is known as vertical analysis.

    3. The *gross margin percentage* is a particularly important item on the common-size income statement. It is defined as follows:

$$\text{Gross margin percentage} = \frac{\text{Gross margin}}{\text{Sales}}$$

The gross margin percentage is a rough measure of the overall profitability of a company's products. In manufacturing companies, the gross margin percentage should increase as sales increase because fixed manufacturing costs are spread across more units.

    4. In addition to horizontal and vertical analysis, stockholders, short-term creditors, and long-term creditors use a variety of ratios to help them evaluate companies. Different ratios are designed to meet the needs of these three different groups.

C. Several ratios provide measures of how well the company is doing from the stockholders' perspective.

    1. *Earnings per share* is an important measure of the annual earnings available for common stockholders. This number is closely followed by investors. The formula is:

$$\frac{\text{Earnings}}{\text{per share}} = \frac{\text{Net income-Preferred dividends}}{\substack{\text{Average number of common} \\ \text{shares outstanding}}}$$

Preferred dividends are subtracted from net income because they are not an expense on the income statement but reduce the earnings that can be distributed to common stockholders.

    2. The *price-earnings ratio* shows the relation between the market price of a share of stock and the stock's current earnings per share. The price-earnings ratio is computed as follows:

$$\text{Price-earnings ratio} = \frac{\text{Market price per share}}{\text{Earnings per share}}$$

Price-earnings ratios tend to be similar for companies in the same industry. One of the biggest factors affecting the price-earnings ratio is future earnings growth. If investors believe one company is likely to have higher future earnings growth than another, they will bid up the price of the stock with a higher expected future earnings growth and hence it will have a higher price-earnings ratio.

3. The *dividend payout ratio* gauges the proportion of current earnings being paid out as dividends. The formula is:

$$\text{Dividend payout ratio} = \frac{\text{Dividends per share}}{\text{Earnings per share}}$$

A company with a high dividend payout ratio is paying out most of its earnings to stockholders as dividends rather than reinvesting the earnings in the company.

4. The *dividend yield ratio* measures the cash yield on the common stockholder's investment. The ratio is computed as follows:

$$\text{Dividend yield ratio} = \frac{\text{Dividends per share}}{\text{Market price per share}}$$

Investors hope to profit from both dividends and increases in market value. The dividend yield measures only the contribution of the dividends. Note that the current market price per share is used in this ratio and not the price the investor originally paid for the shares.

5. The *return on total assets* is a measure of how effectively a company has used its assets. The formula is:

$$\text{Return on total assets} = \frac{\text{Net income} + \left[\begin{array}{c}\text{Interest expense} \times \\ (1 - \text{Tax rate})\end{array}\right]}{\text{Average total assets}}$$

a. Note that interest expense is placed on an after-tax basis by multiplying it by one minus the tax rate before being added back to net income.

b. Interest expense is added back to net income to show earnings *before* any distributions have been made to creditors and stockholders. This adjustment results in a total return on assets that measures operating performance independently of how the assets were financed.

6. The *return on common stockholders' equity* is a measure of the profitability of an investment in the company's common stock. The formula is:

$$\text{Return on common stockholders' equity} = \frac{\text{Net income} - \text{Preferred dividends}}{\begin{array}{c}\text{Average total stockholders' equity} \\ - \text{Average preferred stock}\end{array}}$$

As with earnings per share, preferred dividends are subtracted from net income because preferred dividends reduce the earnings available to common stockholders. The return on common stockholders' equity is often higher than the return on total assets because of financial leverage.

a. *Financial leverage* involves purchasing assets with funds obtained from creditors or from preferred stockholders. If the assets in which the funds are invested earn a greater return than the rate of return required by the suppliers of the funds, then financial leverage is *positive*. Financial leverage is *negative* if the assets earn a return that is less than the rate of return required by creditors.

b. Sources of leverage include long-term debt, preferred stock, and current liabilities.

7. The *book value per share* measures the common stockholders' equity on a per share basis. The formula is:

$$\text{Book value per share} = \frac{\begin{array}{c}\text{Total stockholders' equity} \\ - \text{Preferred stock}\end{array}}{\begin{array}{c}\text{Number of common} \\ \text{shares outstanding}\end{array}}$$

a. Note that the denominator in this ratio is the number of common shares outstanding at the end of the year—not the average number of shares outstanding over the year as in the earnings per share calculation.

b. Book value per share is usually less than market value per share. Market value reflects investors' expectations concerning future earnings and dividends. By contrast, book value measures financial effects of already completed transactions. Because of this orientation toward the past, book value is of limited usefulness.

D. Short-term creditors are concerned with being paid on time and are more concerned with a company's financial assets and cash flows than with its accounting net income.

1. *Working capital* measures the excess of current assets over current liabilities.

$$\text{Working capital} = \text{Current assets} - \text{Current liabilities}$$

Negative working capital signals that current assets are insufficient to cover current liabilities.

2. The *current ratio* is also a widely used measure of short-term debt-paying ability. The formula is:

$$\text{Current ratio} = \frac{\text{Current assets}}{\text{Current liabilities}}$$

The current ratio, as well as working capital, should be interpreted with care. The *composition* of the assets and liabilities is very important. A high current ratio does not necessarily mean that the company can easily pay its current liabilities. For example, most of the current assets may be inventory that is difficult to sell quickly.

3. The *acid-test* or *quick ratio* is designed to measure how well a company can meet its short-term obligations using only its *most liquid* current assets. For this reason, inventories and prepaid assets are not included in the numerator. The formula is:

$$\text{Acid-test ratio} = \frac{\begin{array}{c}\text{Cash + Marketable securities}\\\text{+ Accounts receivable}\\\text{+ Short-term notes receivable}\end{array}}{\text{Current liabilities}}$$

4. The *accounts receivable turnover* ratio measures the relation between sales on account and accounts receivable. The formula is:

$$\text{Accounts receivable turnover} = \frac{\text{Sales on account}}{\text{Average accounts receivable balance}}$$

The higher this ratio, the quicker accounts receivable are collected. This is easier to see if the accounts receivable turnover is divided into 365 days. This gives the *average collection period*, which is computed as follows:

$$\text{Average collection period} = \frac{365 \text{ days}}{\text{Accounts receivable turnover}}$$

As its name implies, the average collection period indicates the average number of days required to collect credit sales. Ordinarily, a short average collection period is desirable.

5. The *inventory turnover* ratio relates cost of goods sold to the average inventory balance using the following formula:

$$\text{Inventory turnover} = \frac{\text{Cost of goods sold}}{\text{Average inventory balance}}$$

The higher this ratio is, the quicker inventory is sold. The *average sale period* measures how many days on average it takes to sell inventory. The formula is:

$$\text{Average sale period} = \frac{365 \text{ days}}{\text{Inventory turnover}}$$

The average sale period can differ dramatically from one industry to another. For example, the average sale period is much shorter in a florist shop than in a jewelry shop. Florists have to sell their inventory quickly or it will perish.

E. Long-term creditors are concerned with both the near-term and the long-term ability of a company to repay its debts.

1. The *times interest earned ratio* measures the ability of a company to pay the interest it owes. The formula is:

$$\text{Times interest earned} = \frac{\text{Earnings before interest expense and income taxes}}{\text{Interest expense}}$$

Generally, the higher the times interest earned, the greater the ability of the company to make interest payments.

2. The *debt-to-equity ratio* relates debt to equity using the following formula:

$$\text{Debt-to-equity ratio} = \frac{\text{Total liabilities}}{\text{Stockholders' equity}}$$

The lower this ratio is, the greater the excess of assets over liabilities. Creditors generally prefer a low debt-to-equity ratio because it reflects a large cushion of protection.

REVIEW AND SELF-TEST
Questions and Exercises

True or False

Enter a T or an F in the blank to indicate whether the statement is true or false.

___ 1. Horizontal analysis uses dollar and percentage changes from year to year to highlight trends.

___ 2. Common-size statements focus on companies of similar size and operations.

___ 3. The current ratio is current assets less current liabilities.

___ 4. Trend percentages in financial statements would be an example of vertical analysis.

___ 5. A common-size statement shows items in percentage form, with each item stated as a percentage of a total of which that item is a part.

___ 6. Earnings per share is computed by deducting preferred dividends from net income and dividing the result by the number of common shares outstanding.

___ 7. If earnings remain unchanged and the price-earnings ratio goes up, then the market price of the stock must have gone down.

___ 8. Dividing the market price of a share of stock by the dividends per share gives the price-earnings ratio.

___ 9. Book value per share is not a good predictor of future earnings potential.

___ 10. The acid test ratio ignores inventories.

___ 11. When computing the return on total assets, after-tax interest expense is subtracted from net income.

___ 12. Inventory turnover is computed by dividing sales by average inventory.

___ 13. If a company's return on total assets is substantially higher than its cost of borrowing, then the common stockholders would normally want the company to have a high debt-to-equity ratio.

Multiple Choice

Choose the best answer or response by placing the identifying letter in the space provided.

___ 1. Artway Corporation's net income last year was $200,000. It paid dividends of $50,000 to the owners of the company's preferred stock. A total of 10,000 shares of common stock were outstanding throughout the year. What was the company's earnings per share for the year? a) $20; b) $5; c) $15; d) $25.

___ 2. Carston Corporation's earnings per share is $3.50 and its market price per share is $28. One million shares of common stock are outstanding. What is the company's price-earnings ratio? a) 43.75; b) 4.375; c) 80.0; d) 8.0.

___ 3. Refer to the data for Carston Corporation in question 2 above. Assume in addition that the company pays an annual dividend of $2.17 per share. What is the company's dividend payout ratio? a) 62%; b) 7.75%; c) 217%; d) 8.9%.

___ 4. Refer again to the data for Carston Corporation in questions 2 and 3 above. What is the company's dividend yield ratio? a) 62%; b) 7.75%; c) 217%; d) 8.9%.

___ 5. Darsden Corporation's net income last year was $800,000; its average assets were $4,000,000; its interest expense was $200,000; and its tax rate was 30%. What was the company's return on total assets? a) 23.5%; b) 25%; c) 16.5%; d) 30%.

___ 6. Kristal Corporation's net income last year was $600,000. The company paid preferred dividends of $200,000 to the owners of its preferred stock. The average total stockholders' equity was $7,000,000 and the average preferred stock was $2,000,000. What was the company's return on common stockholders' equity? a) 12%; b) 4%; c) 10%; d) 8%.

___ 7. Harrison Corporation's common stockholders' equity (i.e., total stockholders' equity less preferred stock) is $24 million. Six million shares of common stock and two million shares of preferred stock are outstanding. What is the company's book value per share? a) $3.00; b) $4.00; c) $6.00; d) $2.40.

___ 8. J.J. Corporation's current assets are $6 million and its current liabilities are $2 million. What is the company's working capital? a) $6 million; b) $2 million; c) $4 million; d) $8 million.

___ 9. Refer to the data for J.J. Corporation in question 8 above. What is the company's current ratio? a) 3.0 to 1; b) 2.0 to 1; c) 0.33 to 1; d) 0.50 to 1.

___ 10. Refer to the data for J.J. Corporation in question 8 above. Assume in addition that the company has $1 million in cash and marketable securities, $1.2 million in accounts receivable, and no short-term notes receivable. What is the company's acid-test ratio? a) 0.8; b) 1.0; c) 1.2; d) 1.1.

___ 11. Proctor Corporation had $25 million of credit sales last year and its average accounts receivable balance was $5 million. What was the company's average collection period? a) 73 days; b) 5 days; c) 20 days; d) 84 days.

___ 12. Larimart Corporation's cost of goods sold last year was $750,000 and its average inventory balance was $300,000. What was the company's average sale period? a) 2.5 days; b) 5 days; c) 146 days; d) 912.5 days.

___ 13. Bresser Corporation's earnings before taxes last year was $42,000 and its interest expense was $6,000. What was the company's times interest earned? a) 12.5; b) 1.25; c) 80; d) 8.0.

___ 14. Nupper Corporation's total liabilities are $320,000 and its stockholders' equity is $400,000. What is the company's debt-to-equity ratio? a) 0.2; b) 1.25; c) 0.8; d) 5.

___ 15. The acid-test ratio: a) can be expected to be less than the current ratio; b) can be expected to be greater than the current ratio; c) could be either greater or less than the current ratio; d) none of these.

Exercises

Exercise 15-1.   The financial statements of Amfac, Inc., are given below for the just completed year (This Year) and for the previous year (Last Year):

Amfac, Inc.
Balance Sheet
December 31

Assets

	This Year	Last Year
Cash	$ 8,000	$ 10,000
Accounts receivable, net	36,000	34,000
Inventory	40,000	32,000
Prepaid expenses	2,000	1,000
Plant and equipment, net	214,000	173,000
Total assets	$300,000	$250,000

Liabilities & Equities

Current liabilities	$ 40,000	$ 30,000
Long-term liabilities	60,000	40,000
Preferred stock	50,000	50,000
Common stock	30,000	30,000
Retained earnings	120,000	100,000
Total liabilities and equity	$300,000	$250,000

Amfac, Inc.
Income Statement
For the Year Ended December 31

	This Year
Sales (all on account)	$450 000
Cost of goods sold	270,000
Gross margin	180,000
Selling and administrative expenses	129,000
Net operating income	51,000
Interest expense	6,000
Net income before taxes	45,000
Income taxes (30%)	13,500
Net Income	$ 31,500

Preferred dividends were $4,000 this year.

Compute the following ratios for this year:

a. Current ratio.

b. Acid-test ratio.

c. Debt-to-equity ratio.

d. Average collection period.

e. Inventory turnover.

f. Times interest earned.

g. Return on total assets.

h. Return on common stockholders' equity.

i. Is financial leverage positive or negative? Explain.

_____

_____

_____

_____

Exercise 15-2.   Cartwright Company has reported the following data relating to sales and accounts receivable in its most recent annual report:

	Year 5	Year 4	Year 3	Year 2	Year 1
Sales..............................	$700,000	$675,000	$650,000	$575,000	$500,000
Accounts receivable.......	$ 72,000	$ 60,000	$ 52,000	$ 46,000	$ 40,000

Express the data above in trend percentages. Use Year 1 as the base year.

	Year 5	Year 4	Year 3	Year 2	Year 1
Sales..............................	_____	_____	_____	_____	_____
Accounts receivable........	_____	_____	_____	_____	_____

Comment on the significant information revealed by your trend percentages:

_____

_____

_____

_____

Exercise 15-3.   Consider the following comparative income statements of Eldredge Company, a jewelry design and manufacturing company:

Eldredge Company
Income Statements
For the Years Ended December 31

	This Year	*Last Year*
Sales..	$ 600,000	$ 500,000
Cost of goods sold......................................	420,000	331,000
Gross margin..	180,000	169,000
Selling and administrative expenses:		
Selling expenses.......................................	87,000	72,500
Administrative expenses	46,800	51,000
Total selling and administrative expenses....	133,800	123,500
Net operating income.................................	46,200	45,500
Interest expense...	1,200	1,500
Net income before taxes.............................	45,000	44,000
Income taxes	13,500	13,200
Net Income..	$ 31,500	$ 30,800

a. Express the income statements for both years in common-size percentages. Round percentages to one decimal point.

	This Year	*Last Year*
Sales..	_____ %	_____ %
Cost of goods sold......................................	_____ %	_____ %
Gross margin..	_____ %	_____ %
Selling and administrative expenses:		
Selling expenses.......................................	_____ %	_____ %
Administrative expenses	_____ %	_____ %
Total selling and administrative expenses....	_____ %	_____ %
Net operating income.................................	_____ %	_____ %
Interest expense...	_____ %	_____ %
Net income before taxes.............................	_____ %	_____ %
Income taxes	_____ %	_____ %
Net Income..	_____ %	_____ %

b. Comment briefly on the changes between the two years.

_____

_____

_____

_____

Answers to Questions and Exercises

True or False

1. T   This is true by definition.

2. F   A common-size statement shows items in percentage form. Each item is stated as a percentage of some total of which that item is a part.

3. F   The current ratio is current assets *divided* by current liabilities.

4. F   Trend percentages would be an example of horizontal analysis.

5. T   This point is discussed in connection with question 2 above.

6. T   True by definition.

7. F   The opposite is true. If the price-earnings ratio goes up, the stock is selling for a higher market price per dollar of earnings.

8. F   Dividing the market price of a share of stock by the earnings per share gives the price-earnings ratio.

9. T   Book value per share is the balance sheet carrying value of completed transactions—it tells little about the future.

10. T   Inventories are excluded because they may be difficult to quickly convert to cash.

11. F   When computing the total return on assets, the after-tax interest expense is *added back* to net income to remove its effect.

12. F   Inventory turnover is computed by dividing cost of goods sold by average inventory.

13. T   If a company's return on total assets is higher than its cost of borrowing, financial leverage is positive. Common stockholders would want the company to use this positive financial leverage to their advantage by having a high amount of debt in the company.

Multiple Choice

1. c   The computations are:

$$\text{Earnings per share} = \frac{\text{Net income} - \text{Preferred dividends}}{\text{Average number of common shares outstanding}}$$

$$= \frac{\$200{,}000 - \$50{,}000}{10{,}000 \text{ shares}} = \$15 \text{ per share}$$

2. d   The computations are:

$$\text{Price-earnings ratio} = \frac{\text{Market price per share}}{\text{Earnings per share}}$$

$$= \frac{\$28.00 \text{ per share}}{\$3.50 \text{ per share}} = 8.0$$

3. a   The computations are:

$$\text{Dividend payout ratio} = \frac{\text{Dividends per share}}{\text{Earnings per share}}$$

$$= \frac{\$2.17 \text{ per share}}{\$3.50 \text{ per share}} = 62.0\%$$

4. b   The computations are:

$$\text{Dividend yield ratio} = \frac{\text{Dividends per share}}{\text{Market price per share}}$$

$$= \frac{\$2.17 \text{ per share}}{\$28.00 \text{ per share}} = 7.75\%$$

5. a   The computations are:

$$\text{Return on total assets} = \frac{\text{Net income} + \left[\begin{array}{c}\text{Interest expense} \times \\ (1 - \text{Tax rate})\end{array}\right]}{\text{Average total assets}}$$

$$= \frac{\$800{,}000 + \left[\begin{array}{c}\$200{,}000 \times \\ (1 - 0.30)\end{array}\right]}{\$4{,}000{,}000} = 23.5\%$$

6. d The computations are:

$$\text{Return on common stockholers' equity} = \frac{\text{Net income} - \text{Preferred dividends}}{\text{Average total stockholders' equity} - \text{Average preferred stock}}$$

$$= \frac{\$600,000 - \$200,000}{\$5,000,000} = 8\%$$

7. b The computations are:

$$\text{Book value per share} = \frac{\text{Total stockholders' equity} - \text{Preferred stock}}{\text{Number of common shares outstanding}}$$

$$= \frac{\$24,000,000 - \$0}{6,000,000 \text{ shares}} = \$4.00 \text{ per share}$$

8. c The computations are:

Working capital = Current assets − Current liabilities

$$= \$6,000,000 - \$2,000,000$$

$$= \$4,000,000$$

9. a The computations are:

$$\text{Current ratio} = \frac{\text{Current assets}}{\text{Current liabilities}}$$

$$= \frac{\$6,000,000}{\$2,000,000} = 3.0$$

10. d The computations are:

$$\text{Acid-test ratio} = \frac{\text{Cash} + \text{Marketable securities} + \text{Accounts receivable} + \text{Short-term notes receivable}}{\text{Current liabilities}}$$

$$= \frac{\$1,000,000 + \$0 + \$1,200,000 + \$0}{\$2,000,000}$$

$$= 1.1$$

11. a The computations are:

$$\text{Accounts receivable turnover} = \frac{\text{Sales on account}}{\text{Average accounts receivable balance}}$$

$$= \frac{\$25,000,000}{\$5,000,000} = 5.0$$

$$\text{Average collection period} = \frac{365 \text{ days}}{\text{Accounts receivable turnover}}$$

$$= \frac{365 \text{ days}}{5.0} = 73 \text{ days}$$

12. c The computations are:

$$\text{Inventory turnover} = \frac{\text{Cost of goods sold}}{\text{Average inventory balance}}$$

$$= \frac{\$750,000}{\$300,000} = 2.5$$

$$\text{Average sale period} = \frac{365 \text{ days}}{\text{Inventory turnover}}$$

$$= \frac{365 \text{ days}}{2.5} = 146 \text{ days}$$

13. d The computations are:

$$\text{Times interest earned} = \frac{\text{Earnings before interest expense and income taxes}}{\text{Interest expense}}$$

$$= \frac{\$42,000 + \$6,000}{\$6,000} = 8.0$$

14. c The computations are:

$$\text{Debt-to-equity ratio} = \frac{\text{Total liabilities}}{\text{Stockholders' equity}}$$

$$= \frac{\$320,000}{\$400,000} = 0.8$$

15. a The acid-test ratio is always less than the current ratio because it contains fewer assets in the numerator but the same amount of liabilities in the denominator.

Exercises

Exercise 15-1.

a. $\text{Current ratio} = \dfrac{\text{Current assets}}{\text{Current liabilities}} = \dfrac{\$8,000 + \$36,000 + \$40,000 + \$2,000}{\$40,000} = 2.15$

b. $\dfrac{\text{Acid-test}}{\text{ratio}} = \dfrac{\begin{array}{c}\text{Cash} + \text{Marketable securities} \\ + \text{Accounts receivable} \\ + \text{Short-term notes receivable}\end{array}}{\text{Current liabilities}} = \dfrac{\$8,000 + \$0 + \$36,000 + \$0}{\$40,000} = 1.10$

c. $\dfrac{\text{Debt-to-equity}}{\text{ratio}} = \dfrac{\text{Total liabilities}}{\text{Stockholders' equity}} = \dfrac{\$40,000 + \$60,000}{\$50,000 + \$30,000 + \$120,000} = 0.50$

d. $\dfrac{\text{Accounts receivable}}{\text{turnover}} = \dfrac{\text{Sales on account}}{\begin{array}{c}\text{Average accounts} \\ \text{receivable balance}\end{array}} = \dfrac{\$450,000}{(\$36,000 + \$34,000)/2} = 12.9 \text{ (rounded)}$

$\dfrac{\text{Average collection}}{\text{period}} = \dfrac{365 \text{ days}}{\text{Accounts receivable turnover}} = \dfrac{365 \text{ days}}{12.9} = 28 \text{ days (rounded)}$

e. $\dfrac{\text{Inventory}}{\text{turnover}} = \dfrac{\text{Cost of goods sold}}{\text{Average inventory balance}} = \dfrac{\$270,000}{(\$40,000 + \$32,000)/2} = 7.5$

f. $\dfrac{\text{Times interest}}{\text{earned}} = \dfrac{\begin{array}{c}\text{Earnings before interest expense} \\ \text{and income taxes}\end{array}}{\text{Interest expense}} = \dfrac{\$51,000}{\$6,000} = 8.5$

g. $\dfrac{\text{Return on}}{\text{total assets}} = \dfrac{\text{Net income} + \left[\begin{array}{c}\text{Interest expense} \times \\ (1 - \text{Tax rate})\end{array}\right]}{\text{Average total assets}} = \dfrac{\$31,500 + \left[\begin{array}{c}\$6,000 \times \\ (1 - 0.30)\end{array}\right]}{(\$300,000 + \$250,000)/2} = 13.0\% \text{ (rounded)}$

h.

	End of Year	*Beginning of Year*
Total stockholders' equity	$200,000	$180,000
Less preferred stock	50,000	50,000
Common stockholders' equity	$150,000	$130,000

$\dfrac{\text{Return on}}{\begin{array}{c}\text{common} \\ \text{stockholers' equity}\end{array}} = \dfrac{\begin{array}{c}\text{Net income} - \\ \text{Preferred dividends}\end{array}}{\begin{array}{c}\text{Average total stockholders' equity} \\ - \text{Average preferred stock}\end{array}} = \dfrac{\$31,500 - \$4,000}{(\$150,000 + \$130,000)/2} = 19.6\% \text{ (rounded)}$

i. Financial leverage is positive because the return on the common stockholders' equity is greater than the return on total assets.

Exercise 15-2.

	Year 5	Year 4	Year 3	Year 2	Year 1
Sales................................	140%	135%	130%	115%	100%
Accounts receivable.......	180%	150%	130%	115%	100%

Sales grew by about 15% per year through Year 3, and then dropped off to about a 5% growth rate for the next two years. The accounts receivable grew at about a 15% rate through Year 3, but then rather than dropping off to about a 5% rate, the accounts receivable grew at an even faster rate through Year 5. This suggests that the company may be granting credit too liberally and is having difficulty collecting its receivables.

Exercise 15-3.

a.

Eldredge Company
Common-Size Comparative Income Statements
For the Years Ended December 31

	This Year	Last Year
Sales...	100.0	100.0
Cost of goods sold.............................	70.0	66.2
Gross margin......................................	30.0	33.8
Selling and administrative expenses:		
Selling expenses.......................................	14.5	14.5
Administrative expenses	7.8	10.2
Total selling and administrative expenses....	22.3	24.7
Net operating income..............................	7.7	9.1
Interest expense...	0.2	0.3
Net income before taxes............................	7.5	8.8
Income taxes	2.2	2.6
Net Income...	5.3	6.2

b. Cost of goods sold and administrative expenses were the two primary areas affecting the percentage decrease in net income. Cost of goods sold increased from 66.2% of sales in to 70.0% of sales—an increase of 3.8 percentage points. On the other hand, administrative expenses dropped from 10.2% of sales to only 7.8% of sales—a decrease of 2.4 percentage points. The net effect was a decrease in net income as a percentage of sales, which fell from 6.2% of sales to only 5.3% of sales. The increase in the cost of goods sold as a percentage of sales is puzzling because sales increased. Ordinarily, cost of goods sold as a percentage of sales should decrease as sales increase because fixed production costs are spread across more units.

Appendix A

Pricing Products and Services

Study Suggestions

This appendix covers three approaches to pricing—the economists' approach, the absorption costing approach, and target costing. You should memorize the highlighted equations in the text. These equations describe how these pricing rules work.

APPENDIX HIGHLIGHTS

A. Some companies have little control over the prices they charge, whereas others have significant discretion in their pricing.

1. Small companies in highly competitive industries that produce standard products typically have little control over the prices they charge. For example, prices for agricultural commodities like corn, wheat, and soybeans are set by the interplay of worldwide supply and demand. Individual farmers have no control over the prices of these commodities.

2. A company that sells a product that is different from the products offered by other companies or that supplies a big chunk of the market typically has some control over its price.

B. *Cost-plus pricing* is the most common approach to setting prices when a company does have some discretion in its pricing. Under this approach, a markup is added to a cost base to arrive at the selling price. The formula is:

Selling price = (1 + Markup percentage) × Cost

What is the cost base? How is the markup percentage determined?

1. In *the economists' approach*, the cost base is variable cost and the markup percentage is determined by how sensitive unit sales are to changes in price.

2. In the *absorption costing approach*, the cost base is the product's absorption costing unit product cost and the markup percentage is a function of a number of factors.

C. The economists' approach recognizes that pricing involves a delicate trade-off. The higher the price, the higher the revenue per unit sold, but the lower the number of units sold. The markup over cost should depend on how sensitive customers are to price. If customers are not particularly sensitive to price, the markup can be high. If they are very sensitive to price, the markup over cost should be low.

1. The *price elasticity of demand*, ε_d, measures the sensitivity of unit sales to a change in price. The formula for price elasticity is:

$$\varepsilon_d = \frac{\ln\left(1+\% \text{ change in quantity sold}\right)}{\ln(1+\% \text{ change in price})}$$

a. The natural log, $\ln(\ )$, can be computed using the LN or $\ln x$ key on your calculator.

b. For example, suppose that a 5% increase in price would result in an 8% drop in unit sales.

$$\varepsilon_d = \frac{\ln(1+(-0.08))}{\ln(1+(+0.05))} = \frac{\ln(0.92)}{\ln(1.05)} = \frac{-0.08338}{0.04879} = -1.71$$

c. The price elasticity of demand is always less than -1. (The reasons for this are technical.) The greater the absolute value of ε_d, the greater the elasticity of demand. For example, suppose a 5% increase in price results in a 10% drop in unit sales rather than an 8% drop:

$$\varepsilon_d = \frac{\ln(1+(-0.10))}{\ln(1+(+0.05))} = \frac{\ln(0.90)}{\ln(1.05)} = \frac{-0.10536}{0.04879} = -2.16$$

d. As in the above example, when customers are more sensitive to price (i.e., there is a greater reaction to a price change), the absolute value of the price elasticity of demand is greater.

e. The above formula may be different from the formula you learned if you took an economics class. While the simpler formula found in most introductory economics texts has its uses, it is not of much help in setting prices.

2. If the price elasticity of demand is constant for a product and the cost of making and selling the product is a combination of variable and fixed costs, the price that would maximize the company's profit is given by the following formulas:

$$\text{Profit-maximizing markup on variable cost} = \frac{-1}{1+\varepsilon_d}$$

$$\text{Profit-maximizing price} = \left(1 + \text{Profit-maximizing markup on variable cost}\right) \text{Variable cost per unit}$$

a. Suppose the variable cost per unit is $1 and the price elasticity of demand is -1.71. The profit-maximizing price is computed as follows:

$$\text{Profit-maximizing markup on variable cost} = \frac{-1}{1+(-1.71)} = 1.41$$

$$\text{Profit-maximizing price} = (1 + 1.41) \times \$1 = \$2.41$$

b. Or suppose the variable cost per unit is $1 and the price elasticity of demand is -2.16. The profit-maximizing price is computed as follows:

$$\text{Profit-maximizing markup on variable cost} = \frac{-1}{1+(-2.16)} = 0.86$$

$$\text{Profit-maximizing price} = (1 + 0.86) \times \$1 = \$1.86$$

c. Note that in the case where customers are more sensitive to price (i.e., unit sales drop by 10% rather than by 8%), the price elasticity of demand is greater and the price and the markup are lower. For example, markups on luxury items are generally higher than on mass-market merchandise because consumers of luxury items are less sensitive to price than other consumers.

d. The computed profit-maximizing price should be used with caution because it assumes that the price elasticity of demand is constant. It should be interpreted as a signal of the direction the price should move in rather than as a precisely accurate estimate of the price at which profits are maximized.

D. The absorption costing approach to cost-plus pricing attempts to set a price without taking into account consumer demand. In this approach, a product's absorption costing unit product cost is used as the cost base. Selling and administrative expenses are not included in the cost base, but rather are provided for through the markup.

1. For example, suppose a product's unit product cost is $50 and the markup is 40%:

Unit product cost	$50
Markup (40%)	20
Selling price	$70

2. The markup percentage may simply be a thumbrule or it may be computed using the following formula:

$$\text{Markup percentage on absorption cost} = \frac{\left(\begin{array}{c}\text{Required ROI} \\ \times \text{Investment}\end{array}\right) + \begin{array}{c}\text{Selling and} \\ \text{admin. expenses}\end{array}}{\text{Unit product cost} \times \text{Unit sales}}$$

For example, suppose that the company's required return on investment is 15%; the company has $100,000 invested in the product; selling and administrative expenses associated with the product are $25,000; anticipated unit sales are 10,000 units; and the unit product cost is $20. Then the markup would be computed as follows:

$$\text{Markup \% on absorption cost} = \frac{(0.15 \times \$100,000) + \$25,000}{\$20 \text{ per unit} \times 10,000 \text{ units}}$$

$$= 20\%$$

3. *The target ROI will be attained only if the anticipated unit sales volume is attained.* There is absolutely no guarantee that the company will earn its desired profit or even breakeven simply because it uses the absorption costing approach formulas to set prices.

E. Some companies use target costing for new products.

1. Under the target costing approach, managers estimate how much the new product can be sold for and then deduct the desired profit per unit to arrive at the target cost. The formula is:

$$\text{Target cost} = \text{Anticipated selling price} - \text{Desired profit}$$

The product development team is given the responsibility to produce and market the product for no more than this target cost.

2. The target costing approach is radically different from the traditional cost-plus approach in which the product is first designed, then costs are determined, and then finally the price is computed with a markup based on desired profits. Unfortunately, the traditional cost-plus approach may result in prices that customers are not willing to pay.

REVIEW AND SELF-TEST
Questions and Exercises

True or False

Enter a T or an F in the blank to indicate whether the statement is true or false.

___ 1. The price elasticity of demand measures how sensitive cost is to changes in demand that occur because of changes in prices.

___ 2. If the price elasticity of demand for a product is –2.00 rather than –1.50, then a given percentage price increase will result in a larger percentage decrease in the quantity sold.

___ 3. The greater the elasticity of the demand for a product, the higher the markup over variable cost should be.

___ 4. Because the profit-maximizing price does not include any allowance for fixed costs, the price may have to be increased to ensure that the fixed costs are covered.

___ 5. If a company has a 20% desired rate of return on investment, then it should add a 20% markup to its products under the absorption costing approach to cost-plus pricing.

___ 6. Both the markup and the cost base under absorption costing approach to cost-plus pricing depend on the anticipated unit sales. (Assume that all units produced are sold.)

___ 7. The absorption costing approach to cost-plus pricing may not maximize profits, but at least it ensures that the company will not lose any money on a product and will earn its required rate of return.

___ 8. Under target costing, the selling price is first estimated and then a target for the product's cost is established.

Multiple Choice

Choose the best answer or response by placing the identifying letter in the space provided.

___ 1. Every 5% decrease in price leads to a 7% increase in units sold for a particular product. The product's price elasticity of demand is: a) –1.60; b) 1.60; c) –1.32; d) 1.32.

___ 2. What is the profit-maximizing price for a product whose price elasticity of demand is –2.30 and whose unit variable cost is $10? a) $23.00; b) $17.69; c) $13.00; d) $33.00.

___ 3. Lerner, Inc. has provided the following data for one of its products:

Direct materials.....................................	$8
Direct labor..	$7
Variable manufacturing overhead.........	$2
Variable selling and admin. expenses...	$3

The company produces and sells 15,000 units of this product each year. Fixed manufacturing overhead cost is $15,000 per year and fixed selling and administrative expense is $30,000 per year. If the company uses the absorption costing approach to cost-plus pricing and desires a 50% markup, the selling price per unit would be: a) $34.50; b) $31.50; c) $27.00; d) $23.00.

___ 4. Justin Corp. estimates that an investment of $800,000 would be needed to produce and sell 20,000 units of a new product each year. At this level of activity, the unit product cost would be $100. Selling and administrative expenses would be $500,000 per year. If a 25% return on investment is desired, then the markup for the new product under the absorption costing approach to cost-plus pricing would be: a) 35%; b) 25%; c) 62.5%; d) 100%.

___ 5. Vintage RR, Inc. is considering a new line of model railroad engines. To compete effectively, the engines would be priced at $45. The company expects to be able to sell 2,000 engines a year at this price. The company requires a return on investment of 20%. The new product line would require an investment of $150,000. The target cost per engine would be: a) $30; b) $45; c) $15; d) $60.

Exercises

Exercise A-1. Karling Furniture recently raised the selling price of its colonial desk from $495 to $529. As a consequence, unit sales fell from 300 units to 270 units per period.

a. Estimate the price elasticity of demand of the colonial desk.

% change in price = $\dfrac{\overline{-}}{\underline{}}$ = _____

% change in quantity sold = $\dfrac{\overline{-}}{\underline{}}$ = _____

$$\varepsilon_d = \frac{\ln(1+\% \text{ change in quantity sold})}{\ln(1+\% \text{ change in price})} = \frac{\ln(1+\underline{})}{\ln(1+\underline{})} = \frac{\ln(\underline{})}{\ln(\underline{})} = \frac{\overline{}}{\underline{}} = \underline{}$$

b. If the variable cost of producing and selling the desk is $280, what effect did raising the price of the desk have on the company's net operating income?

c. Estimate the profit-maximizing price for the desk.

$$\begin{array}{c}\text{Profit-maximizing}\\\text{markup on variable cost}\end{array} = \frac{-1}{1+\varepsilon_d} = \frac{-1}{1+(\underline{})} = \underline{}$$

$$\begin{array}{c}\text{Profit-}\\\text{maximizing}\\\text{price}\end{array} = \left(1 + \begin{array}{c}\text{Profit-maximizing}\\\text{markup on}\\\text{variable cost}\end{array}\right)\begin{array}{c}\text{Variable cost}\\\text{per unit}\end{array}$$

$$= \left(1 + \underline{}\right)\underline{} = \underline{} \times \underline{} = \underline{}$$

Exercise A-2.   Costs relating to a product made by Mackey Company are given below:

Direct materials	$10
Direct labor	$12
Variable manufacturing overhead	$ 1
Fixed manufacturing overhead ($210,000 total)	$ 7
Variable selling and administrative expenses	$ 2
Fixed selling and administrative expenses ($90,000 total)	$ 3

Assume that the company uses the absorption costing approach to cost-plus pricing and a 50% markup. Compute the selling price for the above product.

_____	.....	$_____
_____	.....	_____
_____	.....	_____
_____	.....	_____
Unit product cost		_____
Markup—50%		_____
Selling price		$_____

Exercise A-3.   Speckart Company's required return on investment is 25%. An investment of $800,000 will be needed to produce and market 30,000 units of a particular product each year. The unit product cost will be $50 at this level of activity, and the selling and administrative expense will total $400,000 per year. Compute the markup percentage for the product, assuming that the company uses the absorption costing approach to cost-plus pricing.

$$\text{Markup \% on absorption cost} = \frac{\left(\text{Required ROI} \times \text{Investment}\right) + \text{Selling and administrative expenses}}{\text{Unit product cost} \times \text{Unit sales}}$$

$$\text{Markup \% on absorption cost} = \frac{\left(\underline{\ \ } \times \underline{\ \ \ \ \ \ }\right) + \underline{\ \ \ \ \ \ }}{\underline{\ \ \ \ \ \ } \times \underline{\ \ }} = \frac{\overline{\ \ \ \ \ \ \ \ \ }}{\underline{\ \ \ \ \ \ \ }} = \underline{\ \ \ \ \ }\%$$

Answers to Questions and Exercises

True or False

1. F   The price elasticity of demand has nothing to do with cost.

2. T   The larger the absolute value of the price elasticity of demand, the larger the percentage change in units sold for a given percentage change in price.

3. F   The opposite is true. The more elastic the demand for a product, the lower the markup over variable cost should be. Elastic demand indicates that customers are very sensitive to price and even a small increase in price will have a large impact on the number of units sold.

4. F   If the formula for the profit-maximizing price really provides the price that maximizes the company's profit, increasing the price would result in a decline in the company's profit. If fixed costs are not covered at the profit-maximizing price, the product should be dropped. Raising its price won't help.

5. F   The markup is determined in a more complicated manner than simply marking up cost by the desired ROI.

6. T   Unit sales appears in the denominator of the formula for the markup. The cost base also depends on the unit sales because the unit product cost under absorption costing is an average cost that depends on the number of units produced.

7. F   There is no assurance that the company will break even using the absorption costing approach. If customers do not buy as many units as anticipated, the company may lose money.

8. T   Target costing is used to establish allowable costs, not selling prices.

Multiple Choice

1. c

$$\varepsilon_d = \frac{\ln(1+(+0.07))}{\ln(1+(-0.05))} = \frac{\ln(1.07)}{\ln(0.95)} = \frac{0.06766}{-0.05129} = -1.32$$

2. b

$$\text{Markup} = \left(\frac{-1}{1+(-2.30)}\right) = 0.769$$

Profit-maximizing price $= 1.769 \times \$10 = \$17.69$

3. c

Direct materials	\$ 8
Direct labor	7
Variable manufacturing overhead	2
Fixed manufacturing overhead ($\$15,000 \div 15,000$ units)	1
Unit product cost	18
Markup—50%	9
Selling price	\$27

4. a

$$\text{Markup \% on absorption cost} = \frac{(0.25 \times \$800,000)+\$500,000}{\$100 \times 20,000}$$

$$= 35\%$$

5. a

Projected sales ($\$45 \times 2,000$)	\$90,000
Less desired profit ($20\% \times \$150,000$)	30,000
Target cost for 2,000 units	\$60,000

Target cost $= \$60,000 \div 2,000$ units
$= \$30$ per unit

Pricing Appendix

Exercises

Exercise A-1.

a.

$$\% \text{ change in price} = \frac{\$529 - \$495}{\$495} = +6.87\%$$

$$\% \text{ change in quantity sold} = \frac{270 - 300}{300} = -10.00\%$$

$$\varepsilon_d = \frac{\ln(1 + \% \text{ change in quantity sold})}{\ln(1 + \% \text{ change in price})} = \frac{\ln(1 + (-0.1000))}{\ln(1 + (+0.0687))} = \frac{\ln(0.9000)}{\ln(1.0687)} = \frac{-0.10536}{0.06644} = -1.59$$

b. The impact of the increase in price on net operating income can be computed as follows:

	Selling Price of $495	Selling Price of $529
Unit sales	300	270
Sales	$148,500	$142,830
Variable expenses	84,000	75,600
Contribution margin	$ 64,500	$ 67,230

Assuming that the change in price and quantity sold had no effect on fixed costs, the result of increasing the price was an increase in net operating income of $2,730 ($67,230 − $64,500).

c.
$$\frac{\text{Profit-maximizing}}{\text{markup on variable cost}} = \frac{-1}{1 + \varepsilon_d} = \frac{-1}{1 + (-1.59)} = 1.70$$

$$\frac{\text{Profit-}}{\text{maximizing}} = \left(1 + \frac{\text{Profit-maximizing}}{\text{markup on}}\right) \frac{\text{Variable cost}}{\text{per unit}} = (1 + 1.70)\,\$280 = 2.70 \times \$280 = \$756$$
$$\text{price} \quad\quad\quad \text{variable cost}$$

Because this price is a lot higher than the price that is currently being charged, it would be prudent to raise the price slowly, checking to make sure that profits really do increase after each increase in price.

Exercise A-2.

Direct materials	$10
Direct labor	12
Variable manufacturing overhead	1
Fixed manufacturing overhead	7
Unit product cost	30
Markup—50%	15
Selling price	$45

Exercise A-3.

$$\frac{\text{Markup \% on}}{\text{absorption cost}} = \frac{(0.25 \times \$800,000) + \$400,000}{\$50 \times 30,000} = \frac{\$600,000}{\$1,500,000} = 40\%$$

Appendix B

Profitability Analysis

Study Suggestions

This appendix builds on material in earlier chapters—specifically, the sections on *Segmented Income Statements and the Contribution Approach* in Chapter 6, *Utilization of a Constrained Resource* in Chapter 12, and *Preference Decisions—The Ranking of Investment Projects* in Chapter 13. Review these sections before reading the Profitability Analysis Appendix. Once you understand the material in those sections, you should have little difficulty mastering the Profitability Analysis Appendix.

APPENDIX HIGHLIGHTS

A. Absolute profitability is different from relative profitability.

    1. A business segment such as a product, customer, sales channel, or store is said to be *absolutely* profitable if eliminating that business segment would, without making any other change, increase the total profit of the overall organization.

    2. Even if all business segments are absolutely profitable, managers may still be interested in determining which are the *most* profitable. A business segment is *relatively* more profitable than another if cutting back on the first segment allows expansion of the second segment, with the consequence that the overall profit of the organization increases. Relative profitability is of concern only when some constraint forces the organization to make trade-offs among segments. In the absence of such a constraint, all segments that are absolutely profitable should be pursued.

B. The absolute profitability of a business segment is assessed by subtracting the incremental (avoidable) costs of the segment from its incremental revenues. See the section *Segmented Income Statements and the Contribution Approach* in Chapter 6 for more details.

C. The relative profitability of business segments is assessed using the profitability index, which is defined as follows:

$$\text{Profitability index} = \frac{\text{Incremental profit from the segment}}{\text{Amount of the constrained resource required by the segment}}$$

    1. The incremental profit from a segment is the difference between the incremental revenues from the segment and its incremental (avoidable) costs. The incremental profit from a segment is its absolute profitability.

    2. We have encountered the relative profitability concept before in the section *Preference Decisions—The Ranking of Investment Projects* in Chapter 13. In that chapter, the segments were long-term projects, the constraint was the total amount of funds available for investment in the projects, and the incremental profit from the segment (i.e., project) was its net present value:

$$\text{Project profitability index} = \frac{\text{Net present value of the project}}{\text{Investment required by the project}}$$

    3. The profitability index is used to decide how to best use a constrained resource. First, identify all of the business segments that require the use of the constrained resource. Compute the profitability index for each of them. Then rank the segments in order of the profitability index. Starting at the top of the list with the most profitable segment, move down the list until all of the constrained resource is consumed. All segments above that point in the list are accepted and all segments below that point in the list are rejected.

D. *Volume trade-off decisions* occur when: (1) a constraint forces volume trade-offs among products—producing more of one product results in producing less of another—and (2) fixed costs are not affected by the decision.

    1. In a volume trade-off decision, the profitability index is computed as follows:

$$\text{Profitability index in a volume trade-off decision} = \frac{\text{Unit contribution margin}}{\text{Amount of the constrained resource required by one unit of the product}}$$

    2. We encountered volume trade-off decisions in the section *Utilization of a Constrained Resource* in Chapter 12.

E. An *opportunity cost* is incurred whenever a constrained resource is used. If a constrained resource is used to produce one product, it cannot be used to produce another. The opportunity cost of making a product is the amount of contribution margin given up by not making the other product.

    1. The *marginal product* is the product whose production would be cut back or expanded if more or less of the constrained resource were available.

    2. The opportunity cost of using the constrained resource is the profitability index of the marginal product. In other words, the opportunity cost of using the constrained resource is the contribution margin per unit of the constrained resource for the product whose volume is cut back.

    3. The price of a new product should cover its variable cost plus any opportunity cost. Its opportunity cost is equal to the profitability index of the marginal product multiplied by the amount of the constrained resource that each unit of the new product would require.

REVIEW AND SELF-TEST
Questions and Exercises

True or False

Enter a T or an F in the blank to indicate whether the statement is true or false.

____ 1. If a company has a constrained resource, then there is no point in determining the absolute profitability of its segments.

____ 2. If one product's absolute profitability is higher than another product's, then it is relatively profitable as well.

____ 3. Relative profitability is determined by dividing a segment's margin, net of fully allocated fixed common costs, by its sales.

____ 4. In a volume trade-off situation, the opportunity cost of using a unit of the constrained resource is equal to the profitability index of the marginal product.

____ 5. The price of a new product should cover both its variable cost and its opportunity cost.

____ 6. The opportunity cost of using N units of the constrained resource is equal N times the profitability index of the marginal product.

Multiple Choice

Choose the best answer or response by placing the identifying letter in the space provided.

____ 1. If a segment's incremental revenue is $120,000, its incremental cost is $90,000, and it uses 60 hours of the constrained resource, what is its profitability index? (a) $30,000; (b) $2,000 per hour; (c) $500 per hour; (d) 0.25.

____ 2. If a product's selling price is $25, its variable cost is $16, and it uses 2 ounces of the constrained resource, what is its profitability index in a volume trade-off decision? (a) $9; (b) $4.50 per ounce; (c) $12.50 per ounce; (d) 0.36.

____ 3. Two products at Prime Products Corporation use the constrained resource—a high-cost milling machine. Data concerning those products follow:

	Alpha	Beta
Unit contribution margin	$12	$18
Constrained resource required per unit....	1 minute	2 minutes
Monthly demand	6,000 units	4,000 units

A total of 10,000 minutes on the milling machine are available next month. In order to maximize the company's profit for the month, how many units of product Beta should be produced? (a) 4,000 units; (b) 2,000 units; (c) 2,800 units; (d) 0 units.

____ 4. Refer to the data in question 3 above. In addition to products Alpha and Beta, Prime Products Corporation is considering introducing a new product, Charlie, whose variable cost would be $10 and that would require 3 minutes on the milling machine. The selling price for this new product should be at least: (a) $37; (b) $10; (c) $19; (d) $27.

Exercises

Exercise B-1.   Advanced Concepts, an advertising agency, is considering a number of potential jobs for the forthcoming month. The constrained resource in the agency is the managing partner's time. During the month, 150 hours of the managing director's time are available to work on jobs. Data concerning the potential jobs appear below:

Segment	Incremental Profit	Amount of Constrained Resource Required
Job 1	$ 9,575	25 hours
Job 2	$ 9,854	26 hours
Job 3	$ 6,528	17 hours
Job 4	$ 4,392	12 hours
Job 5	$11,594	34 hours
Job 6	$ 9,870	35 hours
Job 7	$ 7,704	24 hours
Job 8	$ 3,895	19 hours
Job 9	$13,500	36 hours
Job 10	$ 5,772	26 hours

a. Compute the profitability index for each job.

Segment	Incremental Profit (A)	Amount of Constrained Resource Required (B)	Profitability Index (A) ÷ (B)
Job 1	$ 9,575	25 hours	$_____ per hour
Job 2	$ 9,854	26 hours	$_____ per hour
Job 3	$ 6,528	17 hours	$_____ per hour
Job 4	$ 4,392	12 hours	$_____ per hour
Job 5	$11,594	34 hours	$_____ per hour
Job 6	$ 9,870	35 hours	$_____ per hour
Job 7	$ 7,704	24 hours	$_____ per hour
Job 8	$ 3,895	19 hours	$_____ per hour
Job 9	$13,500	36 hours	$_____ per hour
Job 10	$ 5,772	26 hours	$_____ per hour

b. Sort the jobs according to the profitability index and decide which jobs to accept.

Segment	Profitability Index	Amount of Constrained Resource Required	Cumulative Amount of Constrained Resource Required
Job ___	$_____ per hour	____ hours	_____ hours
Job ___	$_____ per hour	____ hours	_____ hours
Job ___	$_____ per hour	____ hours	_____ hours
Job ___	$_____ per hour	____ hours	_____ hours
Job ___	$_____ per hour	____ hours	_____ hours
Job ___	$_____ per hour	____ hours	_____ hours
Job ___	$_____ per hour	____ hours	_____ hours
Job ___	$_____ per hour	____ hours	_____ hours
Job ___	$_____ per hour	____ hours	_____ hours
Job ___	$_____ per hour	____ hours	_____ hours

c. Determine the total incremental profit for the jobs that you have accepted.

Segment	Incremental Profit
Job ___	$_____
Job ___	_____
Job ___	_____
Job ___	_____
Job ___	_____
Job ___	_____
Total........	$_____

Exercise B-2.   Forward Products Corporation has two products that require the use of the company's bottle-neck—a specialized welding machine that is available for 70,000 minutes per year. Data concerning those two products appear below:

	Vrimax	*Kirval*
Selling price	$184.00 per unit	$198.00 per unit
Variable cost	$110.40 per unit	$138.60 per unit
Amount of the constrained resource required	8 minutes per unit	6 minutes per unit
Annual demand	7,700 units	2,800 units

a. Is there enough capacity on the bottleneck to satisfy demand?

	Vrimax	*Kirval*	*Total*
Amount of the constrained resource required	8 minutes per unit	6 minutes per unit	
Annual demand	7,700 units	2,800 units	
Total constrained resource required	_____ minutes	_____ minutes	_____ minutes

b. Compute the profitability index for each product to determine which is the more profitable.

	Vrimax	*Kirval*
Selling price	$184.00 per unit	$198.00 per unit
Variable cost	110.40 per unit	138.60 per unit
Unit contribution margin	$_____ per unit	$_____ per unit
Amount of the constrained resource required by one unit	8 minutes per unit	6 minutes per unit
Profitability index	$_____ per minute	$_____ per minute

c. How much of each product should be produced?

Total constrained resource available	70,000
Less constrained resource required to produce _____ units of _____	_____
Remaining constrained resource available	_____
Less constrained resource required to produce _____ units of _____	_____
Remaining constrained resource available	_____

d. If you plan above is adopted, what would be the total contribution margin for the year?

	Vrimax	*Kirval*	*Total*
Unit contribution margin	_____	_____	
Volume	_____	_____	
Contribution margin	_____	_____	_____

Answers to Questions and Exercises

True or False

1. F If a company has a constrained resource, it is even more important to determine if any segments are absolutely unprofitable. Dropping an unprofitable segment would not only avoid an unnecessary loss, it would free up some of the constrained resource to be used elsewhere.

2. F The relative profitability of two products depends on two factors, not one. In addition to their absolute profitability, relative profitability depends on the amount of the constrained resource each uses.

3. F A segment's relative profitability is determined by dividing its incremental profit by the amount of the constrained resource it requires.

4. T Opportunity cost is determined by what is given up by taking an action. In a volume trade-off decision, if the constrained resource is used to produce more of one product, less must be produced of another product.

5. T If the selling price of a new product does not cover both its variable cost and its opportunity cost, the company would be better off producing more of the marginal product.

6. T The opportunity cost of using one unit of the constrained resource is equal to the profitability index of the marginal product. The opportunity cost of using N units of the constrained resource is equal to N times the profitability index of the marginal product.

Multiple Choice

1. c

Incremental revenue	$120,000
Incremental cost	90,000
Incremental profit (a)...............	$ 30,000
Constrained resource used (b) ..	60 hours
Profitability index (a) ÷ (b)......	$500 per hour

2. b

Selling price.............................	$25
Variable cost............................	16
Unit variable cost (a)	$ 9
Constrained resource used (b) .	2 ounces
Profitability index (a) ÷ (b).....	$4.50 per ounce

3. b All 6,000 units of Alpha demanded by the market should be produced because it is the more profitable product. (See the computation of the profitability index below.) This would require 6,000 minutes of the milling machine time. The remaining 4,000 minutes should be used to produce 2,000 units of product Beta.

	Alpha	Beta
Unit contribution margin......................	$12	$18
Constrained resource required per unit......	1 minute	2 minutes
Profitability index.......	$12 per minute	$9 per minute

4. a The selling price of the new product should at least cover its variable cost plus opportunity cost. The opportunity cost of using the constrained resource is $9 per minute—the profitability index of the marginal product, Beta, from the previous question. Therefore, the selling price should at least cover the variable cost of $10 plus the opportunity cost of $9 per minute × 3 minutes, or $37.

Exercises

Exercise B-1.

a. The profitability index is computed as follows:

Segment	Incremental Profit (A)	Amount of Constrained Resource Required (B)	Profitability Index (A) ÷ (B)
Job 1.............	$ 9,575	25 hours	$383 per hour
Job 2.............	$ 9,854	26 hours	$379 per hour
Job 3.............	$ 6,528	17 hours	$384 per hour
Job 4.............	$ 4,392	12 hours	$366 per hour
Job 5.............	$11,594	34 hours	$341 per hour
Job 6.............	$ 9,870	35 hours	$282 per hour
Job 7.............	$ 7,704	24 hours	$321 per hour
Job 8.............	$ 3,895	19 hours	$205 per hour
Job 9.............	$13,500	36 hours	$375 per hour
Job 10...........	$ 5,772	26 hours	$222 per hour

b. The jobs should be ranked on the basis of the profitability index.

Segment	Profitability Index	Amount of Constrained Resource Required	Cumulative Amount of Constrained Resource Required
Job 3.............	$384 per hour	17 hours	17 hours
Job 1.............	$383 per hour	25 hours	42 hours
Job 2.............	$379 per hour	26 hours	68 hours
Job 9.............	$375 per hour	36 hours	104 hours
Job 4.............	$366 per hour	12 hours	116 hours
Job 5.............	$341 per hour	34 hours	150 hours
Job 7.............	$321 per hour	24 hours	174 hours
Job 6.............	$282 per hour	35 hours	209 hours
Job 10...........	$222 per hour	26 hours	235 hours
Job 8.............	$205 per hour	19 hours	254 hours

The jobs that would generate the most profit for the 150 available hours are Job 3, Job 1, Job 2, Job 9, Job 4, and Job 5.

c. The total incremental profit from the accepted jobs would be $55,443.

Segment	Incremental Profit
Job 3.............	$ 6,528
Job 1.............	9,575
Job 2.............	9,854
Job 9.............	13,500
Job 4.............	4,392
Job 5.............	11,594
Total...........	$55,443

Exercise B-2.

a. The total amount of the constrained resource needed to meet annual demand is computed as follows:

	Vrimax	*Kirval*	*Total*
Amount of the constrained resource required (a)	8 minutes per unit	6 minutes per unit	
Annual demand (b)	7,700 units	2,800 units	
Total constrained resource required (a) × (b)	61,600 minutes	16,800 minutes	78,400 minutes

Because only 70,000 minutes are available, the company will be unable to meet demand.

b. The products should be ranked on the basis of the profitability index.

	Vrimax	*Kirval*
Selling price	$184.00 per unit	$198.00 per unit
Variable cost	110.40 per unit	138.60 per unit
Unit contribution margin (a)	$ 73.60 per unit	$ 59.40 per unit
Amount of the constrained resource required by one unit (b)	8 minutes per unit	6 minutes per unit
Profitability index (a) ÷ (b)	$9.20 per minute	$9.90 per minute

Kirval is more profitable than Vrimax.

c. The optimal plan would be to produce all 2,800 units of Kirval demanded by the market and use any remaining minutes on the constrained resource to produce Vrimax.

Total constrained resource available	70,000
Less constrained resource required to produce 2,800 units of Kirval	16,800
Remaining constrained resource available	53,200
Less constrained resource required by 6,650 units of Vrimax	53,200
Remaining constrained resource available	0

d. By following the above plan, the company would have a total contribution margin of $655,760.

	Vrimax	*Kirval*	*Total*
Unit contribution margin (a)	$73.60	$59.40	
Volume (b)	6,650	2,800	
Contribution margin (a) × (b)	$489,440	$166,320	$655,760